Supporting English Language Learners

A Guide for Teachers and Administrators

Farin A. Houk

HEINEMANN
PORTSMOUTH, NH

Heinemann
A division of Reed Elsevier Inc.
361 Hanover Street
Portsmouth, NH 03801–3912
www.heinemann.com

Offices and agents throughout the world

The author and publisher wish to thank those who have generously given permission to reprint borrowed material:

Figure 5–3 from *Schools That Work: Where All Children Read and Write*, 2/e by R. L. Allington and P. M. Cunningham. Published by Allyn and Bacon, Boston, MA. Copyright © 2002 by Pearson Education. Reprinted by permission of the publisher.

Figures 8–1 and 8–4 are reprinted by permission from *Scaffolding Language, Scaffolding Learning* by Pauline Gibbons. Copyright © 2002 by Pauline Gibbons. Published by Heinemann, a division of Reed Elsevier, Inc., Portsmouth, NH. All rights reserved.

Credits for borrowed material continue on p. 204.

Library of Congress Cataloging-in-Publication Data
Houk, Farin A.
   Supporting English language learners : a guide for teachers and administrators / Farin A. Houk.
      p. cm.
   Includes bibliographical references and index.
   ISBN 0-325-00699-7 (alk. paper)
   1. English language—Study and teaching—Foreign speakers—Handbooks, manuals, etc.   2. English language—Study and teaching—Management—Handbooks, manuals, etc. I. Title.

PE1128.A2H588 2005
428'.0071—dc22   2004030795

Editor: *Lois Bridges*
Production: *Vicki Kasabian*
Cover design: *Catherine Hawkes, Cat & Mouse*
Typesetter: *Kim Arney Mulcahy*
Manufacturing: *Louise Richardson*

Printed in the United States of America on acid-free paper
09 08 07 06 05 RRD   2 3 4 5

For Gabriel and Camilo
mis dos razones de ser

Contents

Preface

We must be the change we wish to see in the world.   —*Mahatma Gandhi*

I have always, since my own days as a schoolgirl, believed in education as the cornerstone of a truly democratic way of life. I certainly didn't call it that; but when I read, wrote, and examined history and the relentless human movements toward liberty, I knew that I was on to something big, something important. Through my own education, I escaped the prescribed parameters of my life; I rose above the limits of my own life and found myself face-to-face with the myriad of possibilities that the world had to offer. And in this, I don't mean that I considered myself some kind of modern-day girl version of Horatio Alger. It wasn't that I knew (or even hoped) that my education was going to bring me riches or prestige or power; rather, I felt free because I was a *thinker*.

Somewhere along the line, and probably not at any one particular time or another, I learned to take control of my life by thinking. I learned to analyze, to imagine, to question, to reason, to challenge, to suggest, to reflect; I learned about a lot of things, and I learned to make sense of that knowledge for myself. I learned to take what I heard and saw and was told, and to put all of that to my own tests of sensibility, logic, and justice. Some people call it critical thinking; it is that, certainly, but I call it being *free*.

This is not to suggest that there is any intrinsic peace in the act of thinking independently; on the contrary, sometimes it feels much easier to *not* exercise your free-thinking skills, to just follow the conventional wisdom, and believe unquestioningly everything you hear. Many times, asking questions and searching for answers brings more grief and distress than the blissful numbness of burying your head in the sand. The peace that I have found and that guides my own life lies, ironically, in the tension created by thinking critically; that space between what *is* and what *should be* is where I find myself as a mother, as a teacher, and as a human being. When we examine the reality of our lives critically, and when we envision a better way of being, we find real hope.

I became a teacher because I wanted to guide children to that same sense of hope. It's not a false hope that says if you jump through these hoops you'll be happy, or if you try hard enough to be just like so-and-so you'll be wealthy. Rather, I wanted to give children real hope, grounded in the fullness of their beings and guided by the magic of their souls. I wanted them to develop the skills and strength to examine their own lives and claim agency over them, to envision something better and to make it happen. I wanted to give children the real hope that comes from capacity, competence, access, and strength. I wanted to help children find the fire inside them that others could never extinguish.

Bilingual education has become a place for me to live in that peaceful tension between what *is* and what *should be.* It's a place where I see all of the realities of life in this country come together: the denigration of public education, racism, classism, a disdain for and mistrust of the "other," a fear of the unknown. It is also a place where I see the wealth of possibilities for what could and should be: an appreciation of the unique gifts of each person, a faith in the capacity of others, a willingness to be humble and take risks for our own good and the good of others, the brilliance and passion and creativity of each human spirit.

As a teacher of English language learners, I live out my hope for all of our students and for all of us. Throughout this book, I reiterate that what I believe to be good practice for English language learners is really good practice for all children. Similarly, I believe that the convictions that guide us in our work with English language learners serve us all, if we could just take the collective leap to embrace them.

There are two fundamental principles that guide my own teaching and that provide the philosophical framework for this book. The first guiding principle comes from the transformative work done at the University of Arizona by Dr. Luis Moll and his colleagues. Every time I heard colleagues talk about how a particular child (and these were almost always English language learners or other minority students) "didn't know anything about anything," or heard a teacher complaining that they had to start from scratch with a child, my hair stood on end. I knew that wasn't right. How can any child who has lived anywhere in this world for five, seven, or ten years not know anything about anything? And beyond individual teachers, I saw programs developed and policies implemented that worked from this deficit model, based on the assumption that certain groups of children just didn't know anything and had nothing to contribute to their own learning.

Dr. Luis Moll's term *funds of knowledge* describes the important bodies of knowledge and skills that individuals, families, and communities possess. These funds of knowledge are skills, strategies, and wisdom generated by groups of people in the course of their day-to-day living, and they are generally either overlooked or simply discounted by mainstream educators. It is my unscientific sense that communities that have traditionally had fewer resources with which to eke out an existence have had to create and nurture a very deep and broad set of skills and strategies in order to survive. It takes tremendous strength, resiliency, resolve, and creativity to make it in an environment where nearly all of the tools for success are kept out of reach.

The failure to recognize the resources that students, families, and whole communities possess has had dire consequences all around. First, and most important, students have been perceived as, at best, empty vessels, to be filled with our "important knowledge," and at worst, pathologically devoid of any worthy cultural or academic knowledge. This paradigm has resulted in massive school failure and underachievement on the part of culturally and linguistically diverse students.

It has also affected us as teachers. There seems to be such a feeling in education that we are in an uphill battle to rescue students (certain groups of children in particular) from themselves. According to conventional wisdom, we contend with their parents' ignorance, their cultural and linguistic deficits, and their lack of motivation or aspirations for the future. I believe it is time for us to bring ourselves back, and remind ourselves that all parents, all families, all communities want nothing more than the success and well-being of their children. The words of Jose Marti ring in my ears, "los niños nacen para ser felices" ("children were born to be happy").

It is critical that educators of all children, and particularly those of English language learners in the United States, embrace the funds of knowledge concept both philosophically and practically. It is important that we take the time to identify, acknowledge, and incorporate the strengths and resources that our students have, and put those gifts to work in the service of their learning. When we approach students in this way, we begin to teach them differently. We say to them, "You are so smart! Let me show you what else you can do with that. . . ." Rather than pitting students against themselves, their families, and their communities, we support children's wide knowledge of the world, and we build on it.

Even though Dr. Moll is a university researcher and professor, he is quick to remind us that all educators can access the funds of knowledge that exist within a student, a family, or a community. The first step is a willingness on the part of a teacher or a school to seek out those resources; we must be willing to accept all of the nonacademic, noninstitutional ways of knowing and negotiating the world. Beyond that, I believe that you will be surprised at how readily you will acquire information about who our students are, what their dreams and strengths and fears and needs are. An afternoon here, a few good questions there, and the doors to our students' lives will open up before our very eyes. It is a little extra work, but the pay-off for our students, and for us as educators, will be breathtaking, and well worth the effort.

The second guiding principle in my teaching and in this book is that of *cultural democracy.* This concept is similar to that of funds of knowledge in that it encourages a more active and meaningful participation in the educational process by students and families. Ramirez and Castaneda (1974) first advanced the idea of cultural democracy in articulating an optimum environment for culturally and linguistically diverse children. They suggest that a culturally democratic environment is one that recognizes and fosters children's connections to their home culture and language, at the same time that it teaches children how to navigate and negotiate the larger mainstream culture. A culturally democratic space encourages children to become *bicultural:* comfortable and confident in their own cultural ways (including their home languages), competent and self-assured in the dominant culture.

Antonia Darder (1991), "in an effort to expand on the emancipatory intent of Ramirez and Castaneda's philosophy of cultural democracy" (62), suggests the need to examine the larger educational and societal constructs that must be redefined in order to effect a culturally democratic education for students. She discusses the need for a fundamental shift in power relationships in schools and classrooms. Rather than a space where one teacher possesses important knowledge that is then conferred upon the twenty-something blank slates who come to the classroom each day, Darder articulates a different vision. She suggests a space where power is both shared and assumed by all participants, teachers and students alike, and is used col-laboratively to involve "students in an active process of empowerment, [to] assist them in finding their voice, and [to] support the development of a spirit of social solidarity" (62).

In my own simple words, then, I believe that much of our work as educators happens before the children ever enter our classroom. Just as I was so empowered by my own education, we must commit ourselves to helping children find that same sense of agency in their own lives. We must acknowledge the resources, the gifts, the strengths that our students bring each day, and we must capitalize on them. We must recognize that we are not only teachers, we are, sometimes more importantly, learners, and we've got to throw ourselves into the teaching-learning process right alongside our students.

Finally, and ironically, we've got to stop having all of the answers for our students. For us, education is a process by which children find their own voice and chart their own course. We cannot and should not do it for them, but we are entirely responsible for guiding them in their journey. We give them the materials, the tools, the love, and the support as they make their own roads in the world.

There are many teachers who see the English language learners in their classrooms as just another drain on their time and energy. There is so much to do as a teacher each day, and they haven't got time to take on the needs or issues of children who just don't "fit in," they say. I appreciate the opportunity to teach English language learners, because it reminds me what I am really here for and it brings me back to the real magic of the teaching and learning process. When we make shifts in our pedagogy to accommodate English language learners, we make changes that benefit all children, because we are forced to acknowledge and centralize the needs of children. Rather than molding ourselves to textbooks, prescribed curriculum, or official mandates, we are reminded by those sweet little faces that we are not math or phonics or reading teachers, we are teachers of *children*.

In my work everyday with English language learners, I am compelled by what Sonia Nieto (1991) describes as "the light in their eyes," that moment when children make the connection, open the proverbial door, and find meaning for themselves in the world. It's what brought us all into teaching, and it's what keeps us here, spellbound, year after year. Together, we venture into this humbling and exhilarating challenge: to meet the needs of our English language learners. Together, we articulate our values and beliefs about education, examine and question our practice as teachers, and we reclaim for ourselves and our students the joy of real teaching and learning.

Acknowledgments

This book has my name on it, but the love and efforts and energy of so many others have gone into its pages.

First and foremost, I am indebted to my two sons, Gabriel and Camilo, who gave up so much time with Mami so that I could write. Thank you for playing sweetly in the sand, sitting on my lap, and giving me kisses on my hand while I typed away at the computer.

To Susan Ohanian, thank you for planting the seed of this book. Your encouragement as a writer is humbling and appreciated.

To Lois Bridges, the best cheerleader/editor anyone could ask for; I am grateful for your ongoing support and kindness.

To Patrick Scott, Katherine Kondylis, Marcela Abadi, Katy Johnson, and Susan Garrett, I am so thankful for your friendship and for your professional brilliance. You are such treasures to me and to the children you teach so lovingly.

And to those of you who have nurtured me personally or professionally, in one important way or another, I am so grateful: Traci Russell; Bob and Dot Houk; Joe Bales; Karen Montes; Happie Byers; Kira Willson; Kelly Warter; Joanne Gallasch; Tilman Smith; Gonzalo Cerna; Pancho and Rita Chavez; Charlie, Maria, and Laura Scott; the staffs of Lister, Webster, and Olympic Hills Elementary Schools; and all of my colleagues at Pacific Oaks College Northwest. My love and gratitude to you all.

1

Challenge as Opportunity

Problems are only opportunities in work clothes. —*Henry Kaiser*

The Children We Serve

It seems as if there are as many different names to describe English language learners as there are children who fit into the category: LEP (limited English proficient) students, LES (limited English speaking) students, ESL (English as a second language) students, SLLs (second language learners), and the list goes on and on. Each year we have more of them on our classroom rosters: children who come to us not only to learn about the Cat in the Hat or about the nine planets in the solar system, but also to develop their ability to use the English language.

This book uses the term *English language learner* (ELL). The term ELL recognizes that there is a wide range of students for whom specialized instruction in language development is crucial for academic success. When we understand that the *English* in English language learner refers to the standard, academic English that is used to communicate in schools in the United States (see Perry and Delpit 1998, or Smitherman 1977, for discussions of "traditional" English versus dialects of English such as Black English), it's possible that more of our students may actually be ELLs than we had previously considered. For many of our students, the term *second language learner* may also obscure the fact that many of our children come to us speaking two or more languages other than English.

The First Generation

When teachers think of English language learners, we tend to think of first-generation students. They are children born in another country and raised speaking a language other than English. They have generally had little if any instruction in English, and have had little experience with it before coming to a classroom in the United States. The level of English dominance among the parents and families of these children can certainly vary, but more often than not, the parents are also just beginning to learn English.

Similarly, ELL children and families have also had different experiences with formal literacy itself. Some families may be highly educated and literate in their first language, and their children may also have developed many important preliteracy skills in that context. Depending on the ages of the children, they may have also had formal education in their first language. Other children will have had less formal education and literacy experience. Their parents may be unable to read and write in the first language, and may have, therefore, been unable to provide a context in which to develop children's preliteracy (at least in terms of reading and writing) skills. Children of any age may come to us for their first formal educational experience. For any number of reasons (refugee status, underdevelopment in the native country, poverty, etc.), these children may not have had access to formal schooling and literacy instruction (Freeman, Freeman, and Mercuri 2002). Consider a few examples:

* Anatoliy is ten years old and has just arrived with his family from the Ukraine. Although he speaks only a few words of English, he speaks Ukrainian, Russian, and Moldavian fluently. He attended school regularly in the Ukraine and has highly developed academic and literacy skills in Ukrainian. His parents have also had an extensive formal education.

* Teresa is seven years old and has recently immigrated with her family from Mexico. Her family speaks Mixtec (an indigenous language) at home, she has a limited command of Spanish (her second language), and very little experience with English. Teresa attended school for a few months in Mexico, but stopped so she could help her family at home. No one in her family reads or writes, and her parents have limited proficiency in oral Spanish.

* Lai is eleven years old. He is Mien (from northern Thailand), and speaks Mien and Thai. He spent most of his life in a refugee camp in Thailand before coming to the United States. His parents do not read or write in any language. His older brother who went to high school in the United States had a very negative experience that was extremely upsetting to his parents. The older brother eventually dropped out of high school.

Second and Third Generations, and Beyond

This group of ELL children is huge, and it continues to grow dramatically. These children were born in the United States, and their parents or grandparents have immigrated from other countries. The child's relationship to the family's heritage language may range from strong to nonexistent. Consider these scenarios:

✳ Adriana is a five-year-old who was born in Los Angeles. She has lived all of her life in a Spanish-speaking community. Her family and all of her playmates speak Spanish. She watches TV and listens to the radio in Spanish. She has been home with her mother for her first five years; her first experience with English will be in kindergarten.

✳ Kimberly is a first grader who was born in California. Her parents' dominant language is Spanish, but as they learn English their Spanish is peppered with increasing amounts of English words. Rather than speaking one or the other, Kimberly speaks "Spanglish," a veritable mix of English and Spanish. She will say things like, "Tengo que hacer mi homework y después voy a ir outside to play" ("I have to do my homework and then I am going outside to play").

✳ Manet is a second grader who was born in Seattle. Some of his older siblings were born in Cambodia; they have a good command of Cambodian, but prefer English and use English with Manet. His parents speak only Cambodian; no one in the family reads or writes Cambodian. Manet responds with a very basic level of Cambodian, and he supplements heavily with English.

✳ Tony is a third grader. His grandmother was born in Vietnam, but his mother was born in California. His grandmother speaks only Vietnamese, and his mother understands some Vietnamese but doesn't speak, write, or read it. Tony speaks only English, and his language reflects his mother's accent and informal understanding of grammar and syntax. His grandmother picks him up from school, but she and Tony aren't able to communicate about much beyond basic logistics.

In our classrooms, we may see these second- and third-generation children falling into a disturbing category: many of them are essentially *alingual*, that is, they do not have mastery of either English or their family's native language.

English language learners come to our classrooms from a variety of cultural, linguistic, and educational backgrounds. We may have one child in one of these categories or we may have only one child who is *not* an English language learner. While the number of ELL children in a classroom or school building may ultimately affect larger program and policy decisions, incorporating best practices for ELL children, even if we only have one in a classroom, will mean better instruction for all students. Read on!

Good News: The Task at Hand

Teachers today face increasing demands from all sides: parents, society, and students themselves. In the age of ever-higher standards, high-stakes testing, and unprecedented federal education mandates, we may feel as though we don't have much time or energy to invest in researching and implementing the best educational practices for our English language learners, particularly if we only have a few in our classroom. It becomes tempting to just keep hoping that the children will mold themselves to fit into our comfortable ways of teaching, rather than the other way around.

The good news, actually the great news, is that a small investment in understanding what works for our English language learners will mean a big payoff for all of our students. The shift in the focus of our teaching required by our ELL children will mean that we will actually be more attuned to the needs of all of our students. We must realize that all children, not just those learning English as a second language, are essentially language learners.

Often, when English is the only language spoken at home, we are quick to assume dominance of that language on the child's part. But research has illuminated the effect that poverty, for example, can have on language development. Factors such as socioeconomic level, level of parental education, homelessness, family trauma, and/or varying levels of family literacy may all contribute to a limited development of vocabulary and deeper language structures (Haberman 1995; Hart and Ridley 1995; Payne 2001). When families suffer serious, long-term hardship or stress, children may miss opportunities for natural language development. They may not receive the conversational stimulation or the variety of world experiences that contribute to a deep, broad understanding of language. Consequently, these children come through our doors with needs very similar to those of children for whom English is a second language. All students, regardless of their background or their level of English proficiency, will benefit from an environment that is specifically designed to cultivate a deep and sophisticated understanding of language.

Good Teaching for All Children

The ideal classroom setting for English language learners (and all language learners!) emphasizes comprehension while it scaffolds language development. As we incorporate those two central goals into our teaching, we will find that we enhance the learning experience for most, if not all, of the other students as well. An emphasis on comprehension means that we do whatever is necessary to ensure that students integrate knowledge and concepts into their own thinking. While this may seem obvious, there are many factors of classroom life that creep into this process and divert our attention from this goal. Time constraints, textbooks or top-down curricula, traditional academic environments ("the way we've always done it"), pressure to get students to perform on high-stakes tests, even our own desire to stick with our lesson plans, may all create a situation in which the needs of some students are marginalized. English language learners are particularly vulnerable to this marginalization. By modifying instruction so that ELL children are able to participate fully in the learning, all children will come away from a lesson with a stronger and deeper understanding of key concepts.

Consider the following example. The teacher is reading Lynne Cherry's *The Great Kapok Tree,* a story in which rainforest animals try to convince a man to spare a great tree that he has been sent to chop down. The teacher plans to read the story aloud, then have the students write independently about what they would do if they were in the man's position. Some students participate eagerly in the read-aloud, others seem overwhelmed by the sophisticated language of the story.

Just before the actions of the man are revealed at the end of the story, the teacher asks the children what they would do. She realizes that some children are unable to articulate a response, and still others seem unclear about what the man's dilemma is. She returns to the beginning of the story and invites children to the front of the class to re-create the story thus far. Students volunteer to act out the parts of the characters; other students elaborate on what each character is doing. She continues through the book, allowing the children to role-play and summarize the story in their own words. By the end of the session, all of the children are able to suggest, with words or actions or some combination of the two, what they might do if they were in the man's position in the story. All students come away with a much stronger grasp of the content and the dilemma of the story. The teacher may have to be flexible in order to give the students sufficient time to record their responses, if she still chooses to have the children write with this lesson. In any case, the level and depth of comprehension among all of the students has been worth the change in plans.

In this example, let's say the teacher modified the lesson in order to enhance the understanding and participation of the English language learners. But many of the other children have also benefited. Gardner's (1983) research on the different types of intelligences reminds us that children learn in different ways: those children who are visual learners have benefited from seeing the story acted out for them, those who are kinesthetic learners have appreciated the opportunity to act out the story, and those who learn most effectively by participating and talking have enhanced their understanding of the text by summarizing it out loud as others role-play it. Those children who may be unclear about some of the vocabulary have also improved their understanding by having some children demonstrate what the words mean and by having others paraphrase meanings with simpler language. Whereas in a traditional read-aloud, only those students who are most adept at processing information aurally (by listening) would have been effectively served, in our modified-for-the-ELL version, many more children's needs are met, and the learning of all of the children is enhanced by the multidimensional presentation.

Becoming Teachers of Children

Effectively teaching English language learners means a shift from teaching content or curricula, to teaching *children*. It means becoming very intentional in our teaching; we train ourselves to be alert to and responsive to the individual needs that students may have, and we allow those needs and learning styles of the children to shape how content is presented and how learning progresses. Making that shift may stretch us in some areas, but will also probably be easier than we think in other areas. In any case, we will be better teachers for having taken the leap.

Creating a Context for Success

Similarly, creating a context within a building in which the needs of English language learners and their families are most effectively met, will also mean a more responsive environment for other students and their families. Again, the shift is away from "what we've always done" or "what the school down the road is doing" to "what do our students and families need." When we open ourselves and our classrooms to the kind of modifications that will ensure the success of English language learners, we will at the same time be addressing the needs of other students and families who may have been underserved by traditional models. In rethinking and reshaping the climate of a school, for example, the opportunity arises not only to incorporate and appreciate the cultures of ELL children, but also to recognize and appreciate the diversity among the entire school population. By creating a space in which difference is an opportunity rather than a challenge, we learn to acknowledge the ways that we are all different; we become proud of the unique contributions that each of us can make.

Learning to become effective educators of English language learners is a tremendous task, but it also presents a transformative opportunity. It challenges educators to become better connected to each other, as teachers, students, administrators, families, and as human beings.

Key Ideas

* In this book, the term *English language learner* (ELL) refers to any child for whom standard academic English is not his or her first language. Generally, these children have some kind of relationship to a language other than English, although other children might also be identified as needing specialized instruction in language development.

* ELLs have varying levels of experience with and proficiency in the non-English language. Some are highly proficient in their first language, and others may only understand the language, without speaking it themselves.

* There are wide differences in the experiences of ELLs in terms of formal schooling opportunities that will affect their needs in the school system.

* ELL children are widely diverse. There is no one profile for an English language learner, and each child has his or her individual needs. Their one commonality

is the need for thoughtful instruction designed to maximize language and academic development.

* Best practices for language development for ELLs are just that: highly effective strategies for language development. *All* children benefit from these successful strategies for developing language.

* Making even small changes in classroom practice to accommodate ELLs will mean enhanced experiences for *all* children. The bigger the changes, the more you will accommodate the varying strengths and needs that all children have.

* Making even small changes in how we manage school systems in order to accommodate the needs of ELLs and their families will mean enhanced experiences for *all* students and families.

2

School Climate

We are constantly invited to be who we are.   —*Henry David Thoreau*

A Scenario: "School Is a Family Event"

When you walk into Options at Lincoln Elementary School in Olympia, Washington, the whole school is there to greet you. Every classroom teacher, each student, even their families are there with welcoming smiles, ready to receive you as the newest member of their school community.

No, they haven't all interrupted their important school business; rather, the entire front hallway of the school is covered with family pictures. Every family in the school is represented, under a personalized photograph of each classroom teacher. Every year, before school starts, the school hires a photographer to attend the back-to-school barbecue. The photographer takes casual family photos of all the families in the school (and almost all of them make it to the barbecue!) that will later be displayed under their teacher's picture in the front hallway.

Principal Cheryl Petra observes that this is another expression of Lincoln School's belief that families must be integrated into the fabric of school life. More than a belief, she says, "It's an attitude." It's an attitude conveyed constantly to staff, students, and families when they hear her mantra in the hallways or in the staff room or at assemblies: "School is a family event."

When new families come to Lincoln, Cheryl makes it a point to connect with the family on a personal level, and if she needs to, she uses interpreters to be able to sit down and talk with families. She also tries to match a staff member with the family as its advocate. The staff member becomes the contact person for the family, a real name and face of someone who's looking out for them.

Lincoln is a community that has emerged and strengthened around clear, common goals. School is a place where children become intellectuals; beyond teaching content standards in reading and math, Lincoln has developed a more fundamental curriculum, based on *thinking goals* and *thinking behaviors*. Throughout the curriculum, teachers have articulated objectives such as developing empathy, curiosity, and flexibility in thinking; distinguishing point of view; sequencing, evaluating, and goal setting. Teachers focus on encouraging those habits of higher-level thinking in all aspects of the curriculum.

And the curriculum is one that emerges from the students who come to Lincoln every year. Rather than following a packaged program, teachers know that they're expected to develop a curriculum that is relevant to the students in their classroom. It's hard work, but teachers have realized and have truly come to believe that it's the only effective way to teach their students. They know the standards backward and forward, but they also have a plan that they believe in for getting students to meet them.

The culture of Lincoln is so focused on recognizing individuals as important members of the community that nearly all of the issues that usually marginalize English language learners and their families from school settings are absent. Teachers know all children and families personally; they take time to know about the family, what their strengths and struggles are, and what their gifts and needs are. Teachers have high expectations for all students; issues that come up with students are taken up by Lincoln's "culture of questioning." Rather than wallowing in problems, staff members question each other about possibilities. Instead of "He's late to school all the time," you'll hear "I wonder why he's late every day" or "Let's find out what that family needs to be able to get here on time."

The attitude at Lincoln is exhilarating; students, families, teachers, and staff members engender community and success wherever they gather and connect. All students and families, English language learners or not, are embraced as essential, integral threads in the Lincoln fabric.

The Discipline of Magic

Schools that work successfully with English language learners have what seems to be a magical combination of hope, vision, and commitment. As you walk into one of these buildings, you breathe in the presence of the students, the staff, and the community. It's as if the air itself is buzzing with energy, excitement, and purpose. It's clear that there are shared goals and ambitious plans for reaching them.

But the "feel" of a positive, successful school is not an abstract. Rather, there are specific components that can be developed and implemented within a building to create that magical atmosphere of excellence and success.

Creating the School Community

Just as a loving family is the best place to nurture a child, a warm, caring, school community is essential in cultivating confident and competent students. English language learners in particular need an environment that is supportive and risk-free (Krashen 1981), and that simultaneously guides them toward excellence in all aspects of their lives, including language and academic learning. The attitude in effective schools is that everyone has a gift to offer; children need the best of what each one of us, families and educators, has to give.

Establishing Cultural Democracy

A school community that strives to be relevant for English language learners must build itself on a foundation of *cultural democracy* (Ramirez and Castaneda 1974). A culturally democratic environment is one that allows each individual to express and cultivate his or her own culture, while at the same time learning to negotiate the wider mainstream culture. In a culturally democratic school, students are guided and supported in the process of becoming both bilingual and bicultural. While we typically think of a bilingual child as one who speaks English and another language, we cannot forget that many of our students come to school speaking other non-standard forms of English, such as Ebonics or patois. Whether teachers provide a formal structure for children to maintain their home languages, a culturally demo-cratic school provides encouragement and recognition for *home* languages, whatever they may be, and instructs children in the language of schools and the language of power, standard academic English.

Similarly, culturally democratic schools embrace and affirm each child's culture (August and Hakuta 1997; August and Pease-Alvarez 1996), and the attendant "funds of knowledge" (Moll, Amanti, Neff, and Gonzalez 1992), and at the same time teach children how to negotiate the larger, mainstream culture (Darder 1991). Students are encouraged to examine and engage in the larger social and political discourse, the intersection between their own lives and the external forces that shape them, in order to become knowledgeable and powerful agents of change for

themselves and others (Freire and Macedo 1987). Again, all children at all levels must be instructed in meaningful, critical participation in the larger society; for second language learners, it is as fundamental as reading and writing.

Embracing a philosophical framework of cultural democracy in a school thus serves two purposes: first, it recognizes children as whole human beings, with all that they bring from themselves and their families; secondly, it reminds us that we need not be threatened by or seek to stamp out children's home languages and cultures. We must first believe, and then communicate to them that those languages and cultures, along with the families and communities that breathe life into them, are indispensable to their development as positive, productive human beings (Christian and Genesee 1998).

Turning Vision into Practice

How and where do we make the leap from the theory of cultural democracy to a building that buzzes with the life and energy of its students and teachers? How do we go about creating a school environment in which each child feels capable and enthusiastic, ready to tackle multiplication, multisyllabic words, or the life lessons of *Strega Nona*?

Reflecting Families

First, it's important that the lives of students and families are reflected physically in the school. Pictures of families, signs in all of the languages of the school, and

spaces for families to gather all make for an atmosphere that is inviting and affirming for both students and families. And by drawing from the actual present community of the school, we make no mistake in representing families' cultures and languages: we give students and families space to define and express their own unique identities.

At the same time, however, it is important for staff to do their own work to know who the children and families in the building are. Learning about students' cultural and linguistic backgrounds should be a routine part of the school year. Just as it helps us to know what children are interested in, what motivates them, it is essential to know about their families, their culture, and their language resources. Teachers need to know whether their students are Russian or Ukrainian, why they may be from Mexico and may still struggling with the Spanish language, why some Vietnamese families don't speak to each other, what their route may have been from Southeast Asia to the United States, or why some Eastern Europeans may reject the Russian language. Asking a Puerto Rican family how long they have been in this country may be a simple oversight to us, but to a family it reflects a pervasive indifference and disrespect on the part of the staff and school.

When culture and language are put into broad, universal terms, all children can better understand themselves and others. The idea is not to put the Latino students on the spot and have them tell you about how they cook beans and rice with mom at home, the idea is to recognize and discuss culture in a way in which all children can learn about themselves and share that knowledge with others. Schools and classrooms that focus on larger themes such as "families" or "storytelling" provide a general framework into which children can plug in the details of their lives. Everyone has culture: all of us have ways of living, being, loving, and learning that are both unique to ourselves and similar to others. It is important to have this conversation out in the open among students, families, and staff, in both formal and informal ways, so that we begin to build genuine respect and community within a school. Once this process is underway, we have also set the stage for all community members to engage in the critical dialogue necessary to examine other, more global aspects of our lives.

Further, when you know who your students are, you are better able to address their needs in the classroom and in the school. No child is an empty slate: all children possess literacy and knowledge that they have developed in their home lives. By tapping into this knowledge, you can then build on it. Choosing to believe that some children "don't know anything," either because they don't speak English or because their families have limited formal schooling, puts everyone in a difficult situation. Teachers who think they are working with a blank slate are actually working against all that a child knows, and may even exacerbate a child's academic problems by creating behaviors that detract from a student's learning process. Students are not only cut off from the knowledge that they have brought with them from home, they are clearly made to understand that what they do know counts for nothing, leaving them two steps behind in both confidence and capability. Expanding on Cummins' (1981) common underlying proficiency (CUP) theory of language even further (he asserts that when children have learned concepts in one language, they need not relearn them in the new language, see Figure 11–1), skills children have learned in one setting need not be discounted in another setting. Children who have learned to translate for parents in the grocery store, take care of younger siblings at the park, sort and wash clothes properly, or organize dinner when mom is working have learned many important concepts that they can transfer into the school setting. Teachers must recognize what resources children bring to the table, and put them to use as our formal work begins.

There are different ways that schools go about learning who their families and students are. Some schools provide regular forums for parents to educate staff about language and cultural issues in the form of staff meetings, teacher inservice days, or parent–teacher education nights. Other schools bring in community members or organizations to teach staff about different communities. Again, the best way to learn about families is to hear it directly from the families themselves; this way you avoid all manner of generalizing or stereotyping inaccurately, and you allow for the unique paths that particular families have taken. In some buildings, teachers have created ways within their classrooms to learn about children and families. Conference time can be a starting point for this, but this research must be ongoing, beginning on the first day of school, and the knowledge must not be limited to teachers: principals, support staff, office staff, all members of the school community should be learning together. Some buildings have chosen to adopt schoolwide themes that allow for the discussion of language and culture, and engage all students at all levels. Broad themes such as music, art, life cycle, neighborhood, family, and others, all allow children (and teachers!) to carve out and define their own particular cultural niche, as well as learn about others. Such themes are ripe for participation by everyone in a school, and set up an equal playing field on which both similarities and differences can be examined and embraced.

Setting High Expectations

Schools that find success with English language learners are schools that *expect* success with English language learners (Berman, Minicucci, McLaughlin, et al. 1997). The attitude in these schools is "I know you can, let me show you how." Part of the magic in schools like this is that teachers, principals, support staff, families, and most important students all truly believe that excellence is within their grasp (Carter and Chatfield 1986; Costa and Kallick 1995; Garcia 1994). For them, it's just a matter of finding the right path, the right combination for each student to develop his or her gifts. Everyone perceives the task as absolutely doable, as long as each person takes full responsibility for his or her part. Here, there is no time wasted in shifting blame: it's not parents' fault, it's not student's lack of motivation, it's not the teacher's fault; rather, the job of helping all children, and particularly English language learners, do their best is *our* collective responsibility.

Recognizing Students' Hard Work

When you walk into a school that values all of its members, you see evidence of students' challenging and creative work. It is a valuable investment to spend time creating spaces where students' work can be displayed carefully and respectfully, and to maintain ongoing exhibits of children's work. It is a source of pride for students and teachers to see their hard work on the walls each day. Sharing work in this way also creates a powerful sense of community among those who see it each day: teachers, students, and families see and appreciate the hard work that others are doing; they learn from the work of others; they find points of intersection in their lives and work; and they feel like important, contributing members of a vibrant learning community. Anyone who enters a school that looks like this says, "Wow! These kids are smart! They work hard!"

Lincoln Elementary School includes in their mission statement a commitment to celebrate students' hard work, and they take it very seriously. Displays of student

work are careful, intentional, respectful, and celebratory. Visitors can look at student displays and get a sense of the process of the work and the objectives of the projects. Recognizing student achievement in such a way gives our work purpose: as students learn, they enter into the larger conversation of ideas, of possibilities, of discovery. Their work becomes vibrant and meaningful.

Schools with "magical" climates never pass up an opportunity to celebrate what students are doing. They write about it in newsletters, they broadcast it on the in-house television channel, they relay it to parents in the hallways as they pick up their children, they hold Monday morning assemblies to highlight it, and they have "Nights" and "Fairs" throughout the year to showcase student learning.

Valuing Bilingualism and Biculturalism

Beyond all of the district and state standards placed on educators, schools that are responsive to English language learners establish goals of their own. The specific goals of becoming bicultural and bilingual are important for schools to articulate (Christian and Genesee 1998). Apart from the benchmarks in each subject area, educators must strive to develop whole, well-rounded, compassionate, and competent children. We know that bilingualism provides important social and cognitive benefits to children; we want our high schoolers to become bilingual, why not our kindergartners as well? In asserting bilingualism as a schoolwide goal for all children, we give an important boost to children who are already faced with two languages: we take what could easily be a struggle and we turn it into an unequivocal asset for children.

In encouraging children to be powerful members of the larger society, we must simultaneously encourage children to embrace their own cultures and identities (Darder 1991) as we teach them to navigate the larger society. In between those two points, we push children to question, negotiate, challenge, think critically, and imagine new possibilities. Schools must encourage our ethnically and linguistically diverse students to become fully bicultural as well as bilingual.

As schools begin to recognize the linguistic and cultural resources that children and families bring to school with them, and begin to embrace them as capable, enthusiastic learners (whether they seem to be on that particular day or not!), the residue of the ineffectual, indifferent school structure will begin to fade. Rather than complaining about how parents don't read to their children, we will hear how children pass on family stories of war, sacrifice, journeys, and birthdays to their younger siblings. Rather than lament linguistic deficits, we will appreciate families who support their children's language development, regardless of the language. When we hear the third-grade teacher talk about how far behind a child is, we will share how far the child has come, and how the child's language has grown exponentially in his time at the school. Rather than reciting the never-ending list of what kids can't do, teachers and staff will begin to spend their time identifying and capitalizing on the gifts that all children have, and will become collaborative problem solvers. If a school finds the will, it will also, inevitably, find the way.

Living by a Schoolwide Vision

Lincoln is a community committed to learning, kindness, and celebration.

Schools committed to success for their English language learners must develop a comprehensive vision for the purpose and direction of the school (Berman, Minicucci, McLaughlin, et al. 1997). The vision should reflect the values and goals of each member of the school community, from the tiniest kindergartener to the principal, from the music teacher to the parents. It must be broad enough to provide a philosophical framework, and specific enough to provide more direct guidelines for decision making in all aspects of school life. In some schools, this means a mission statement; other schools have further elaborated on an educational philosophy statement in place of or to support a mission statement (Berman, Aburto, Nelson et al. 2000).

Such a vision necessitates collaboration among all invested parties: administrators, students, teachers, families, and community members. A collaborative process ensures that the needs of each constituent group are represented and addressed, and also creates a sense of shared responsibility, where everyone is enriched by and accountable to the school's vision.

The process of creating a vision for a particular school is so important for English language learners because it is a time for the school to commit itself to the particular needs of *all* children. Again, when we make paradigm shifts in order to better serve ELL students, we are more effectively serving all students. There are several essential elements in this kind of a school vision.

A meaningful school vision must reflect a belief that all children are capable of excellence in their academic and personal lives. The school must be a place where children learn to understand the world, as well as act responsibly and productively in it. *All* students must be seen as possessing important gifts; the school commits itself to discovering and nurturing those individual gifts for the benefit of the students themselves, the larger community, and the world.

Secondly, a school community must make a commitment to cultural democracy (Darder 1991) within its walls. In such a place, everyone becomes a learner and everyone a teacher. Rather than a trickle-down, banking approach to education, where knowledge is held by those at the top and deposited into the empty vessels that come through our doors each day, knowledge is created within the constructs and for the purposes of the community. The school becomes a place where teachers and students share in the teaching and learning process, they create and discover knowledge together, on their own terms and for their own important purposes. As educators, we help our children learn about the world, we help them define their own place and purpose in it, and we encourage them to cultivate and express their own unique identities. We commit ourselves to supporting children in their own bicultural and bilingual development.

Successful schools of English language learners also commit themselves to a collaborative schooling process (Darder 1991). It becomes fundamental to such a school to have the full participation of students, teachers, parents, staff, and community. All are seen as indispensable components of each child's education. A school's vision must reflect this belief, and there must be further elaboration, in the vision statement or in the schoolwide plan, for facilitating this collaboration.

All of these concepts are essential in creating a meaningful, dynamic context for English language learners, but I want to stress the importance of spelling these guiding principles out. It is important that a school take the time to articulate its belief system in a public way. Such a document becomes important in the definition of a community: it reminds us and others of who we are, the important job we are here to do, and how we go about doing it. It is also important to focus on these beliefs as the school makes instructional and policy decisions. That way, all decisions large and small, from choosing classroom materials to making hiring decisions, can be evaluated in terms of how well they match up with the guiding principles and values of the school. It's a way to keep our ideals clear and our daily actions relevant.

Effective Leadership

Finally, the importance of a principal who embraces and demonstrates a commitment to meeting the needs of English language learners and their families cannot be overstated. The head administrator sets the tone of the school in no uncertain terms for students, staff, and families. Principals must first provide high expectations for staff and students, and then must provide support for reaching those goals. The attitude of the principal toward primarily staff but also for students is "I know *we* can, how can I support you?"

The principal is the one who steers the ship, keeping the school pointed in the right direction, using the guiding values and principles of the school to keep everyone on course. At the building level, the principal must constantly keep these questions in mind: How is this decision an opportunity to live out our values? How can I partner with families and community in order to better support our students? What are the barriers to staff and student success, and what can I do to minimize them?

At Lincoln Elementary School, Cheryl Petra has established what she calls a "culture of questioning." She says that by framing challenges as questions, rather than as condemnations, you win "ten seconds of innocence." That is, rather than spelling out "problems" that people are likely to get defensive about, posing the issue as a question evokes an entirely different emotional and intellectual response.

And while the staff lives within this "culture of questioning" in their work with students and each other, families and students are also invited into that same "culture." Teachers use that same language with students, in order to provoke the same level of thinking and problem solving.

This kind of questioning is necessarily based on purpose. Wallowing in problems distracts from our purpose; when we are clear about our intentions and goals, it's natural to talk and think about how to proceed in meeting them. At Lincoln, all staff members are clear about their purpose: to foster learning at the highest possible levels, to make a habit of kindness, and to celebrate ourselves and our hard work. They hear the principal repeating this mission constantly, they teach it to their students, and they share it with parents. Purpose and vision are in the air, present in the daily life of the school.

Finally, Cheryl Petra articulates the role of leadership to "inspire" teachers, students, and families. She believes that part of her job is to be "genuinely engaged and excited" about the work being done in her building. She finds ways big and small to celebrate the successes that teachers and students and families are realizing each day. And her attitude is infectious: anyone who walks in to Lincoln takes it on. They can't help but become part of the excitement, part of the purpose, part of the magic happening each day in every classroom.

Key Ideas

* Children, families, staff, and administrators all feel part of a hard-working, productive learning community.

* Children, families, staff, and administrators feel equal ownership of the school.

* All members of the school community feel like success is within their grasp; school is the place where we find tools to achieve our possibilities.

* The linguistic and cultural resources that children and families bring to school with them are integral to their development and success as learners. Schools must identify and capitalize on those strengths.

* All members of the school community are both learners and teachers; all have knowledge to share, and all have much to learn.

* Bilingualism is a valuable goal for all children.

* Biculturalism is critical to the identity development and academic success of English language learners. Students must explore their own identities and the larger society, and become active agents in negotiating the intersection between the two.

* Each school must articulate its commitment to these goals, in the way that is appropriate for that particular community.

* School administrators embrace these goals, and take the lead in steering the community away from deficits and indifference, toward hope and possibility for all students.

3

Developing a Schoolwide Plan

We are what we repeatedly do. Excellence, then, is not an act, but a habit.

—*Aristotle*

Schools and school districts looking for success for their English language learners must have a plan. For too long, schools and districts have tried alternately to ignore the "problem" of ELL students or to blame students and communities for school failure. Educators who are committed to effectively serving their English language learners must create, develop, implement, and continuously reevaluate a comprehensive, research-based plan for academic success.

A Scenario: A School District Transformed

When "Proficiency" Isn't Very Proficient

When Kathy Larson and her colleagues in the Woodburn, Oregon, school district began to look carefully at the success of the English language learners passing through their schools, they knew they had some hard work ahead. The district had for years been using an English immersion model, where students who spoke a home language other than English were placed in all English classrooms and pulled out of class for ESL services.

The students seemed to follow a disturbing pattern: even among students who reached "proficiency" in English (measured as level O on the Language Assessment Scales), students seemed to head directly from the English immersion program into a Title I remedial reading program. And as the students got into middle school and beyond, they began to fall even further behind academically. Kathy Larson, now principal of Heritage Elementary school in the Woodburn district notes, "The kids did what ELLs in English-only programs typically do: they mastered basic English, but they never developed the depth of language that they needed to continue academically."

The Search for a Solution

The district staff began to study what could and should be done to better serve their ELL students. They began with a review of the research relevant to their students: they studied second language acquisition theory, language and literacy development, cultural and linguistic dynamics, anything that would give them insight into the experiences and needs of English language learners. From there, they developed a profile of the school they wanted to become; they identified the elements of a successful program that they wanted to incorporate into their schools.

District teams began to search out and visit schools across five states. As they observed program after program, they narrowed their vision down, until they decided to develop and implement a late exit program. This model would provide children with home language literacy development, with increasing amounts of exposure to English, until students received formal English literacy instruction in fourth and fifth grades. At that point, the model would move to "maintaining" home language, while continuing English language and literacy development.

As the district began to explore the options for their English language students, a groundswell emerged from the community: parents wanted their children to receive support and instruction in their home languages. The community's appeal for a viable biliteracy option for their students became stronger and clearer.

A Vision Becomes Practice

Educators spent an entire year designing the programs that would start with kindergarten cohorts in the district's four elementary schools. A tremendous amount of energy was spent in overcoming the standard obstacles: finding bilingual, bicultural teachers, and finding appropriate curricular materials in Russian and Spanish, the primary languages among the district's ELL population. The district established a resolute recruiting program, which evolved into a "Grow Your Own" program; promising candidates (often former teachers in their native countries) were supported through credentialing programs as they worked in schools. When Russian early literacy materials could not be found, the district worked with publishing companies to translate materials. Kathy Larson notes that the district took on the task of planning and designing the new programs with no outside grant or funding support, "It didn't really cost anything over what we were already spending; it was just a matter of reallocating energy and resources."

With the program well underway, the district took on several outside consultants to provide program evaluation and technical support. One of those consultants stayed on as the district's bilingual coordinator, and provides ongoing technical assistance: "We are always fine-tuning." says Kathy. One remarkable change came as the first cohort was preparing to relegate first language development to "maintenance" and transition into a primarily English program. Parents made clear that they didn't want to simply maintain the first language; they wanted to continue home language development alongside English language and literacy development. Again, the district found a way to support students' bilingualism and biliteracy beyond the elementary years.

The changes undertaken by the district have rippled out to all aspects of the school system, and their effects have created nothing less than a total paradigm shift. Families and communities have become much more integrated into their children's education; responsiveness on the part of the district has created steadfast loyalty within the community. Even native English-speaking families have begun to push for bilingual, biliterate experiences for their children.

Teachers, for their part, have realized that team teaching is the only option for supporting their students effectively; Kathy notes that a grade-level team may have teachers teaching in three different languages, but they are working together to figure out how to teach Oregon state history to their fourth graders. The district has established a heavy emphasis on content knowledge development, using GLAD (Guided Language Acquisition Design) strategies to develop language through content studies.

The Woodburn community has articulated and strengthened its commitment to bilingualism, biliteracy, and the academic success of its children. Through this process, parents and families have become advocates for their students and partners with schools. And the proof is in the pudding: over the last few years, the Woodburn investment has paid off with a steady decrease in dropout rates, as well as steady increases in parent involvement, attendance, and academic achievement.

Common Problems, Uncommon Solutions

Initially, the Woodburn story is pretty typical: English language learners who seem to be moderately successful in an English immersion program, and who then go on to struggle as they reach middle and high school. But from there the story becomes decidedly distinct, and exhilarating in its promise as an example to other school systems seeking to be more efficient with English language learners. The Woodburn example illustrates a number of essential components to creating and implementing an effective systemwide program for English language learners.

Success as the Only Option

The first critical ingredient in the Woodburn transformation was an unwavering commitment to improve the academic opportunities and success of the district's English language learners. Rather than blaming students or families for the students' dismal performance, the school district took responsibility for identifying and remedying the school-based problems. And the comprehensive, sustained investment in finding a successful approach for English language learners reflected the district's belief that success *was* indeed possible. Schools and districts looking for better results among English language learners must first *believe* that academic success is possible (no more lip service!) and then commit themselves fully to achieving it (Carter and Chatfield 1986; Costa and Kallick 1995; Garcia 1994).

Reflecting on the Research

Secondly, the Woodburn district committed itself to finding a *research-based* solution to the academic problems of its English language learners. Teams of teachers and district personnel reviewed the literature relevant to the demographics of the students being served. Each component of the newly evolving plan was guided by and grounded in supporting research. There are any number of publishing company salespeople ready to convince schools that they've developed the magic formula for ELL success, but educators must hold instructional practices and materials accountable to solid research.

Woodburn district staff also allocated a considerable amount of resources toward the effort to design and implement the new plan. Many, many educators worked for a full year before the first kindergarten cohorts began, researching, observing, designing the program, and gathering appropriate staff and curricular materials.

While they would have surely appreciated some instant relief from the bleak situation of their English language learners, educators knew that a madcap leap into a hastily designed program would ultimately mean an ineffective program.

Thinking Outside of the Box

Furthermore, educators approached challenges as problems to be solved rather than barriers to progress. The difficulty in finding educators that were a cultural and linguistic match did not mean that the district settled for unqualified or inappropriate substitutes (often a downfall of well-intentioned programs); rather, they were persistent in finding creative ways to meet their staffing needs. When literacy materials were hard to find, the district invested time and creativity into producing developmentally, culturally, and linguistically appropriate materials.

Schools looking to develop a comprehensive, effective plan for their students must approach the unique difficulties of their situation creatively and resolutely. Rather than wishing that students or families were one way or another, a successful school system assesses its needs and designs accordingly. If a school has multiple languages, that cannot impede the development of an appropriate, effective plan. If a school has a highly transient population, that factor must be acknowledged and accommodated in the planning process. Educators cannot simply throw up their hands and say, "Well if the students . . . if the families would just . . . ." Whatever the unique circumstances and demographics of our schools happen to be, there *is* a solution. Schools that have a *will*, do find a *way*.

I have a Dream that one day I am in College.

Success Takes Time

The Woodburn school district also committed itself to student success over the long haul. Rather than patting themselves on the back and moving on after the first kindergarten cohorts started their year, the district continued to evaluate and reflect on the progress of its program. Outside observers and evaluators continued to provide district educators with feedback and guidance. Schools and educators continued to make improvements to their program in order to meet students' needs and enhance student achievement. And success was continuously measured in terms of student performance on academic assessments. Currently, eight years into this process of transformation, ELL students as a collective group in high school have met state and federal standards for English Language Arts (from the Woodburn School District website 2004).

Schools looking to improve performance among English language learners must be willing to invest in a long-term plan. There is no short-circuiting the time necessary to develop the depth and breadth of language necessary for long-term academic success. It's critical that schools develop ways to measure student growth toward language and literacy goals, even though achievement of those goals may still be far off. If we've based our program on solid time-tested theory and strategies for language and literacy development and have designed our programs accordingly, students *will* meet the goals we've set for them if we give them the time and support to do so. Even though programs will constantly be revising and fine-tuning, staying the course with a thoughtful, well-designed program will allow students to realize the positive outcomes that we planned so carefully for.

If You Are an Island

At this point it is important to recognize that in order to make long-term meaningful changes for English language learners, there must be some institutional support. That is, there may very well be a few classrooms or one school or even a few schools that are attempting to create a more successful experience for ELLs, but that are limited by the next level of policies. For example, it's difficult for several schools in one area of town to individually meet the needs of students from eight or ten language groups. Creative thinking at the district level, however, might mean some different decisions about services and staffing in order to establish greater intentionality at each school. Opting to house a dual language program at one school, for example, would likely attract most of that language group's students to a well-designed bilingual program.

The point is that real change for ELLs must be systematic; it must be incorporated into the fabric of the larger school district. Anything else is simply an afterthought, and undermines the efforts of individual educators or even schools who may be trying to improve their practice and their students' achievement. It is critical for educators to network and collaborate; building a collective political will among students, educators, and families may be the first step in making meaningful policy changes at higher levels, in order to impact academic performance at the local level.

A Recipe for Success

School systems looking to develop a more effective plan for the academic success of English language learners need, therefore, to base their efforts on four preliminary components.

Data

Schools must have extensive data on student performance. It's not enough to know that students are "failing." What skills are they lacking? What skills do they have? What is the school doing right? What are the areas that schools needs to improve on in order to improve overall achievement? Schools also need information about students. Who are the students in the school? What kind of educational, cultural, and linguistic backgrounds do they have? What do cultural norms say about the roles of school and home? About academic expectations?

Research

Schools need to spend time reviewing research that pertains to their particular academic, cultural, and linguistic needs. What are the best instructional practices for the areas that students are weak in? What does research say about school design for high-poverty schools or high-ELL schools? What does the research say about the relationship between home and school in high-ELL schools? What strategies and approaches have been successful with populations similar to the population at your school? Before we invest resources, staff time, and students' one shot at an education, we've got to know *what* has worked and *how* it's worked.

Successful Models

Once we've examined needs and relevant research, it's important to see what successful programs actually look like in practice. Observing schools that have met the needs of similar populations will give tremendous insight into the creation of a new program. While each school is certainly unique, connecting with other educators who have gone through the same process gives us valuable information about how to proceed.

Goals for Students

It's interesting to note how the goals for students in the Woodburn district shifted over time (they are currently in their eighth year after restructuring). Initially, the district was simply interested in improving students' performance in English, so that they could access the academic curriculum more effectively. But as time went on, the reality of what children were capable of doing, parent expectations, and the long-term possibilities for language acquisition converged to expand the academic and linguistic goals for students. When the first cohort of kindergartners reached middle school, it was clear that they didn't need to abandon their first language development; they were capable of continuing first and second language development simultaneously and successfully. Consequently, a smaller movement within the district that had always advocated a dual immersion approach became a tidal wave; suddenly, bilingualism and biliteracy became realistic, attainable, even necessary goals for all children. As a plan for English language learners is created, it's important to be clear about what the goals are. Do we want them to transition to English as quickly as possible, even if that transition may be shallow and limited? Do we want to maintain first language literacy for the purpose of facilitating English language development? Do we want children to become bilingual and biliterate, fully competent and capable in two languages?

What Are the Options?

At this point, it's important to provide an overview of the different models that exist to serve English language learners. The model a school adopts will correspond with the data collected about its students, the research relating to the students, and the specific academic and linguistic goals for students. Regardless of the model adopted (and not having a model is its own default model), the practices and strategies outlined in the rest of this book are effective for the language and literacy development of all children.

This discussion of instructional models may contribute to the larger discussion in your school or district about how to best serve English language learners.

Early-Exit and Late-Exit Transitional Programs

The goal of these programs is to bring children to English proficiency as quickly as possible. These programs recognize the utility of first language development in developing both content knowledge and second language literacy. The first language is a medium for instruction until the second language has developed enough to support content instruction in the second language (English). At that point, literacy and content skills transfer to support full instruction in English. In an early-exit program, children are transitioned into English within two or three years. A late-exit program generally begins transitioning into English-only toward the end of elementary school (Faltis and Hudelson 1998).

Pullout ESL Services

With this model, students are placed in all-English classrooms and are pulled out of class for varying lengths of time for specialized instruction (Peregoy and Boyle 2001). This specialized instruction may or may not utilize the student's first language. ESL services also vary widely in the level to which they are connected to regular classroom instruction, and in whether they are content-based or based purely in the acquisition of discrete literacy concepts. This is generally considered a remedial service for English language learners, and students that transition out of these programs consistently demonstrate low levels of language proficiency and academic achievement (Thomas and Collier 2002).

English Immersion, or Sink-or-Swim

This model places English language learners into an all-English classroom with little or no additional support. This is the regular classroom setting from which students are occasionally pulled out for ESL services. English language learners are expected to "fend for themselves" (Samway and McKeon 1999), and teachers generally make no special instructional modifications to develop language or content proficiency beyond the regular instruction provided for all students.

Structured Immersion

In this model, the medium of instruction is generally English. Teachers, however, are generally bilingual, and support their students' use of the first language in order to negotiate meaning in English (Samway and McKeon 1999). The goal of this kind of a program is strictly English proficiency, with no attempt to either maintain or develop the second language.

Sheltered English, SDAIE (Specially Designed Academic Instruction in English), or GLAD (Guided Language Acquisition Design)

These approaches generally share the goal of developing content knowledge using instructional methods that are designed to be comprehensible to English language learners (Peregoy and Boyle 2001). The language acquisition goal is centered strictly on English acquisition, with no provision for first language maintenance. Hands-on, experiential learning, thematic units, and focused development of academic language and vocabulary are often components of this kind of instruction. Thomas and Collier (2002) note in their five-year study of bilingual models and student achievement that even the highest-quality ESL content programs "close [only] about half of the total achievement gap."

Two-Way Immersion or Dual Language Immersion

This model promotes as its goal bilingualism and biliteracy for native English speakers and for native speakers of the target language (Spanish, for example). Classes are made up of equal numbers of native English speakers and native speakers of the target language, allowing all children to be both teachers and learners of a language. Programs are either 90:10 or 50:50. In a 90:10 model, kindergarteners spend 90 percent of their time devoted to language and literacy development in the target language, with 10 percent of their day devoted to oral English language development. The percentages continue to converge each year, until third or fourth grade, when the day is divided equally between languages. It is at this time that formal literacy instruction in English also begins. In a 50:50 model, children are either developing literacy simultaneously in both languages beginning in kindergarten, or they are receiving native language literacy instruction first, to which they later add literacy in the second language. Within either of these models, a dual language immersion program emphasizes language acquisition and development through content study, and works toward full biliteracy for all children.

In a number of long-term studies, two-way immersion programs have produced significant academic results for both native English speakers and English language learners (Christian 1994; Lindholm 1990; Lindholm and Gavlek 1994; Lindholm-Leary and Borsato 2001; Peregoy 1991; Peregoy and Boyle 1990; Thomas and Collier 2002). In fact, in Thomas and Collier's (2002) five-year study, native

Spanish speakers in a 90:10 two-way immersion program equaled or outperformed native Spanish speakers in other models, and native English speakers educated in a 90:10 two-way immersion program equaled or outperformed native English speakers educated in English-only classrooms. They note that the strongest predictor for academic success in English is the amount of formal schooling in the first language. The more effective the formal academic instruction in the home language, the greater the level of eventual transfer of language and concept proficiency to English (Cummins 1979).

Key Ideas

* Schools committed to the academic success of English language learners must develop and implement a comprehensive plan for language and academic achievement.

* A schoolwide plan must be long term, research-based, and grounded in educators' high expectations for student success.

* A schoolwide planning process should begin with collecting of community-specific data, which is followed by a review of research, observation of successful programs, and an articulation of academic and linguistic goals for students.

* There are a number of program models available to serve English language learners that vary widely in terms of instructional strategies, program structure, and long-term success with English language learners.

* Two-way immersion programs or dual language immersion programs have demonstrated long-term success in producing high levels of language proficiency and academic achievement.

Staffing and Staff Development

The ultimate measure of a man is not where he stands in moments of comfort, but where he stands at times of challenge and controversy.

—*Martin Luther King Jr.*

S chools are made up of people. In any school looking to improve instruction and achievement among its students, investments in human resources are the most critical. In schools serving English language learners, it is all the more essential that the staff of a school be specially tailored and trained to meet the needs of students.

A Scenario: Matching Up Challenges and Solutions

Identifying Needs, Developing Resources

The Bilingual Preschool Through Third Grade (BP–3) Teacher Education Program is a federally funded grant, administered through Pacific Oaks College Northwest in Seattle, Washington. The program was created by a group of teacher-educators at the college who recognized two parallel trends in the education of children of color and English language learners: first, that there were not enough certificated educators from those two communities who had the credentials to teach in the public school settings where the students were. So often, discussions in public schools around how to best serve bilingual and bicultural children end with "We can't have that kind of a program, we don't have the staff for it" or "And where are we going to find that many certificated bilingual teachers?"

Secondly, there were many capable, experienced individuals from within those communities who were talented, dedicated teachers, lacking only a formal credential. There were many people working around Washington and Oregon who had been educators in their home countries, many had years of experience working in Head Start programs, and many worked in preschool or private school settings where they had developed an extensive knowledge of child development and the particular needs of children of color and English language learners. All they lacked were the material resources to matriculate and complete a credentialing program.

The BP–3 grant sought to match up abilities with an existing need. The program began in the spring of 2002 and provided tuition and resource support for thirty-two teacher-candidates. The candidates were a mix of dominant Spanish-speakers, balanced bilinguals, and dominant English-speakers. Participants were African American, Latino, and European American. The program was designed according to a two-way dual immersion model; that is, half of the courses were presented in English and half in Spanish, and students from each language group were supported in developing their own bilingualism, biliteracy, and biculturalism. The program was designed to meet whatever academic needs the candidates had: they were supported in their own literacy development as they learned theory and best practices relating to English language learners. The program is currently in its third and final year (with plans to create and support another cohort in the future), and has been a remarkable success. Thirty-two new teachers, grounded in relevant theory and best practices, themselves, bilingual, biliterate, and bicultural, are ready to take on the challenges and joys of public school teaching!

Training That Counts

An essential element of the BP–3 program, in fact, an essential part of all teacher training through Pacific Oaks College, is a class called "Social and Political Contexts of Human Development." While this class teaches about the many societal influences on human development, it is primarily designed to encourage teacher-candidates to examine their own personal place within that larger context. Issues of power, privilege, oppression, bias, and inequality are discussed, particularly in terms of their effects on children and the educational system. This is a class where the hard questions come up and don't go away. It is an integral part of teacher training at Pacific Oaks, because of the belief that each of us approach the outside world grounded in a complex web, the intersection of all of these societal influences with our own personal life experiences. When we enter our classroom each day, we bring with us the sum total of all of our experiences, good, bad, and in between. We see the world through the lenses of our own lives, shaped as they have been—and all of our lives have been—by the forces of racism, classism, sexism, and other manifestations of power and oppression. This class at Pacific Oaks is not about assigning blame or proclaiming righteousness; its purpose is to examine the ways that the social and political contexts of our larger society play out within the art-covered walls of our own classrooms.

Staffing: Two Levels of Preparation

There are two important components of a comprehensive plan to create a staff of educators ready and able to work successfully with English language learners: first, the staff must, as much as possible, reflect the community that it serves. Staffing decisions reflect each school's commitment to the success of English language learners. Even though schools may have to negotiate with district hiring policies or even union pressures, it's critical that schools find the right staff for their students. Secondly, it is crucial that staff who work with English language learners in any capacity be trained in the social, political, linguistic, and cultural dynamics of education. This critical examination of larger societal influences on children's education will provide a more meaningful and transformative experience for all children, but for English language learners, it is an indispensable part of preparing to be their teachers.

Reflecting the Cultural and Linguistic Diversity of Students

There are many reasons why it is important to have a staff that reflects the demographics of a given school. First and foremost, it is crucial for children to have someone that they are able to communicate with freely and relate to culturally. Regardless of the language goals for children in a particular school, it is important for them to have someone who can support them socially, emotionally, and academically. When little Carla is sobbing in the cafeteria before school, it's not the time to insist that she use her English; it is time to hear and understand what is happening to her so that we can meet her needs and get her ready for learning.

Again, even if our language goals for children are only focused on English language development, it is important to have staff that can support children academically as well. A staffing plan for a school will likely reflect the needs of the program they have adopted to serve English language learners (i.e., more bilingual staff in a dual language program, etc.) but even in an all-English academic setting, it is necessary to have staff from the same culture and language groups as the students. This is because bilingual, bicultural staff members can provide the critical link for children learning to negotiate the larger, mainstream culture as it intersects with their own lives. Bicultural educators have experienced the process of navigating two cultures and two languages; they are grounded in the linguistic and cultural dynamics of the community, and they also understand the "codes of power," that is, how one is required to act and speak in order to access power in this society. Bilingual educators are often more able to teach children of color and English language learners the "rules of the game," as well as ways of living and thinking that minimize the impact of bias on children's lives (Darder 1991).

Bilingual, bicultural educators can contribute significantly to the staff's knowledge of and ability to serve groups of children. These staff members can educate others around language and culture issues, can advise about particular situations with students, can be called upon to mediate student–student or student–teacher conflicts, and can also be a critical point of connection between schools and families. Consider this example: Adriana was a new kindergartner, having spent two years in the school's Head Start program. She had never talked much during her years in Head Start, and her teachers sensed a delay in her skill development. They also complained that she was absent for long periods of time, during which her family sent her to Mexico to be with grandparents. On the first week of school with her bilingual teacher, the teacher noted significant impairments in the child's Spanish language skills; she was extremely difficult to understand in Spanish. The teacher was able to work with the speech therapist in order to provide specialized speech services for the child, and was able to translate concepts in speech development and support for the parents. Additionally, there was finally some conclusive information about what the child knew and didn't know, because there was a teacher who could assess her accurately. The teacher was also able to suggest that rather than her absences being problematic, a good dose of affectionate Spanish immersion in her early years was probably just what the child needed.

Taking Opportunities, Creating New Ones

Ideally, we would have school staffs that reflected perfectly the population of the student body. Keep in mind that it is important to take advantage of the opportunities that *do* exist, while simultaneously striving to create new opportunities. There are many places that bilingual staff can fit into a school: as certificated teachers, as paraeducators, even in the office. What a difference it makes for second language families to walk into a school and find someone in the office that they can communicate with. If that is the best you can offer your students and families at the moment, do it. As schools hire new staff members in any capacity, that is the time to think about how to create a staff that is most relevant to English language learners. Is there a bilingual applicant? Is there someone who has experience with English language learners? Is there someone who demonstrates a commitment to bilingualism and biculturalism? That is the time to express clearly the values that a school has come to embrace and to look for a good match.

Additionally, schools committed to better serving their English language learners need to seek out resources for their schools. Frequently, a staff will have one or more outstanding bilingual paraeducators who function in many of the same capacities as regular classroom teachers. Find ways to encourage those people in becoming certificated teachers. Districts often have programs to support continuing education, grants are available for tuition support, even offering the scheduling flexibility to allow that person to continue to work as they pursue their studies can make the difference. These ideas are also applicable for parents or other community volunteers. There are many immigrants to this country who were educators in their own countries, but do not have the credentials that transfer. For those, and for any other community members who demonstrate an ability and willingness to educate children, encourage and actively support them in their journey to become certificated teachers (Darder 1991). The BP–3 program is a significant example of an effort to develop the kinds of teachers that English language learners need.

An Unnecessary Paradox: Teacher Needs Versus Student Needs

At this point, a caveat for those of you shifting uncomfortably in your seat. This is the place where a lot of teacher support for bilingual, bicultural education breaks down. Rather than face the possibility that others might be better equipped to serve English language learners, we begin to dream up reasons why it couldn't really work at our school, or why our kids don't need it, or some other reasons why, when push comes to shove, we won't do it. First, we remind ourselves of our purpose: we are here to guide and challenge children to be the best that they can be. Education, ultimately, is not about teachers, it is about learners. While we sometimes get very adept at disguising our own fears and needs by putting them in student terms, we need to gently remind ourselves and each other that we must make decisions based on what is best for our students.

Secondly, there is room for us all. Each of us has strengths that children need, and not one of us is an expert in everything. Our students need the best of each of us. In thinking about transforming education to effectively serve English language learners, we must begin to think about restructuring both our educational system and our schools. Remember, we are talking about developing *bi*lingual, *bi*cultural, intellectual, confident children. They need a little (actually a lot!) of what each of us has to offer. All of our students, English language learners or not, also need us to model for them the process of working together and negotiating difference, conflict, and power. When teachers from the dominant culture and bicultural/bilingual teachers collaborate to provide a meaningful educational experience for students, we offer them a powerful message of hope and possibility (Darder 1991).

Taking Risks

Beyond ethnic, class, or linguistic considerations, the most important element in becoming an effective educator of English language learners is a profound dedication to transformative, liberatory education for students, and a deep commitment to professional growth as their teachers. Having a bilingual, bicultural staff member or two does not guarantee that your school is providing a culturally relevant education for children; it's possible to have individuals from the same community as students who can actually work against a liberatory experience for those students. Similarly, it is necessary to guard against tokenism, having one person who makes a school feel like it's done its work in becoming relevant to a particular community, at the expense of a broad, comprehensive effort to create a responsive environment. It also doesn't count if there are bicultural, bilingual staff in a school if their participation in school matters is limited or silenced. At the same time, there are many mainstream, European

American teachers who have committed themselves to the process of critical reflection, and have challenged themselves to ask the hard questions and find some honest answers. The next section of this chapter addresses the ways that staff can begin to enhance their abilities to work effectively with English language learners.

Staff Development

Effective and relevant staff development is crucial for schools and teachers seeking to better serve English language learners. There are particular areas of training and development that are critical for schools and educators to address if they are to become more responsive to students learning English. As I continue to try to demonstrate throughout this book, an investment in this specialized training will benefit not just English language learners, but all of our students.

Grounding Our Practice in Theory

First, it is important that teachers be grounded in solid theory relating to second language acquisition, language development, and early literacy development. These theories will not be detailed in great depth here; rather, a list of references is included for your study. The point to be made here is that it is essential that anyone who works with English language learners has a basic understanding of the cognitive and linguistic processes that those children are experiencing. And as learning, literacy, and language development (first and second) are developmental processes, it is important that educators at all levels be familiar with these theories, so as to better understand the performance of their students.

For example, if we understand Cummins' (1981) dual iceberg theory, which states that children build new language learning on the foundation of prior language knowledge (see Figure 11–1 for a graphic of this concept), then we know we can't start from scratch with an eighth grader who has just entered the country. The student probably has an extensive understanding of content and literacy concepts in her first language, and we can focus our energies on mining that knowledge and putting it to work for us in building new concepts and new language skills. If we have a good grasp of Cambourne's (1988) work about conditions of learning, we will understand why a balanced literacy approach is essential for early English language learners. We will be able to provide those conditions of optimum learning through our curriculum, and can effectively evaluate what we are offering our students in order to identify gaps (see Chapter 9 for a more detailed explanation of Cambourne's conditions for learning).

Turning Theory into Action

It is important to spend significant time translating that theory and research into best classroom practices for English language learners. What's most critical here is establishing a *process* for learning and incorporating best practices into your classroom repertoire. You probably won't be able to read through this book once and change your practice effectively. Rather, meaningful change in classroom practices requires a sustained, focused, collaborative process that allows teachers to learn, reflect on, and analyze their work with children. A structure for staff collaboration is an important place to start this process of understanding and integrating best practices. Grounded in theory, educators can talk together about best practices: share what they have tried, what they're thinking about, and encourage each other in attempting new strategies. But it is important not to just talk; educators know that learners learn best by doing.

Joyce and Showers (1988) found that teachers need five components in order to make meaningful change in their classroom practice: theory, modeling, guided practice, feedback, and peer coaching (sounds a lot like what we try to offer our students!). Excluding any of these steps effectively limits the scope and permanence of change in a teacher's practice. While inservices, guest speakers, book discussions, or other formats might be effective ways to learn new theory, teachers need a more comprehensive approach if they are to effectively incorporate new ideas.

It is important to develop a risk-free (that means *not* open for evaluation!) mechanism within a school to allow teachers to do more active learning; much of this work can be guided and undertaken by teachers themselves. Together, on a regular basis, teachers can work through the theory around their students' needs. Working collaboratively toward improving practice, teachers can demonstrate lessons for each other in classrooms, they can provide flexibility for each other so that colleagues can practice new strategies with smaller groups, and they can observe each other as they try out new strategies with children in order to engage in constructive dialogue (as opposed to constructive criticism). The subsequent element of this ongoing action-reflection cycle is a follow-up dialogue about how strategies are evolving and meeting students' needs and what can be done to improve further.

Teachers as Resources

Each teacher possesses unique skills and insights; as teachers develop particular strengths, schools should recognize and utilize those teachers as models in those areas. It's important to recognize your own expertise: once you have some good theory under your belt, you can combine that with your intimate knowledge of your students and their needs. Of course, if your building is lucky enough to have some-one whose job it is to support schoolwide instruction (instructional facilitator, liter-acy coach, they have all kinds of names), certainly utilize that person as much as possible. But it is important to begin to trust yourself as an educator, and to begin to enter into the critical, collaborative dialogue with other educators about what the theories and best practices look like in other classrooms.

Language and Culture Are Inseparable

Beyond purely academic achievement, it is urgent, if we are to become effective with English language learners, that we educate ourselves in the larger issues that sur-round bilingual and bicultural education. On a basic level, it is important for teach-ers and entire staffs to become familiar with the relationships between language, culture, identity, and cognition. We cannot hope to effectively educate English lan-guage learners if we continue to view their academic experiences as purely language-driven. Language is an essential part of culture and identity. When we deny chil-dren's first languages, we deny their very wholeness as human beings. When we speak as if we have to "start from scratch" when they come into our classrooms, we deny families and communities as sources of culture, knowledge, and wisdom.

We must master ways of integrating home cultures into our children's education. When we study the elements of story, invite parents in to tell stories, or even ask children to retell stories they've heard a lot around their families. When we study the life cycle, invite old and young and even in-between family members in to talk about their experiences. Have children reflect on the differences between their lives and those of parents, grandparents, even older brothers or sisters. We make our own lives easier by building on what children already know and the strengths that they have already developed, and we simultaneously provide children with that sense of belonging and competence that they must have in order to truly learn.

Grounding Our Philosophy in Theory

Meaningful change usually doesn't happen as the result of a mandate. Schools and teachers must develop a belief system based on the available research. It is well worth the investment of time and resources for schools or groups of teachers to spend time reviewing and discussing the relevant research. If teachers don't under-stand the social and political consequences of home language loss, they won't feel the urgency to support home language development (Handscombe 1989). If teach-ers have a good sense of the value of their students developing a strong bicultural identity, they will necessarily begin to reflect that in their practice (Cummins 1981,

1986, 1994; Darder 1991). If educators understand the cognitive benefits of being bilingual, they will begin to advocate in all sorts of big and small ways for their students (Baker 1995). As educators of English language learners, it is essential to have a sense of *why* we do this important work, before we can really master *how* it's done.

Rethinking Roles, Remodeling Structures

And while there is much to learn about our students, it is critical that educators also begin to look at themselves. When it comes to the social and political issues that impact our students' education, teachers have a tendency to remove themselves from the equation. "It's not about politics," they say, "it's about learning English." It is important that educators examine the dynamics of power within their own classrooms and schools. These days, the majority of teachers are still white, middle-class women, and ever-growing numbers of students are English language learners, students of color, or students who live in poverty. Teachers have a lot of power in a classroom or school setting, and unless this is acknowledged and managed they risk using it to re-create, however unwillingly, the pervasive inequality of the larger society and to disempower our students (Giroux 1981, 1983; Gramsci 1971).

Teachers may feel like they are just being themselves, or they are just doing things the way everybody does them. We do need to be ourselves, but we also need to be careful that we are not giving our children the message, subtly or overtly, that our values are really the only ones that matter, or that our way of living is what students should aspire to. Like fish in water, it is oftentimes difficult for middle-class European Americans to separate out their own culture, in order to identify how it is different from other cultures.

There are many resources that shed light on cultural differences, and should be used by educators working to create an affirming context for English language learners. Peggy MacIntosh (1988) has done an in-depth review of "white privilege," and gives excellent insight into the differences in experience between white Americans and more marginalized groups. She writes, "My schooling followed the pattern my colleague Elizabeth Minnich has pointed out: whites are taught to think of their lives as morally neutral, normative, and average, and also ideal, so that when we work to benefit others, this is seen as work which will allow 'them' to be more like 'us.'" Ruby Payne (2001) has done extensive research into what she terms the *culture of poverty,* and illuminates the tremendous differences between middle-class norms and those of people living in poverty. Often, what educators perceive to be the values and beliefs that all people do or should live by conflict with the values and beliefs that others hold.

There is no time to be wasted feeling guilty or feeling righteous; there are children who need us. All educators need to do this important work, for ourselves and for our students. When we begin to examine the ways that power and oppression are played out within our classrooms and schools, we will have taken the first step in creating a more just, more meaningful, and most important, more successful environment for all of our children, English language learners included.

Teachers Becoming Learners

Finally, it's essential that all those who work with English language learners become culture and language learners themselves. For those educators who are learning a second or third language, use it! And for those who are English speakers only, take some classes! Regardless of the level of proficiency you attain, you will be an asset to your students. Ideally, you will achieve nativelike fluency and will become an important link for families and students in navigating their school experience, and advocating for or providing native language support. And even if you can't get it straight which phrase means "good morning" and which means "good night," you will have taught your students, families, and colleagues some very important lessons, and you'll learn a few yourself.

When you take the risk and attempt another language, you put yourself on more of an even plane with your English language learners and their families. You may even need to employ their expertise in your own learning. That's a powerful message, and a huge step in shifting power in a classroom or school. You model lifelong learning, and you remind everyone that each of us has strengths to share and more to learn. There is also no better way to understand the process of learning a second language, as your students are doing, than to try it out. When you experience the frustration, the I'm-not-in-control-of-everything-anymore feeling, the blank stares of people who have no idea what you're talking about, and then when your heart leaps because you've actually communicated with someone, you develop an empathy with your students that is irreplaceable, and will necessarily begin to be reflected in the experience you provide your students.

Finding the Right Path

There is much, much work to be done, and although we can look to some guiding principles about staffing issues and staff development there are no hard- and fast-rules. It will be your job to determine what makes sense for your unique setting, and then to take the plunge!

Key Ideas

∗ As much as possible, school staff should reflect the cultural and linguistic backgrounds of its students.

∗ ELL educators must be trained in the social, political, linguistic, and cultural dynamics relevant to the students that they serve.

∗ As schools take on new staff in any capacity, they should work toward a bilingual, bicultural staff.

∗ Schools and school systems should develop mechanisms for recruiting and training promising paraeducators, parents, and community members to become certificated teachers.

∗ English language learners need educators of any background who maintain a deep commitment to a liberatory educational experience for those students, and a commitment to ongoing critical reflection and professional growth.

∗ Educators of ELLs need a solid understanding of second language acquisition, language, and literacy development, and must then translate that theoretical knowledge into classroom practice.

∗ Those who work with ELLs in any capacity must explore the relationships among language, culture, identity, and cognitive development.

∗ School staffs must establish a research-based system of beliefs for educating English language learners.

∗ All educators who work with ELLs should become culture/language learners as well.

5

School Resources

In creating, the only hard thing is to begin: a grass blade's no easier to make than an oak.   —*James Russell Lowell*

A Scenario: A Library at the Center of a Community

The school library at Webster Elementary School in west Long Beach, California, is much more than a place to check out books. There certainly are books to check out: thousands of titles, including over two thousand Spanish titles of all genres and many others in Samoan, the two dominant languages of the school besides English. But librarian Melody Hubbard has invested time, energy, and enthusiasm to create a library that offers more than books. She wants the library to be a place where kids fall in love with books and with reading itself. She is passionate about helping students discover the joy and power of reading. Even though the fifth graders roll their eyes a bit when she starts in on another sermon about the difference reading can make in their lives, they know she lectures out of love and stellar expectations for each one of them. "When you're born, you can't choose your family or your neighborhood, but if you are a reader, you can decide your own future," she tells them.

Melody is dedicated to helping children develop a relationship with books. She takes the time to know children as individuals and doesn't rest until she helps kids discover the kinds of books that are right for them. During library time, Melody teaches students the typical skills of navigating the library, accessing books, and finding information on the computer. But the library is also a continuation of the literacy and language development that happens in the regular classroom, and Melody provides endless literature-based activities for the students to improve their vocabularies and language skills. She recently sponsored a schoolwide "Synonyms for *Said*" contest, in which she had students mine the books they were reading for more interesting synonyms for the word *said*. Children may spend their library time reciting poetry, researching a topic of interest, performing a selection for reader's theatre, or simply reading favorite books.

And the library is never empty. Children are able to come in before school, after school, even during lunch if there is not a class scheduled. Melody gives these kids even more individual attention, calling many of them "future librarians of America," teaching them as much as they want to learn, and appreciating them for their unique talents. Often kids bring back their books before their regularly scheduled library time because they can't wait to get a new one.

The library is also a hub for parents and community. Melody has transformed one parent's request to borrow books into a lending program with over one hundred parents who borrow books on a regular basis. Melody encourages parents to read in their native language, helps them find books that their children will be interested in (or a cookbook that the parent might be interested in!), and talks to them about developing language and literacy with their children. "I talk to them as another parent; I tell them things that I tried when my kids were little, and listen to them as they talk about their own kids," she says. Parents are regular visitors to the library before and after school; they will often bring in their younger children and spend time reading and talking over books together. Melody notes that many parents who were initially intimidated by the school are now regular visitors to the library. Many of them have even become featured readers during the schools yearly "Read Across America" celebration.

The Webster school library is so much more than just a library. It is a place for people to gather, a place for people to explore their own interests and passions, a place for children and adults alike to savor the joy of learning together.

Appraising the Resources of Your School

There are many ways that a school can be creative with its resources, whether they are meager or abundant, in order to maximize effectiveness with English language learners. It's important to begin first by taking good stock of all of the resources available in the school. Whether you feel like there are lots of resources or not enough, materials that are organized around a specific purpose become exponentially more valuable. Further, once a school begins to take inventory of what resources are available, staff can begin to identify what the real material needs are and how to go about meeting them.

Books

School libraries. ✳ The previous scenario from Webster Elementary School is a wonderful example of how a school library can become an integral part of a vibrant school learning community, especially for English language learners and their families. The school library presents great opportunities to become a hub for student and community learning; investing creatively in that opportunity is a powerful way to demonstrate a school's commitment to literacy and learning as core values. A well-designed and well-managed library can be a dynamic force in cultivating powerful readers (Applebee, Langer, and Mullis 1988).

There are three components of the school library that can be put to work for the enhanced learning of English language learners: the books, the space, and the librarian. First, it is important that the library be filled with an extensive collection of high-quality reading materials from all genres. Fiction, nonfiction, magazines, newspapers, poetry, reference books, and even comic books—a good library should have it all. The breadth of books available in the library cannot be underestimated. There has been a great deal of research (Anderson, Wilson, and Fielding 1988; Cunningham and Stanovich 1998; Elley 1992; Krashen 1993; Neuman 1999; Neuman and Celano 2001) relating the quantity of reading materials available to students to the development of vocabulary, literacy skills, and love of reading. These researchers point out the correlation between access to an extensive and varied source of reading materials and literacy development. It is critical that schools have a wide variety of books available to students at all times. This need becomes even more amplified for groups of students who tend to lag behind in literacy performance; schools with English language learners or students living in poverty need to be particularly deliberate about establishing an extensive library collection. Neuman (1999) and Elley (1998) describe "book floods," the inundating of learning environments with large numbers of reading materials, as having a remarkable impact on children's language and literacy development, particularly in areas where access to reading materials had traditionally been limited.

Secondly, why not rethink the use of the physical library space in order to maximize its effectiveness for English language learners and their families? Could the library be available to students and families before school? After school? Are there other people in the school (parents?) who could facilitate library use at these other

times? In many schools, children arrive at the school campus well before the day begins. Rather than having these children out in the rain, wandering aimlessly through the hall, or sitting idly in the cafeteria, could they be invited into the library for some quiet, self-selected reading? Could older students be paired up to read with younger students before school, giving them both a relaxing way to practice reading? Some schools offer parents the opportunity to check out books themselves from the school library, further encouraging before or after school visits by children and their families.

Finally, the role of the librarian cannot be overstated. Librarians have a special role fostering an interest in and a joy for reading. As we witnessed in the example at the beginning of this chapter, the librarian at Webster played a key role in promoting books and reading among students and their families. She made the library a place that people loved to go to, and she helped them connect to books and resources that enriched their lives. This is the essence of teaching and learning; our job as educators is to create a space and an opportunity for children to discover the power that reading and knowledge can have in their lives. A skilled, passionate, and dedicated librarian can allow children to experience that magnificence every day when they come to the library.

Classroom libraries ✳ No matter how well stocked a school library is, there is no substitute for an extensive classroom library as well. All children, and particularly English language learners, need to have constant, uninterrupted access to interesting, accessible, and familiar texts. Classroom libraries, like school libraries, should have a wide variety of texts: fiction, nonfiction, magazines, poems, songbooks, shared read-

ings (chants and poems), big books, almanacs, dictionaries, and so on (Cullinan 2000; Dreher 1998; Fielding, Wilson, and Anderson 1989). Texts should be as varied as the children's reading levels; a kindergarten classroom would, for example, need to have a variety of easy, patterned texts, alphabet books, shared reading poems and chants, counting books, and so on, along with all of the other interesting reading choices. A second-grade classroom would likely have some easier, predictable, but still age-appropriate texts for emerging readers, and would also contain a range of picture books, chapter books, lots of nonfiction text, reading-to-learn texts, and so on.

It makes sense to have some classroom library books leveled according to independent reading level, so that all children can find books that are "just right" for them. It's not feasible or even sensible to level an entire classroom book collection, but having maybe a quarter or a third of the total books leveled allows children to always find something right for them. Oftentimes, as we begin to level books, we also notice a gap in our collections: we may be missing books at the very early levels, for example, and we then know that we need to collect books from that particular level.

The beauty of a rich classroom library is that children begin to have relationships with particular books. When particular titles are always available, children will go back to them over and over, and will at the very least, come to love and "own" those titles; ideally, kids who spend time with books they love will, with each rereading, push themselves a little further with the text. An example is the kindergartner who "read" *One Fish, Two Fish, Red Fish, Blue Fish*, over and over, day in and day out. What really attracted her to the book were the whimsical illustrations, and the fact that the book had been read to her several times before. As her letter–sound knowledge and her sight-word knowledge increased, she was eventually able to begin to identify certain words in the text, and was able to begin to navigate the actual printed words on the page, using her newly developing base of sight words to anchor herself in the text. Fast forward six weeks, and you've got a child who can read an entire book independently; and most important, she *loves* to read it. If the teacher had had to return that book to the library after a week or so, that bond between child and book might never have developed.

The same is true for books that are read aloud in a classroom; it is essential that those titles be available to children at all times. Even children who cannot read a book that has been read to them independently enjoy pulling those books out and retelling the story, acting out the parts, taking on the role of the characters, and so on. Oftentimes, children will push themselves to work on a book that is beyond their independent reading level, because of their interest in it and their familiarity with it. Again, a good classroom library facilitates a loving relationship between children and books.

This is not to say that every classroom must contain every imaginable title. All teachers will still look to school libraries, public libraries, and book rooms to supplement classroom reading stocks. But it is essential for all students, particularly those who are learning English as a second language, to have a core collection of appropriate, fun, and interesting reading materials available at all times (Bissett 1969; Gutherie, Schafer, Vaon Secker, and Alban 2000; Morrow and Gambrell 2000).

Book rooms ✳ A well-stocked book room is another way to get appropriate books into the hands of students. Book rooms generally have a large stash of texts, organized by reading level, genre, or theme. Having sets of books allows teachers to check out titles appropriate for small, guided reading groups. These books are available to teachers on a check-out basis for classroom use. While the format and management systems of book rooms vary, the purpose does not: to provide classroom teachers with another resource for reading materials, particularly leveled materials that can be matched appropriately with readers (Mace 1997; Routman 1991).

At Lister Elementary in Tacoma, Washington, the book room is a tiny closet off the main hallway, but it is filled with basket after basket of leveled reading books (using the Fountas and Pinnell leveling guide), baskets of poetry, books about seasons or butterflies or gardens, big books, baskets of songbooks, and books on tape. Initially, classroom teachers were asked to contribute the majority of their levelable classroom texts (Rigby, Twig, PM Starters, and so on) for the book room cause. The books were then leveled, organized, and placed in the book room so that all teachers could have equal access to them. While there was some initial grumbling about giving up books that teachers had had in their classrooms, the result was a well-stocked, well-organized room that allows teachers to find just the right texts to meet students' needs. The book room also served to remedy the inequity of classroom resources between veteran teachers and new teachers.

Teachers now use this collection of leveled texts as the foundation for their classroom guided reading programs (Fountas and Pinnell 1996). Many teachers also draw from this collection in order to create stashes of "just right" books for students. In the classroom, children are taught to identify books that are "just right" for them; that is, books in which they can read and comprehend most of the words and concepts, but that also give them a bit of reading "work" to do in the text. Kids might keep "just right" books in individual book boxes, and teachers might have baskets of "just right" books out for children to select from (a K–1 classroom, for example, might have baskets of books at reading levels A–E for readers to choose materials from during reading time).

A book room is just another tool that can be mobilized and put to use for the purpose of providing children with appropriate, interesting, and challenging reading materials. It is a prime example of creating a resource from thin air: when a school takes stock of books that it has, organizes them for a purpose, and creates a system for sharing those resources sensibly, the value of those books, even if the quantity of them is relatively low, increases immensely for all students.

Family lending libraries ✳ Finally, it's important for schools to think about opening up their resources, whatever they may be, to families. Many schools, as in the previous example from Webster Elementary, have opened up their school libraries to families, by creating systems for parents to check out books as well as students. This is brilliant for three reasons: first, it puts more reading materials within the reach of students. In general, English language learners, their families, and communities tend to have access for fewer libraries and fewer books; the more reading materials that flow their way, the better. Secondly, giving parents opportunities to check out books gives them an easily accessible, specific way to support their child's language and literacy development. Parents who check out books from a school library will probably take them home and read them to their children, or at least see that they are read. Finally, offering the school's library collection to families makes an important statement about the school's commitment to the community. Giving families access to the school library tells parents, "We trust you, we need you, you are an important part of your child's education." What a powerful way to build a school-family-community bridge!

For schools with high populations of English language learners, native language lending libraries for families can be valuable. Particularly in schools that do not offer home language instruction to students, lending libraries with native language materials are a nice way to support children's home language development. One school took some of the Title I money that is earmarked for parent involvement and purchased reading materials in the six major languages of the school. They bought children's picture books, chapter books, song and craft books, and where available, parenting books. Those books then became available for check-out to parents twice a week. Future plans for that lending library include purchasing subscriptions to native language periodicals, so that parents can gather in the Parent Room over a newspaper or magazine from their native country.

And if schools do provide native language instruction as a part of their regular program for English language learners, a home lending library is a great way to further support language and literacy development. Many of the families from Webster Elementary who checked out books in Spanish each week had children in the school's dual immersion program. They were able to support their child's academic progress and love of reading through the books available from the school library. A family lending library creates an important role for families in their children's education; by offering native language books to take home, we encourage parents to participate in and support their children's educational growth, regardless of their English language proficiency.

A family lending library is a great springboard for engaging all families in dialogue about their role in their children's education, the importance of first language development, the way that children learn language and develop literacy, second language acquisition and what it looks like, how to create a home environment that supports literacy development, the possibilities are endless. Whether a school offers native language instruction, it is crucial that parents of English language learners develop an understanding of how their children will best become proficient academically, why it is important that children maintain their first languages, and how parents can support their children's overall growth. A native language lending library is a great place to start that conversation.

Hands-on Learning

One way that a school can really pull together to support teaching and learning with English language learners is by creating stocks of hands-on materials for teachers to use in their classrooms. Using real objects, called *realia*, boosts students' understanding of content and concepts tremendously (Cunningham and Allington 1999). And, as usual, English language learners aren't the only ones who benefit from a more hands-on approach: children living in poverty, children whose families have been too stressed to prioritize their development, children who learn kinesthetically, or children who have just had limited life experiences for one reason or another, can all benefit from having a more hands-on experience in school.

Using real objects ✳ Just as we create libraries and book rooms to house collections of books, creating a collection of real objects can help teachers enhance comprehension during lessons. When we read *The Little Red Hen* (Galdone 1974) to students, they love to see what grains of wheat really look like, they love to poke their cheeks with the stalks of wheat, they love to let the flour run through their fingers. And soon enough, as we read, they are wagging their fingers along with the characters, "Not me! Not me! Not me!" When we read *Agatha's Feather Bed* (Agra Deedy 1991) to students, many of them ask about the fabric that Agatha describes at the beginning. Silk, cotton, and wool are hard for children to really understand without actually touching them.

As we work with English language learners, we come across so many things that children either haven't had experience with, or don't have the language for. One kindergartner was telling a story about her mother cooking: "She was going like this [she pretends to squeeze something with her hands], and it was yellow and I tasted it, and I did like this [she puckers up her face and crosses her eyes]." A lemon! Even a plastic lemon from the kitchen set would make the connection for her, and open the door to so much language: *lemon, rind, pulp, peel, juice, sour, squeeze, tart, pucker*!

A good stock of realia isn't as hard as you might think: plastic fruits and vegetables, unusual stuffed animals (koalas, emus, and platypuses for *Koala Lou* [Fox 1988]), spices to smell, fabrics of different textures, tools, plastic plants and flowers, binoculars, bee hives, a fuzzy blanket for *Owen* (Henkes 1993), birds' nests, molted snake skins, shells, teapots, corn husks, a black pot for *Strega Nona* (De Paola 1975), the list is really endless. Kids who are learning English need to match words to objects, and kids who are developing vocabulary need to match even more words to objects. When the text refers to a "mug," drag a coffee cup out to show them!

Picture files ✳ Another component of your realia stock can be a high-quality picture file, since it's not feasible to bring in every kind of object kids will want to know about. That way when you want to show kids what a plow is, or a cornfield, or a dock, or a highway overpass, you can access a picture of it to show to children.

Obviously, it takes a bit of work to create an organized stock of real objects and quality pictures. But once you begin to move in that direction, you will find all kinds of things to add to the collection, you will run across perfect pictures of one thing or another, and your newly created resource will expand. Schools that have done schoolwide themes or curriculum mapping could also easily develop picture files or realia based on selected themes. A running inventory of objects and a clear system for check-out and return are essential. The important thing is that objects be stored carefully and in a way that provides easy access for all staff. Beyond that, it won't be long before you start to see the payoff in your classroom: lessons will be more comprehensible, language development will move more quickly, students will understand more of what is being taught, and most important, kids will be more engaged in learning. Nothing like clutching your own fuzzy blanket to give you empathy for *Owen*!

Time: The Invisible, Elusive Resource

Finally, it's critical to address the most intangible and one of the most important resources of all for students: time. For English language learners, time is of the essence; these students are doing two jobs at once, learning a new language and developing concept and content knowledge, and they don't have a minute to waste.

Every second counts ✳ First, it's important to think specifically and realistically about how time is spent during the school day. As in all effective schools, instructional time must be protected. When Allington and Cunningham (2002) subtracted the time eaten up by "settling in" and "packing up" routines, intercom announcements, attendance and lunch counts, candy sales and book order money collections, transitions to lunch and recess, testing, and so on, a five- or six-hour instructional day was suddenly reduced to three or maybe four hours of instructional time. Even that time is then cut by other valuable, but nonacademic classes such as P.E. and music (although this can be mitigated by intentionally training those teachers to become language-through-content teachers as well). Struggling learners, special education students, and English language learners often receive even less meaningful instructional time, as they transition to other classrooms to do activities with other staff members who often have less training than classroom teachers.

Take an English language learner from one or two classrooms in your school, map out their daily and weekly schedule, and calculate how much time that student spends doing academic work guided by a certificated teacher. It may be a way to begin to think about how students' time is used during the school day, and how you can improve your classroom planning to improve instruction.

Allington and Cunningham provide many provocative suggestions about how to improve the way we use time with our students. Taking care of housekeeping tasks before the instructional day begins; releasing children to pack up at, not before, the final bell; creating "safe" blocks of instructional time, that are not interrupted by specialists, assemblies, or announcements are all ideas for using time more efficiently.

Assessing the payoff ✳ In terms of English language learners specifically, there are some additional concerns related to the use of time. These students often spend a tremendous amount of time in two areas: being pulled out for ESL services and being tested. Is it possible for ESL staff to work in classrooms with students, rather than pulling them out? This generally provides more relevant support for students and is a much more efficient use of student time. At the very least, transitions to and from ESL classes could be examined: could they meet closer to students' classrooms? Could they go to ESL class directly from recess?

The payoff for students spending time in these classes should also be assessed (see Chapter 3 for a discussion of the comparative value of different program models). Is it worth sacrificing time for students to go and do rote, unrelated activities, just because we call it ESL? See Allington and Cunningham's (2002) scenario about a student pulled out of class daily for remediation, and substitute an English language learner for the remedial student (Figure 5–1). Or could teachers be trained to provide support for students within the regular academic context of the classroom?

Cutting summer losses ✳ Finally, research has shown that struggling students—and we know that these are very often English language learners—suffer significant academic losses during the summer months (Allington and Cunningham 2002; Cunningham and Allington 1999; Entwistle, Alexander, and Olson 1997; Hayes and Grether 1983). While struggling readers appear to progress at a similar rate as their peers during the school year, they actually lose ground during the summer, while

Why should Ronald lose 20 to 25 minutes of instruction each day (1½ to 2 hours every week) just to go down the hall to complete workbook activities with an untrained teacher aide? By the time Ronald packs up and leaves his classroom, travels down the hall, greets the aide, waits for other children to arrive, and finally gets his vocabulary workbook from the aide, 10 to 12 minutes have passed since he put away his classroom work. The vocabulary workbook is the least effective way to develop vocabulary, and the aide offers no instruction; she is not allowed to "teach." Ronald works on some words that are not in his reader, his library book, or even his science book. When his pull-out session ends, it will take him another 10 to 12 minutes to pack up, say good-bye, travel back, and get re-engaged in classroom instruction. Ronald is scheduled for a half-hour of remediation, but he is actually "unavailable" for classroom instruction for 40 to 45 minutes each day, and he typically works about 20 of the 30 minutes for which he is scheduled. Given these time realities, the activities monitored by the aide need to be a lot more effective than his classroom lessons just to keep Ronald from falling farther behind. But they won't be, and Ronald won't get better at reading this year.

FIG. 5–I ELL students lose precious instructional time transitioning to ineffective pullout services.

their more advantaged peers (i.e., white, middle-class) continue to grow. Thus, the gap between struggling learners and more advantaged students grows each year, regardless of the hard work done during the school year.

In talking about resources, it's important to think through this research, and examine the implications for your school. Could school resources be opened up to students during the summer months? At the very least, it seems feasible that schools could look at how to give children access to books over the summer months, whether through an extended check-out system, or a summer check-out program. For English language learners, who are generally surrounded by fewer reading materials, this could be an invaluable support.

More ambitious schools could look at a summer program that provided fun, low-key, but still academically oriented activities on the school campus during the summer months. Many schools do use Title I funds to support a summer school; such a program could be in place of or in addition to a summer school program. When making decisions about resources, however, we know that kids don't need elaborate programs to make gains in language development, reading, or writing. They *do* need time, a comfortable place, and quality materials. Allocating resources to provide children with those components seems like a wiser investment than a highly staffed, expensive summer school program. Remember: kids learn language by using it purposefully! They learn to read by reading!

Using Our Resources Efficiently and Effectively

We could probably never have enough resources to meet all of the needs of all of our children all of the time. It's crucial, especially when we begin to look at our work with English language learners, that we use our *available* resources as wisely as possible. And you can bet that when a school begins to take a good look at what is available, and begins to organize around a specific purpose, resources will appear where none had existed.

Key Ideas

* Schools should begin by doing a thorough inventory of available materials, which can then be organized for maximum use with our English language learners.

* In the school library, the books, the space, and the librarian are all important resources that can be used to enhance the experiences of ELL students.

* Classroom library collections should be extensive and permanent.

* Every school should have an organized, easily accessible book room, well stocked with texts leveled to match readers.

* Allowing families to check out books from the school library or from a separately maintained collection is a great way to integrate families into the literacy development of their students. Native language lending libraries are a nice way to support the maintenance and development of students' first languages.

* Schools can establish depositories of hand-on materials to support content learning in classrooms.

* It's critical to evaluate the use of time during the school day for English language learners. For ELL students, every second counts!

6

Family and Community Involvement

It is no use saying, "We are doing our best." You have got to succeed in doing what is necessary.   —*Sir Winston Churchill*

A Scenario: One School, Two Worlds

On one end of the building, the early childhood wing, which is dominated by Head Start classrooms, one parent volunteer is preparing paint pots and arranging paper on an easel, another is guiding children through the process of setting the tables for lunch, and another is sitting with the group listening to the teacher read *The Very Hungry Caterpillar* (Carle 1969). All of the teachers in the classrooms know the parents by their first names, and several of the teachers speak Vietnamese, Spanish, or Cambodian, predominant languages among the families served by this particular program.

Around the classroom, there are pictures of families, pamphlets and flyers for parents in different languages, a parent lending library with books in several languages, health and nutrition information, and other helpful resources for parents. Alongside children's work on the walls and counters there are brief but clear explanations describing the activities and learning objectives to parents and other adult visitors.

Later in the day, many parents will be back for a workshop about supporting early literacy learning at home. At the first parent night of the year, teachers ask parents for input about the content of parent nights. What are parents interested in learning about? What activities would they like to do together? What do they need support with? This year, families requested help in supporting their children's learning at home, help with discipline, and fun and easy activities to do with their kids at home. Families come to each monthly meeting, drop their kids off at the on-site child care, share a meal, and participate in the activity, through a translator if necessary.

The other half of the building is home to a regular K–5 public school; nearly four hundred students, many of them graduates of the Head Start program, come for classes each day. In this world, however, the presence of parents is virtually undetectable. Absent are the family pictures, the student work displayed for parents, handy resources for families, or signs in different languages. But more important, the staff on this end of the building is mired in a vicious cycle of indifference: there is no real effort to include parents in their children's education, parents don't participate, and therefore, staff feel justified in their criticism and exclusion of families. It's a cycle that won't go away by itself; on the contrary, the mistrust, misunderstanding, and dampened morale only become more deeply entrenched over time.

This is a painful, but valuable scenario to examine. The very common refrain that parents just aren't interested in parent involvement is refuted in this scenario: in the first situation, parents are eager and active participants, and in the second, those very same parents are alienated and apprehensive. Why the stark contrast? This chapter explores the dynamics of and possibilities for meaningful parent and family involvement.

Embracing the Need for Meaningful Family Involvement

It is essential to begin by establishing family involvement as absolutely critical to student success, especially when those students are English language learners. Research on the general student population has shown time and time again an indisputable correlation between family involvement and student achievement (Chavkin and Gonzalez 1995; Comer 1988; Henderson 1987; Revicki 1981; Walberg, Bole, and Waxman 1980). Considering the unique needs and vulnerabilities of English language learners in the public school system, this connection between families and schools becomes all the more urgent. The greater the linguistic and cultural differences between family and school, the more important it is for schools and communities to collaborate in order to bridge those differences. In the case of ELLs specifically, there is considerable evidence that a strong home–school connection supports greater student achievement (Aspiazu, Bauer, and Spillett 1998; Jones and Velez 1997; Lucas, Henze, and Donato 1990).

Once we have solidly embraced the notion that children benefit when their parents are involved in their education, we arrive at the task of facilitating that involvement. In considering how to generate involvement on the part of ELL families, two fundamental principles guide our thinking.

Recognizing Parents as Partners

First, we must begin to recognize parents and families as indispensable resources in the education of their children. Cotton and Wikelund (1989) assert that "Too often, because of the discontinuities between teachers/administrators and the communities in which their schools are located, school personnel tend to view the parents and surrounding community as needing to change and having little to offer" (5). Just as the "deficit model" undermines our work with children in the classroom, it also poisons our work with families and communities.

We must presume that all families, no matter how limited their English is, no matter how limited their formal schooling has been, no matter how many jobs they are required to hold to make ends meet, *all* families want to and, even more importantly, *can* contribute to their child's success in school. That premise changes distinctly the role of the school in parent involvement; rather than dictating the parameters of family involvement and expecting parents to fit themselves in somehow, we focus our energy on identifying and developing capacities that families already possess, and putting those strengths to work for the benefit of students.

One Size Doesn't Fit All

Secondly, we need to acknowledge that meaningful involvement in their children's education is going to *look* different for different families (Scribner, Young, and Pedroza 1999; Trumbull, Rothstein-Fisch, Greenfield, and Quiroz 2001). The traditional, white, upper-middle class version of parent involvement is based on the PTA model, where stay-at-home moms work with schools to raise and allocate money, promote school events, and support teachers in classrooms.

There is, however, a whole range of possibilities when it comes to families being involved with their children (Ascher 1988). Parent and family involvement is informed by many factors: availability of time, lack of money or transportation, other family obligations, or limited or negative experiences with formal schooling, among many others.

In the case of English language learners, family decisions about involvement in school are often shaped by the distinct cultural context that parents come from, which dictates what a proper home–school relationship looks like. When teachers at Lister elementary school in Tacoma, Washington, surveyed families and community members about what expectations for family involvement were, Eastern European, Latino, and Southeast Asian parents overwhelmingly suggested that their role as involved parents had to do with grooming children at home, physically and psychologically, to be ready for learning at school. Many families put an enormous amount of energy into their children and their education through these home-based efforts (Scribner, Young, and Pedroza 1999).

In terms of parent involvement, our expectations as (generally) mainstream American public school educators may look very different from expectations that people bring with them from other cultural backgrounds. At the risk of generalizing inaccurately, many of the cultures from which our ELL students come prescribe very distinct roles for teachers and families, with a clear separation of responsibilities. Home is the domain of the family and school is the domain of the highly respected and trusted educators (Carger 1997; Chavkin and Gonzalez 1995; Espinosa 1995). Many parents said that initiating interactions where they might be perceived as questioning teachers or trying to influence educational decisions would feel unnatural and disrespectful (Chavkin 1991; Chavkin and Gonzalez 1995; Espinosa 1995).

It's Our Responsibility

Keeping that in mind, as well as the fact that coordinating home–family collaborations falls naturally within our regular professional obligations as educators, it's important that schools take responsibility for this aspect of our students' education. It is unacceptable to expect families to follow norms that they are not aware of, and then to criticize them for not following them. If we believe that it's best for children that their parents be involved in their learning, we've got to take absolute responsibility for facilitating the process. It's what we do each day with children: we decide on the results we want, and we try everything we can think of until we get them.

In most cases, families are already involved in their children's learning; it's simply a matter of recognizing and appreciating what that looks like for different families. Even if parents are not chaperoning field trips, they may be scrubbing their children and feeding them and sending them to school ready to learn. Even if families are not involved in fund-raising, they may be urging their children each morning to obey the teacher and follow the rules. Even if mothers are not volunteering to supervise recess, they may be putting their children to bed at a reasonable hour so that they can be alert in the morning. Even if parents are not making copies for teachers, they may be stressing to their children the importance of a good education.

Lopez (2001), in a case study of a Texas family that had high-performing children, found that the parents consistently encouraged their children to be serious and diligent in their education. He stated that the family's goal "was to teach the children to appreciate the value of their education through the medium of hard work" (430). The father used his own life as a migrant worker as an example: he constantly reminded his children that they could either work hard in school or work hard in the fields. Lopez calls this kind of nontraditional, but invaluable form of parent involvement the "transmission of sociocultural values" (430).

As educators, we've got to be less judgmental and more flexible in our thinking. All parents and families have strengths that can be utilized for the benefit of their students. It's up to us to seek out those resources, strengthen them, and put them to best use. It's up to us to acknowledge and appreciate the ways that parents are and can be involved, from the most basic getting-kids-ready-to-learn level, to the more sophisticated taking-charge-as-a-leader level. We need the best of all families, and our students do, too.

Components of a Successful Program for Family Involvement

Successful programs for family involvement, especially in schools with significant numbers of English language learners, seem to include focused efforts in four areas: creating an inviting physical environment, creating effective home–school communication, involving families in school decisions, and providing services and/or education for parents.

Creating an Inviting Physical Environment

Just as we work deliberately to create classroom environments for students that create enthusiasm and energy to learn, it is important to create school environments that generate excitement and interest among families (Scribner, Young, and Pedroza 1999). As you open the door at Atkinson Elementary in Portland, Oregon, you are drawn in by music that plays throughout the day in the front entryway. There are vibrant displays of student work ready to pull you in any direction. Teachers and staff members rushing to meet children are never too busy to wish you a good day. Before you know it, you're wandering around, admiring student work, chatting with staff members, watching as students get busy with their learning.

It's important that parents and families feel welcomed into the physical space of the school. Families should feel like the school is an integral part of the community, another place where they gather and interact with other community members. Parents should be able to walk in the door and find a way to be engaged in the goings-on of the building.

A successful school environment is also one that plans for the logistics of family circumstances and schedules. Often, parents who would gladly be more present in their child's school are prohibited by issues of transportation, scheduling, or child care for siblings (Chavkin and Gonzalez 1995; Inger 1992; Scribner 1999; Sosa 1997). When schools make efforts to eliminate those kinds of barriers, they send a strong message to families about how important their presence and participation in the school is.

Strategies for Making Families Feel Welcome

* Designate a greeter. Recruit a staff person to stand at the door fifteen minutes before and fifteen minutes after the school day, as parents are dropping off and picking up their children. It's amazing how far a warm "Good morning" can go, and even more amazing how far a "Buenos días" or a "Dobroye utro" will take you.
* Beyond an official greeter, set a norm in your school that *all* staff members will greet family members as they encounter them. It's important to acknowledge families when we see them and demonstrate our open invitation to them.
* Create inviting displays of student work in the main entry of the building. Give parents a reason to hang around and admire what their children are doing. Celebrate that hard work!
* Represent *all* families in a public, celebratory way. Remember the displays of family pictures at Lincoln Elementary in Chapter 2? What a way to give families ownership of a space! At another school, large maps of the world were displayed and parents were encouraged to put their names on little flags and mark where their families came from originally. The maps served as a place for people to share their history with others, and also got staff members and parents and students talking to each other on a personal level.
* Provide a space for families to gather. This doesn't have to be fancy, but it should be pleasant and comfortable. A room designated for parents would be best, where people could gather, sit, drink coffee or tea, post and read announcements in different languages, or meet fellow parents. If your

building doesn't have a spare room, how about some comfortable chairs in the entry way? How about an interactive bulletin board designed just for families? How about some native language periodical subscriptions so that parents could gather and talk over the latest news from the homefront? The first step is for families to actually be present in the building and to feel comfortable there. Whatever physical space we can create for that to happen in will be well worth the investment.

Effective Home–School Communication

Every school that has developed meaningful family involvement has realized the importance of good home–school communication. With families of our English language learners, where language is often a barrier to communication, it also becomes a barrier to effective participation by parents and families. If we want to include families of English language learners, we are going to have to be creative and persistent in our efforts to facilitate meaningful communication.

First and foremost, schools must develop a mechanism for translation (Chavkin and Gonzalez 1995; Inger 1992; Sosa 1997). Whether schools have staff that can be called on, community translators who are available, district interpreter services that can be accessed, there must be a formal, steady, and reliable process for translating information for parents. Using students or even family members is not necessarily a reliable resource for translation. Sending notes in English, talking slow, talking louder, or reducing important messages to simple words or gestures ("Antonio,

BAD!" or even "Antonio, MALO!") do not ensure effective communication. These meager attempts to communicate with families make a strong statement about how much you value real dialogue with families.

Translation must also be available in written and oral formats. Given the history of immigration and refugee patterns in the United States, there are significant numbers of ELL families that may have had limited formal schooling in their own countries, and may not be fully literate in their own languages. The most effective way to get information to families of English language students is either face-to-face or over-the-phone contact, in the parent's primary language. Having written material translated is a good first step, but it is not likely to reach all families.

Additionally, it is critical that schools develop a comfortable and workable framework for *two-way* communication with families, especially with English language learner families who may not tend to initiate contact with schools and teachers. In order to best meet the needs of our English language learners, we first need to know them and understand what their needs are. We need information from families and parents, and we've got to ask directly for it. The goal in this chapter is not to dictate what your two-way communication will look like; what makes sense in one context won't necessarily work in another. Rather, each individual school will need to think about what the necessary components of effective home–school communication might be, in order to come up with a workable, effective plan.

Strong lines of communication are valuable for families of English language learners for many reasons. Obviously, schools have a lot of important information to impart to parents, but we also need a lot of information from families in order to best serve their children. Parents give us the context for their children and the family; they tell us what their expectations of education are, how are children taught and disciplined in the home, what the cultural norms that define how children interact with adults are, what a traditional home–school relationship looks like, how the family and the teacher can support each other, how the child's language development is progressing, and so on. Schools need this valuable information in order to mediate the cultural and linguistic disconnect between ELL families and schools, and in order to reshape the school so that it more appropriately serves English language learners and their families.

Strategies to Develop Meaningful Home–School Communication for ELL Families

* Work toward a staff that matches the language needs of your school population. If you have a large number of Spanish-speaking families, for example, you need teachers and paraprofessionals and office staff who speak Spanish.

* Contract with community service providers to provide translation services. A steady relationship, where translators become familiar with how the school works and who families are, is best.
* Connect new families immediately with a contact person. When a Cambodian family enrolls in a new school, for example, introduce them to someone in the school that can facilitate communication between the family and the school. Let parents know who they can call with questions, and who will be contacting them to give or solicit information.
* Phone trees are a great way to call families, in the native language, with information about school events and needs. Identify people who can call families on a regular basis to provide or solicit information. These people could be staff members or parent volunteers. This helps families develop a trusting relationship with one or two people at the school, and gives them the one-on-one personal contact that really makes a difference. You may need parent permission in order for nonstaff volunteers to access phone numbers; if this is the case in your district, ask for that permission up front, when parents enroll, so that you can begin a relationship with families right away.
* Conduct home visits periodically throughout the year. How about holding in-home conferences rather than school-based conferences?
* Invite parents in to the classroom or the school on a regular basis to celebrate student work. In this way, we normalize the presence of parents and families in the classroom and school. Regular occasions for celebrations are nice for developing relationships between teachers and families.
* Set aside specific times (during teachers' work days or weeks) for home–school communication. This time could be used for making phone calls, writing notes, visiting parents at home, or conferring at school.
* Create a panel of interested parents from different linguistic and cultural groups. This group could work with school staff to facilitate home–school communication, providing information to both parties and mediating cultural differences and questions that arise. This group could also be key in articulating exactly what *parents* want parent involvement to look like, and making that happen.
* Provide numerous opportunities for parents to give input to the school. These could be parent nights at the school, where parents are included in generating a body of knowledge that will be used to work with students. During a parent night about how to support literacy at home, for example, spend time helping parents identify literacy activities that they may already be doing at home. This input could also be solicited in the form of surveys or questionnaires.

* Engage families in direct dialogue about potential differences between home culture and the mainstream, public school culture. During a parent night, for example, one school began with different groups brainstorming and sharing about their traditional expectations for schools, teachers, parent involvement, children's behavior, and so on. As groups shared their own cultural information (teachers were another group and shared the public school perspective), differences and sources of potential problems became clear. There could then be a dialogue about how those conflicts could be avoided in the future.

* Share linguistic and cultural information collected from families with *all* staff members. It's important that all staff members get to know families, and become aware of possible cultural conflicts that may arise.

* *Listen* to families. If they drop their kids off at the curb and never come in, listen to that message. If they don't respond to written information sent home, listen to that message. If they congregate in the lobby after school and chat with each other, listen to that powerful message. If parents are spending time at the school and always have younger children with them, listen to that message. It is the responsibility of the school to listen and be responsive to families, not the other way around.

Involving Parents in Decision Making

In order to have a school that is truly responsive to the needs of families, including English language learner families, we must incorporate them into the fabric of our schools. Schools must seek out ways to include parents in decision making at all possible levels (Kuykendall 1992). This component of effective parent involvement is intertwined with the communication component; each feeds into the other. When there is effective communication and families have a strong presence in the school, they may begin to find themselves in conversations about school decisions that are being made. And when parents are involved in the decision-making process, they are able to provide valuable information about the needs and wishes of families.

Because of the possible differences between the home cultures of ELL students and the school culture, it is important to solicit the help of those parents in shaping the course and daily life of the school. This does not mean parading families in to "tell us what we should do"; rather it is part of a commitment to the larger value of cultural democracy. As professional teachers, we are an integral part of the education of children, but we are not the only experts. We need to ask for the expertise that all families have about their children, particularly when children come from a different cultural context than that of the school, and we need to incorporate that information into those children's school experience.

In all aspects of parent involvement, but especially when we talk about parent leadership, it's important to remember that this level of involvement will not be a match for all parents. Many families (and not just ELL families) will not feel comfortable in seeking out such a role in the school. We need to make it as easy and painless for parents to have a say in the day-to-day happenings of the school, and we need to search out and encourage those parents who might be more interested in taking on a more formal role.

Strategies for Involving Families in School Decision Making

* Make sure that there is a parent represented on your school council. This is required for Title I schools, and makes good sense for all schools that are truly committed to real family involvement. In some schools, a representative from each classroom sits on the school council.
* Facilitate a parent group. This could be a PTA group, a booster club, any kind of a regular, sanctioned group of parents who come together to support and influence school decisions. The critical piece, especially in schools that have smaller populations of English language learners, is ensuring that such a group truly represents all parents, and works for the benefit of *all* students.
* Include parents in interviewing and hiring new staff members. This is a great way to ensure that the commitment to parent involvement will continue as new staff members join a school.
* Establish groups of parents who come together to speak to particular issues in the school (Levin 1987). A group of parents who meet on a regular basis with staff members to strategize about discipline, for example, might produce some solutions to discipline problems that school staff had not considered. Discipline is a particular area ripe for cultural differences between families' traditional expectations of school discipline and what American public schools expect in terms of discipline.
* Don't offer to include parents in the school decision making until your school is fully prepared to listen to what parents have to say. Parents should not be "included" to rubber stamp school decisions, or to provide affirmation for school staff about decisions made with no real input. Allington and Cunningham (2002) remind us not to respond to every bit of family input with "We tried that once" or "We can't afford that." Oftentimes, when families, especially ELL families, are asked to give input into decisions, that input is never really considered if it doesn't match what we were already planning to do.

Sometimes what we hear from families, particularly those that live in the cultural and linguistic margins, does not feel so warm and cozy. If we're committed to best serving our students, we've got to ensure that those voices are a natural, integrated part of our decision making and our daily school lives.

Providing Services and Education to Families

Nearly all successful parent involvement programs have some component for providing services or education for family members. Whether it's helping families meet their daily needs, addressing health issues, or helping parents better support their children at home, schools can play a vital role. Offering such services to families is one way to initiate a home–school connection. Providing services that parents want or need is at the very least a way to simply get them into the building, and that is a first critical step in building family–school relationships. At best, it shows our commitment to the well-being of the students we serve, and a recognition that we must work collaboratively with families to that end.

Allington and Cunningham (2002) suggest the concept of "school-linked services," where schools would partner with other service providers to offer necessary services to families on the school campus. They offer this scenario:

> Imagine that the mother of a first grade student walks her son to school and brings his baby sister along. While she delivers her son for another day of classes at the school, the young mother stops in the see the school nurse to have her daughter's temperature checked and a throat culture taken. Then she moves to the satellite Women, Infants, and Children (WIC) office to be recertified for continued participation before dropping her daughter off at the on-site day care room. Next, she spends two and one half hours in an adult education program where she works on her high school GED. The focus of her literacy development activities, however, is children's books and family stories rather than the more traditional skills workbook. That afternoon, after having lunch in the day care room with her daughter, she works in her son's classroom as a paid assistant, practicing her reading skills by introducing little books to small groups of children. This paid internship is part of a planned educational program that will lead to a Child Development Associate (CDA) certificate jointly planned and funded by the state Department of Social Services, the Department of Labor, Head Start, and Title I. (208)

Amazing! What a way to show families that we are committed to their well-being and to that of their children.

And while this scenario may seem way beyond what your school is ready to take on, many of these services may not be as difficult to coordinate as first imagined.

Spend a bit of time to research what services are already being provided in the local community. Is there a high school or community college looking to offer students credit toward early childhood education that might staff an on-site day care for parents? Is there a family support center that might use the school space to offer some of its classes or services? Are there adult education classes that might be held at the school in the evenings?

One easy way to begin providing services to families might be to just relocate many services that are already being offered into the school building. At one school, staff members heard that the local Ukrainian church was holding Saturday Ukrainian language classes for children. The school offered, and the church members were more than happy to use the school facilities rather than the damp basement of the church.

Obviously, coordinating these kinds of school-linked services takes effort, organization, and commitment. Begin by designating one person or a small group within a building to spend some time researching and formulating possibilities for school-linked services. For best results, find a way to compensate staff to focus specifically on the issue of developing and implementing school-based services. It is too big of a job for staff members to do within their regularly scheduled workday, and the results will be meager and incomplete. Incorporating parents into this process might be another way to identify available, effective services and ease the workload on teachers.

Beyond partnerships with community service providers, schools need to find their own ways to provide education and information to parents. Some schools hold parent meetings, others provide school-day workshops, others offer evening classes for parents to come and learn about a particular topic. Each school has to take stock of what areas they want to work with families in, what needs and wishes parents have expressed, and what kind of format makes sense for their context. The important thing is that family education efforts be ongoing, be based on what families have requested, and be interactive in nature.

Strategies for Providing Services and Education to Families

* Partner with community service organizations to provide services to families. Know what services are offered and find ways to incorporate them into the life of the school.
* Offer building space to community service providers. If space is an issue, before or after school hours might be best for service providers to work with families. In fact, Allington and Cunningham (2002) suggest that outside-of-school time might even be better for reaching families and for providing continuity of services.

* Offer space and resources to less official community organizations, such as cultural groups who need a space to practice music or dance, or groups that want to encourage first language development and maintenance. One school coordinated an after-school story hour in Spanish, and provided books for parents to come and read to groups of children. Sometimes making an offer of space or resources up front will inspire community members to organize themselves around a particular area of interest.
* Foster mentoring services. This could be parent mentors for other parents, community mentors for parents, parent mentors for students, or community mentoring for students. In any case, this is a nice way to provide one-on-one help for students and families, to build culturally and linguistically relevant partnerships, and to integrate communities into the school for the purpose of supporting students and families.
* Offer classes and workshops based on families' needs and interests. Classes could be about anything from parenting to cooking to ESL for parents. These might be during the school day, in the evenings, or even on week-ends. They could be run by staff members, community experts, or parents themselves. Remember, in order to attend these classes, families need reasonable notice, need to be contacted in their first language, may need transportation, and may need child care. Many families simply *won't* be able to participate without those arrangements. A nice snack or even a light meal also goes a long way to encourage attendance. Schools that receive Title I funding can access funds earmarked for parent involvement for just such activities.
* Arrange times during regular school hours that families can join their children and at the same time learn ways to help support their children at home. One school offered a schoolwide read-in to celebrate Dr. Seuss' birthday. Families joined their children during the school day for relaxed, recreational reading; teachers took the opportunity to demonstrate for parents ways to foster and scaffold recreational reading at home.

Key Ideas

* Schools must embrace as a guiding principle that meaningful parent and family involvement is critical to the academic success of English language learners, and that it is the responsibility of educators to initiate and facilitate this involvement.

* All parents and families have strengths that can be put to use in the service of their children's education.

* Family involvement will look different for different families. Schools must recognize the tremendous continuum of support that families can and do provide.

* An inviting physical environment is the first step toward integrating families into the school setting.

* Meaningful, two-way communication between families and schools is critical.

* Parents and families of ELL students should be involved in meaningful decision-making processes in the school setting.

* Schools should strive to offer families an array of services and educational opportunities. Partnerships with community agencies are one way to make this happen within a building.

7

Classroom Environment

There are no great things, only small things with great love.

—*Mother Theresa*

A Scenario: Knowing Each Other

Each year, Marcela Abadi starts the year with her first and second graders the same way. Although the activities may vary, the focus for the first two months of school is always the same: getting to know each other as individuals. This year, one of the class' earliest endeavors was the shoebox project. Marcela went first, modeling for the children how they would put together and present to the class a shoebox that represented them as individuals. She collected artifacts from her life and her house, and brought them in to present to her students. The box was full of artifacts that told the story of who Marcela is, who and what she loves, what she enjoys doing with her time, and important experiences that she has had. This particular year, she brought, among other things, a picture of her son, Amiel, recently off to college, a miniature bicycle to show how she enjoys getting around, and a drawing of the sailboat her husband recently acquired for relaxing trips around Puget Sound. The other artifacts revealed Marcela's love for traveling, cooking, and gardening, her Jewish and Colombian heritage, and her admiration for the recently deceased Queen of Salsa, Celia Cruz. She shared each of the artifacts with the children, giving a little explanation or story along with each. The children, captivated, saw their teacher in a new, vibrant light.

One by one over the first few weeks, the children took turns at bringing their shoebox in and sharing it with the class. The children's artifacts shed light on their individual joys and passions, their unique histories and experiences. They watched each others' presentations, spellbound, learning the ins and outs of each of their classmates. No longer was the classroom full of random faces. Instead, the room came alive with artists, rock collectors, scientists, big sisters, readers, gardeners, musicians, dancers, and star gazers. The children learned about where different families came from, how they celebrated together, how different families lived their everyday lives together. There were differences to be sure, but mostly, the room became full of folks that shared an amazing amount in common. And that was just the point.

Marcela spends the first few months of school building the classroom community. She knows that children do their best learning when they feel like important, integral members of the class. She wants the children to know and care about each other, the same way they know and care about her. When kids are connected, she says, they support each other as learners, they have fewer conflicts, and they develop a stronger sense of themselves as individuals.

To this end, the children spend the first months of school writing about themselves, reading their work to others, doing presentations about one aspect of their lives or another, creating art about themselves, graphing their commonalities and differences, composing poetry about friends and family; the children ease themselves into the rigor of academic learning through a topic that they know better than any other: themselves. By November, you can walk into Marcela's classroom and breathe in the charm and character of her class. There are self-portraits, poems, posters, photographs, charts, graphs, and homemade books everywhere. The class has become a family, a group of distinct personalities who've forged a strong bond for the purpose of learning.

Through these efforts, Marcela establishes herself as another one of those distinct personalities. She is the teacher, certainly (there's no doubt about who's in charge!), but she also reveals herself to the class as a real person. Marcela presents herself as a human being, one who makes mistakes, laughs, takes risks, and learns right alongside the students. She lets the children know that even though she knows a lot, she is always learning new things, and she knows that the children will teach her as much as she will teach them. Marcela uses her own experience as an English language learner to demonstrate the reality that we are all learners and experts in different areas. Through her own mistakes with the language (few and far between as they are!), she teaches the children how to handle differences and weaknesses kindly and constructively. She communicates her expectations that the children always be kind and constructive with each other. And as they go about the important business of first and second grade, they rise magnificently to the occasion.

Turning Children into Partners

In this age of "scientifically proven" pedagogy, it's important to keep in mind something that any good teacher, on his or her hardest day, always knows: good teaching is an art. We certainly avail ourselves of the multitude of research around learning theories, language acquisition, and literacy development, but the art of our work becomes vitally important when we begin to factor in the ever-changing, ever-dynamic variable: the students. There is no scientific formula for this part: each child, with his or her own unique set of life experiences, with his or her own distinct way of looking at the world, takes a slightly different path.

The only sensible way to manage such delightful chaos is by transforming the twenty-something distinct personalities in the classroom into willing and capable partners. As we build a viable learning community in the classroom, we cultivate children who eagerly take responsibility for their own learning, who know how to support others in their learning, who can negotiate conflict, and who feel intrinsically the value of challenging themselves. If we take the time to create such a community, our job is halfway done.

Children Need the Support of a Community

Learning Is a Social Activity

Though it may sound touchy-feely to talk about community as central to the education of, in this case, English language learners, there is a great deal of research that converges to support this assertion. First, we know that knowledge, and language, in particular, is socially constructed. Vygotsky (1962) offers us the concept of the *zone of proximal development* (ZPD), which is at the heart of teacher–learner interactions. The ZPD is the distance between what children can do independently and what they can do in collaboration with teachers or more competent peers. Cummins (1994) describes the ZPD as "the *interpersonal* space where minds meet and new understandings can arise through collaborative interaction and inquiry" (45).

In addition, most of Cambourne's (1988) conditions of learning can only be met within the context of social interaction. It is in a group setting that language and literacy learners receive many *demonstrations* about how to use language. The group is where learners are *expected* to *use* their developing skills authentically and purposefully, and it is where they receive constructive *feedback* about how to refine their skills.

For English language learners, the importance of a supportive learning community is even greater. Because English language learners are learning to negotiate the social skill of communicating, either orally or in print, it's critical that they have a social context in which to develop those skills. Long and Porter (1985) have advanced what is called the *interactionist theory of second language acquisition*. This theory suggests that language learners acquire language most effectively when they interact with target language speakers for the purpose of communication. Children's language development is guided and shaped by these interactions; others provide comprehensible input to the learners, children are motivated to participate in the communication, and errors are naturally corrected as ELLs negotiate meaning (Peregoy and Boyle 2001).

The Need for Equal Membership

For English language learners, the learning community must be more than simply a place where they learn and practice communicating in a new language. For ELLs to learn most effectively, they must feel like whole, integrated members of the community. Ogbu's (1978) research reveals the association between how students are perceived and valued by the larger community and their academic success. The more marginalized a child's community is by the larger society, the greater the classroom difficulties are likely to be. Krashen's (1981) hypothesis about the affective variable in language learning tells us that in order to incorporate new language skills, learners must have positive perceptions about the target language and its speakers. Children who are weighted down by anxiety, hostility toward a language or its speakers, or other emotional distress related to the language learning make stunted, if any, progress (Brown 1987; Cloud 1994; Gardner and Lambert 1972; Krashen 1982).

Classrooms That Mirror Oppressive Societal Structures

American classrooms and schools have been, from the beginning, based on what Paulo Freire (1970, 1985) has called the "banking" system of education, which states that students are simply empty vessels, to be filled up with the valuable knowledge that educators confer upon them. Traditional American pedagogy is rooted in the idea that teachers must prepare children to move on and assume their roles within American society. In the context of a society that is built on inequities and race, class, and linguistic stratification, schools and classrooms begin to take on the role of training students for their corresponding roles. Consciously or not, schools and classrooms operating on the historical fundamentals of educational "meritocracy" (where the hardest workers get the rewards), tracking (intentionally or otherwise), intelligence testing, standardized testing, and traditional curricula (everything from Columbus to Shakespeare), begin to mirror the larger society (Darder 1991). Left unchallenged, the stratification so entrenched in the larger society re-creates itself within our classrooms.

Just as ethnic and linguistic minority communities have been disempowered in the greater American context, students from those communities are equally susceptible to being rendered "voiceless" (Cummins 1994; Fine 1987; Giroux 1991; Walsh 1991), literally and figuratively, within a parallel classroom community. The level of educational success that English language learners achieve corresponds to the extent that a classroom works to reverse typical societal patterns of marginalization within its community (Cummins 1994).

Classrooms That Challenge Oppressive Societal Structures

An effective classroom context for English language learners is one that presents a direct challenge to the systems and structures that have traditionally silenced English language learners and inhibited their success. It is not enough to *care* about the children that you work with. We must realize that, whether we like it or not, there are varied and powerful forces playing themselves out in the lives of our children; it is part of our obligation to them to acknowledge and confront that reality. In order to effectively educate English language learners (and *all* children) we must create a classroom context that actively and purposely counters the influences that limit our children.

Jim Cummins (1984) has suggested the term *student empowerment* to incorporate the overlapping factors of linguistic/academic development and identity development. He asserts that while the development of a "confident cultural identity" is a valid end in itself, it is also the means to greater academic participation and progress for English language learners. He says that students "who are positively oriented towards both their own and the dominant culture, that do not perceive themselves as inferior to the dominant group, and that are not alienated from their own cultural values" realize significantly greater academic achievement. Cummins (1986) urges, therefore, an educational context, in this case, the classroom, that validates, encourages, and promotes students' cultural identities, not only because it is the right thing to do, but also because it will result in greater academic success among our most vulnerable students.

Creating Cultural Democracy

Ramirez and Castaneda (1974) used the term *cultural democracy* to describe an environment in which every member is encouraged to explore and express his or her unique cultural identity. Within a culturally democratic context, the traditional rules that place cultures within a hierarchy, some superior and others inferior, are abandoned. Rather than being centralized within one particular person or one particular set of cultural norms, power is shared and assumed by all members equally. In a culturally democratic classroom, each student's linguistic, cultural, and life experiences are viewed as resources to be utilized in the service of future learning. Each child is encouraged to learn within his or her unique cognitive and communicative styles, and is encouraged to explore new ones as well. We support the development of biculturalism among our students, where each child, grounded in his or her own context, learns to effectively negotiate the larger society and culture.

Darder (1991) expands on this concept of cultural democracy by infusing it with a collective challenge to oppressive practices. She suggests that within a cultural democracy, educators must develop within students the "capacity for critical thought," whereby students become fully engaged in reading, interpreting, analyzing, and acting upon the world around them. The notion of "voice" becomes both literal and figurative, inseparable in the discussion of how to enhance learning for English language learners. Henry Giroux (1988) encourages educators to "create the conditions where students come together to speak, to engage in dialogue, to share their stories, and to struggle together within social relations that strengthen rather than weaken possibilities for active citizenship" (200–201). Central to Paulo Freire's (1970) theories on effective, meaningful education is the link between "reading the word" and "reading the world"; both must be integral parts of any sincere efforts to develop language and literacy, particularly among traditionally marginalized groups.

True Multicultural Education

Similarly, Sonia Nieto (1999) advocates for what she calls "multicultural education" for *all* children. This vision of education puts the classroom in the middle of the larger, global context, and prepares students to navigate, negotiate, and impact the world around them. She describes multicultural education as a framework that "can lead to the creation of richer, more productive learning environments, diverse instructional strategies, and a more profound awareness of the role culture and language can play in education" (2). Multicultural education, she articulates, is characterized by seven traits: it is antiracist, it is important for all students, it pervades every aspect of the schooling process, it educates for social justice, it is a dynamic process centered on the ever-changing needs of students, it is the foundation for basic education, and it is critical pedagogy (3).

Critical pedagogy becomes, therefore, the cornerstone of an effective educational environment for English language learners. Within a critical pedagogy, the experiences, learning styles, linguistic backgrounds, and cultures of students become central; all aspects of the learning process are shaped around these variables. From the way that knowledge is generated and constructed, to the way time is used in the classroom, to the content of the curriculum, to the way students are encouraged to interact with others, it is the needs and strengths of the students that determine these structures. But this alone is not enough. Critical pedagogy compels us to move ourselves as educators and our students to the next level, to find the greater purpose and relevance in our teaching and learning. In order for our students, in this case, English language learners, to become truly literate and educated, they must be encouraged and instructed in a way that cultivates their own agency in their lives and in their world. English language learners will only learn to effectively speak and "read the word" by effectively learning to "read the world" as well.

Creating an Effective Learning Community

How do we create an appropriate classroom environment for our students? Similar to the discussion of school climate in Chapter 2, highly effective classrooms seem to have a magical energy about them. When you walk into one of these classrooms, you can feel the challenging, exciting work that the students are engaged in. You see student work all over the walls, you see children working together on projects, you hear an animated, purposeful buzz of student talk. In these classrooms, learning, knowledge, and discovery permeate every moment of activity during the school day. The kids can't help but learn, and they seem to enjoy every minute of it.

It's Up to the Teacher

Many different elements come together to create this classroom magic. Central to the effectiveness of any classroom is the teacher. Teachers create the atmosphere in a classroom; they structure it according to their beliefs about teaching and learning, and if there are changes to be made in the classroom structure, they are the ones to make them.

The first and most critical step is for teachers to fully embrace the idea that all of their students are gifted in one way or another, that all have the potential to be important contributors to our world, and that each one of them wants to be the best that he or she can be. No child wants to fail. Every child wants to be successful and to live his or her life to the fullest. And every child has strengths that can be built on. If teachers don't believe this about each and every one of their children, they shouldn't be teaching them. Teachers should always ask: "Would I want this for my child?" Educators of English language learners have got to be sure that they are above the rhetoric that insists that English language learners have too much stacked against them to ever be very successful in the larger context. Teachers of ELLs need to have high expectations of their students; it's the first essential step toward realizing them.

As we think about our expectations for our students, we've got to be willing to take our classrooms out of the vacuum, and place them appropriately in the larger societal context. Think long and hard about your school and about your classroom. Who are the children in your community and in your class? How does the larger society perceive the students in your classroom? How have the issues of race, ethnicity, gender, class, linguistic diversity, and immigration intersected to shape the lives of your students? What are the societal factors that may limit student success now or in the future? What resources do the students in your class have access to, and which resources are out of their reach?

You may find that you don't have the answers to some of these questions. If that's the case, you'll need to do some homework. It may be that simply sitting with other colleagues to discuss these issues will bring you closer to these answers. Almost certainly, you will need to do some research among the families in your classroom. Unless your classroom population is for some reason significantly different from that of the rest of the school, much of this work can take place at the school level, although it must still be localized within each particular classroom. What's important is to familiarize yourself with the students and families in your classroom, and to begin to tap into the realities of their daily lives and their future possibilities.

It's important to work on constructing this knowledge base about *all* of the children in your classroom, not just your English language learners. We are all part of the larger societal context; if we are to begin deconstructing the hierarchy implicit in that larger society, we've got to be clear and honest about where each of us falls on that social ladder. We want children to be powerful not because they are rich or white or their parents are fancy lawyers; that is a false, unearned power that doesn't hold up to much scrutiny. Our job is to create children who are powerful because they are thinkers; power that comes from critical thought and reasoning is not easily disregarded.

Examining Power Dynamics

As we push our thinking, we begin to find ourselves in the middle of a conversation about the dynamics of power in the classroom. And that's just as it should be. As teachers, we hold all of the power in the classroom (although sometimes it certainly doesn't feel like it!). If we're committed to the well-being and academic success of English language learners, we've got to make sure that the oppressive structures and practices of the larger society don't replicate themselves inside of our classrooms. It's our job to create an environment in which English language learners feel empowered to find their "voice" (literally and figuratively) and to take control of their own learning.

For the teacher who wants to rethink power relationships in the classroom, here some guiding questions:

* How and when do children in the classroom get to make choices about their learning?
* What is the process for deciding how time and space are used?
* Does the teacher merely transmit information to children, or are children involved in the social construction of knowledge?
* Who decides the curriculum? How and when are children able to make curriculum decisions?
* Who does the most talking during the day? How much of the day does the teacher spend talking at the group?
* Are children regarded as teachers in the classroom? Are children encouraged to help other children? Is the teacher willing to learn from the children?
* How and when can children question or challenge the teacher?

* Does the teacher assert herself as a learner of some sort (i.e., second language learner, piano student, and so on)?
* Is there real conversation in the classroom, or is the raise-your-hand format the only option?
* Do children get the opportunity to share their strengths with the group?
* Are children encouraged to take responsibility for their learning and their classroom, or are they totally dependent on the teacher?
* Are all children encouraged to participate meaningfully or is it the same children every time?

Negotiating Teacher Authority and Student Empowerment

Clearly, teachers are responsible for making sure that their students develop skills in particular areas. Teachers must be accountable to supervisors for the growth and progress of their students. Obviously, children cannot make every decision in the classroom. Every successful classroom has a set of clear rules and norms for behavior and performance that are necessary for living and learning together. But a classroom should be structured and managed in a way that provides for participation from all students, rather than silencing and stifling particular children. It's up to the teacher to set this up.

In the example at the beginning of this chapter, Marcela makes clear at the beginning of each year that the children are together for a very important purpose: to learn. No one has the lock on knowledge, not even the teacher. Marcela sets a tone in which everyone has something to learn and everyone has something to teach. Children in her class understand that they are responsible for and capable of effecting the success of all of the members of the community.

Not only does Marcela set this tone, but she also makes sure that everyone is accountable for living by it. She encourages children to question her, and discusses issues with children openly and honestly. Her students know that she is thoughtful about the decisions she makes with them, and she is willing to hear about how those decisions affect children. Marcela knows that this approach builds trust with her students, and it also keeps *her* accountable to the vision that she has set up for the class.

Marcela makes sure that children are responsible for the effect that their actions may have on others; she never allows children to mistreat each other. She believes that her initial work in building the classroom community wards off the majority of conflict between students, but when the occasional conflict does arise, she doesn't let it go for a second. Marcela emphasizes the way that discord divides the community and distracts from the important learning to be done. She gives children the chance to speak for themselves, and encourages them to think through the causes and solutions to their problems. It is a labor-intensive process to begin with, but as the year goes on, children are more and more able to manage and resolve their own disputes with each other, and the time spent in this area becomes negligible.

As they nurture the growth of community relationships, strong teachers of English language learners also take time to nurture children individually. For ELL students, this one-on-one attention may be all the more critical because of language anxieties in the large group, and the possibilities for isolation that exist if there are relatively few ELL children in the environment. Any successful teacher knows that there are some children who take a little bit more of our time and love before they are willing to branch out on their own.

Taking an Antibias Approach

Effective teachers of English language learners make a valuable investment of energy in creating an antibias environment. An antibias approach takes as a given that we all come together with our own biases and preconceptions about others. Teachers as well as students, raised within contemporary American society, have absorbed the fear and mistrust of the "other" cultivated by our mainstream culture, each of us to different degrees. An antibias environment does not condemn us for this, but challenges us to identify and confront our own biases and those of others. Integrating an antibias viewpoint into a classroom does not simply mean dealing with prejudice and injustice as it arises, although that is certainly imperative in a classroom that wants to counter bias; antibias is a comprehensive, proactive approach that teaches children to recognize and appreciate the strengths and differences of others (Derman-Sparks 1989).

In Marcela's classroom, bias is confronted openly and quickly, but she also reinforces the ideas of differences and commonalities on a daily basis, throughout all of her curricular activities, in a way that draws children together and encourages them to value each other. There is open, natural, and constant reflection about the sources of difference and conflict, truth and perspective, justice and injustice.

Strong Teachers Mean Successful Classrooms

In summarizing the characteristics of effective teachers of culturally and linguistically diverse students, Diaz Soto (1997) cites the extensive research (Garcia 1988;

Haberman 1995; Ladson-Billings 1994; Lucas, Henze, and Donato 1990) and asserts that those teachers demonstrate

* An unshakeable belief in the children and their abilities to learn
* An ability to communicate to the children that the teacher is clearly on their side
* High expectations with no excuses
* An orientation toward the community: its strengths, its culture, and its people
* A willingness to consult adults who are members of the children's racial or ethnic group
* A political interpretation of the community, its context in the large society, and the debilitating consequences of powerlessness and poverty (10)

Considering the Curriculum

Beyond the critical role of the teacher, Faltis and Hudelson (1998) remind us that "what students talk, read, and write about matters" (101). Simply put, curriculum for English language learners must be relevant to their real lives. Paulo Freire (1970) has referred to using "generative themes," Sylvia Ashton-Warner (1963) has called it "teaching organically," and Jones and Nimmo (1994) use the term "emergent curriculum" to refer to the concept of using children's lives and experiences as a primary source for curriculum content.

When children are able to read and write and learn about topics relevant to or reflective of their lives, their motivation to push themselves swells. For English language learners, this concept of generative themes is even more critical. English language learners most often come from distinct cultural circumstances and have traditions, experiences, histories, and ways of thinking that are not necessarily reflected by mainstream American culture. It is essential that teachers, the majority of whom are still grounded in this dominant culture, provide opportunities for children to explore culturally relevant themes in the classroom.

Children who have a personal connection to what is being studied are able to draw on resources and background knowledge that might otherwise be rendered insignificant. If a class is researching and writing about neighborhoods, for example, a child could be encouraged to use her own experiences to think about how neighborhoods work, how they evolve, what constitutes a neighborhood, how they serve the needs of people, and so on. The student could use her own neighborhood as a lens for studying the concepts, and could also draw on the expertise of family members, friends, and neighbors to deepen her understanding of the concepts being studied.

A Curriculum That Creates Thinkers

Intentionally using themes straight from the students' lives lays the groundwork for children to learn to "read the world" and "read the word" simultaneously (Freire and Macedo 1987). It's hard to be a high-level thinker about issues that you don't have much familiarity with, especially if you have to do it in a second language. But when children are given the opportunity to explore themes that are central to their lives, they become eager to push themselves in all kinds of ways. Not only do they want to read and write and listen and talk about something, we also encourage them to share and develop their *thinking*. They become excited about debating, about engaging in dialogue with others, about asking questions and being persistent about seeking answers. Children are connected in all kinds of ways to the larger world; they already know a lot about how it works and about how it impacts their lives. When we connect school learning with students' real lives, suddenly, their work in school becomes urgent and important. Students begin to see the way that education can impact their lives, and the way they can use it to make an impression on the world.

The writing curriculum from Lucy McCormick Calkins and her colleagues at the Teachers College Reading and Writing Project at Columbia University (2003), *Units of Study for Primary Writing*, is a great example of how children can further academic skills using their own particular experiences and histories as the basis. Not only does this guide teach the art of writing in a very explicit, developmental way, it also teaches children to recognize, articulate, and expand on their own rich lives. Kids who tell you that they have boring weekends and never do anything interesting at home worth writing about learn to see the magic and emotion in helping to prepare a meal with a parent. Calkins and her colleagues help us help children realize how rich and provocative their lives are with a little examination. A child whose conversation never seemed to go beyond cartoon stories learns to extract the excitement and anticipation and giddiness of being on a plane as it's landing in Cambodia for his first trip back. The affirmation that children feel when they are able to express what's important to them is very often the catalyst that turns them into writers who all of the sudden can't match up their letters and sounds fast enough to get their ideas on the paper.

Let Them Talk!

Central to an effective classroom environment for English language learners is the language itself. Specifically, classrooms must be designed so that children are immersed in and using the language purposefully all the time. Particularly in classrooms where there is no specific model for language learning, where children are learning and learning through English as a second language, children must have ample opportunities to use language in meaningful ways in order to expand their language capacity (Bruner 1978). Although opportunities to read and write must be plentiful, English language learners need to be surrounded by meaningful, comprehensible oral language (see Chapter 10 for more on the importance of oral language development).

Read-alouds, shared readings and writings, and interactive writing all offer access to oral English, but I want to suggest the importance of student *talk* in the development of language and literacy for ELLs. Simply put, children who are learning a new language need to be speaking and listening to that language all day long. Research shows that children involved in conversation engage in what Peregoy and Boyle (2001) call the "negotiation of meaning," the process by which speakers and listeners struggle to understand and be understood. Within conversation, English language learners prompt more competent speakers to modify their language until it becomes comprehensible (by asking for clarification, making a confused face, and so on). Long's Interaction Model (1981) suggests that the give-and-take between more and less competent speakers in a conversation is where language acquisition happens most naturally and easily. The negotiation that takes place in this setting includes both comprehensible input (Krashen 1981) and comprehensible *output* (Swain 1985), both critical ingredients for language learners.

Teachers are traditionally so resistant to allowing children to talk in class. Whether we feel like what we have to say is more important, or we worry about them being off task, or we fear a collective degeneration into chaos, it seems to be in our teacher blood to stifle children's talk. But if children are going to learn a language, they've got to practice it as much as possible. They've got to talk, talk, talk!

The difference is in making talk productive and purposeful. What's needed is *comprehensible invite* (Faltis 1997), that is, the opportunity for students to "participate in discussions and other social activities to make sense of the ideas and concepts and to have opportunities to use language in ways that are authentically associated with those ideas and concepts" (Faltis and Hudelson 1998, 97–98). So as children are reading and writing around their generative themes, they also need to be discussing, questioning, and challenging others around these same topics.

Giving children an important purpose for their talk is the first step to making talk in the classroom manageable and productive. When children are excited about learning and discussing something, they will usually keep to the task at hand. Additionally, if children are accountable to others about their talk, they will likely invest more into it. If children are expected to share back with the group, for example, about what they've discussed with a partner, they're more likely to be purposeful with their partners.

Including a time for talking with a regular reading, writing, or content activity is a good way to contextualize student talk. It can be as simple as, "Talk to your neighbor for a minute about what you might like to read today during Reader's Workshop," and then, "Before you come back to the carpet, tell your neighbor a bit about something you read this morning." Once you begin to look for real opportunities for children to talk, you'll discover many ways that children can practice language purposefully and manageably. Here are some suggestions:

* Ask all of the children to repeat another student's response. "Did you hear what Resep just said? Tell your neighbor the great idea that Resep just had."
* Give children partners during whole group times. This opens up opportunities for children to talk with partners for different purposes. "Talk to your neighbor about how the weather outside looks today" or "See if you and your neighbor can brainstorm three new words that have the prefix *re-*."
* Assign children partners during read-alouds. You can then ask partners to summarize, clarify, or discuss at different points during the read-aloud. "Tell your neighbor what you think is going to happen next" or "Talk to your neighbor about a time you've felt worried like Wemberly" (Cole 2003).
* Ask children to tell or retell a story to their partner as you hold up the book and go through the pages. This can be done before reading a book or after

having read it once; it can also help jog children's memories while reading stories over more than one session.

* Give children explicit instruction in how to carry on meaningful conversations around different topics (Cole 2003). This kind of teaching allows children to pursue their own learning whenever and wherever the opportunity presents itself. Children need to be able to know how to structure and navigate communication independently.

* Schedule times during activities for children to stop and talk to classmates about what they are reading, writing, or learning.

* Ask children to talk to each other about what they are or will be doing, throughout the day. Even as children line up, you can say "Whisper to your neighbor one thing that you need to remember as you're walking in the hallway."

* Set aside time at the beginning of the day for children to catch up with each other about interesting things that have happened recently. Many teachers do this in a morning meeting format, but there are certainly other options.

* Set aside time at the end of the day to reflect together about the events and happenings of the day.

There are endless opportunities for children to talk throughout a school day, and it is critical for children who are developing a new language to do so. In a raise-your-hand-and-say-the-answer format, very few children have the chance to speak on any given day. The more student talk can be placed within a conversational context, where children are talking with a partner or a small group, the more we can maximize the opportunities for all children to talk and enhance their language skills (Cole 2003).

Grouping Students for Collaborative Work

This leads us directly into how we can group children in order to maximize their opportunities for learning and language development. While there are certainly occasions where a whole-group setting makes the most sense (for a read-aloud, for example), the large majority of children's days can be organized around activities in partners or small groups. There are several reasons why this format is ideal for English language learners.

Children need ample opportunities to participate: they need to talk, they need to handle materials, they need to ask questions of their peers, they need to discuss ideas and new concepts, and so on. The more time children can spend in partnerships or in small groups, the more time each child is directly engaged as an active learner. Also, while this may not be the case for everyone, for many English language learners, as well as African American and Native American students, a collaborative learning setting is more of a cultural match than a format in which children are working individually or competitively (Au 1993). It's important to know your students and to know which learning styles and formats are most appropriate for them.

There are lots of different ways and lots of different reasons to group children; you will need to identify the ways that will work for your classroom. The following are some things to think about when grouping English language learners in the classroom.

* Try to create opportunities for children to mix with different kids all day long. If some kids are together during math groups, try to create different configurations for reading or science groups, for example. Different partners give English language learners different experiences, and ELLs need as many varied language experiences as possible.

* Don't be quick to pull ELLs away from other speakers of the same first language. You may believe that they need to be around English speakers only, and speak only English in order to learn the language more quickly, but Cummins' (1981) "counterintuitive principle" tells us that this is not the case. Children need the support of other children who are like them, socially, culturally, and linguistically. Learning for ELLs must be meaning-based, and very often, children can help each other with meaning enough so that they can negotiate the language more successfully.

* Don't be quick to push ELLs to work with other children from similar linguistic backgrounds. Often, teachers put children together thinking that one will translate for the other, and that no other support is subsequently necessary. Young children may have a hard time translating even if they are proficient speakers of both languages, and often times, we miscalculate language proficiency levels among children. When a child with a more distant relationship to the Vietnamese language is paired with a student that has just arrived, for the purpose of language support and scaffolding, we may become frustrated with the students' lack of progress and productivity. While these children can provide mutual support in other ways, it is our job to create the classroom structures for language support and scaffolding.

* Know your students well. Which students are introverted, and might benefit from being around someone who is more open and verbal? Which students work well together? Which students know how to explain things articulately, and who would best benefit from this? Which students have very limited

vocabulary? Which students can patiently and clearly negotiate misunderstandings? Which students are skilled as teachers, as opposed to just doing for other students? How can you make best use of children's strengths and gifts, for the benefit of other children?

✳ Provide children with ongoing, explicit instruction about how to work effectively in a group setting. This means teaching children about the different roles of a group, how to ask for and clarify information, how to divide up tasks, and so on. We can't assume that students already know how to work in groups together; the level of success that students reach in a group setting will directly reflect the amount of time that you have spent in teaching them how to work cooperatively.

Let Them Play!

The final component in a successful classroom environment for English language learners is one that is essential for all students, but that is left out of the educational experience for most children, not just ELLs. That final ingredient is good, old-fashioned *play*. Even older students need a regular self-directed time in which they can explore their own interests with a variety of materials. For those of you indignant at the thought of taking time away from serious academic work to *play*, let me qualify that statement by saying that effective classrooms for English language learners make time for purposeful, self-directed, language-rich, often content-based play that supports social and conceptual development (Owocki 1999; Van Hoorn, Nourot, and Scales 2002; Wasserman 1990). Better?

Patricia Cunningham and Richard Allington (1999) suggest that all effective classrooms for children include a daily period of time during which children can choose their own activities, materials, and purposes. They say that the time gained by tightening up routines is time that can be used for self-directed learning, during which children explore topics and activities that are interesting to them; they suggest that this time pays for itself as students are more productive throughout the rest of the day. Debbie Miller (2002) advocates for a "work activity time." This time, she says, is "the perfect time for children to synthesize and apply their learning in new contexts, either independently or with their peers; it's the time when children can put into practice what they've learned during other parts of the day" (103).

The fact that English language learners are learning a new language along with academic content makes it all the more necessary that they have a regular, predictable time in which to put their new content and language learning to use for their own important purposes. Cambourne's (1988) conditions of learning remind us that

learners need to assume responsibility for their own learning, and they need time to use their newly acquired skills for authentic purposes. A self-directed, "play" time is the perfect time for children to relax, enjoy each other's company, and support each other's language and learning while they have fun. During play, children happily push themselves into their ZPDs (zones of proximal development); when they are engaged in pleasurable activities, they soak up and retain language more effectively than at any other time.

During a class called "Play, Language, and Literacy" through Pacific Oaks College Northwest, the two instructors tried to convince students of the importance of "play time" to language development. They arranged centers similar to what would be found in primary and even intermediate classrooms: a library corner, a science area, math manipulatives, dramatic play, even a playdough and water area. As the students engaged with the materials (as adults, not as children!), the instructors roamed around and recorded vocabulary words they heard being used, or new words that students could have been using (i.e., *traffic* for *a lot of cars*). Those who had been unsure of the utility of spending class time for play were more than convinced when they saw the hundreds of words that were generated within about forty-five minutes of play.

Good, purposeful play, where a mix of children with varied language proficiency are engaged together, is one of the most effective spaces for language learning. A time for self-directed activities also allows children to explore their own interests, express themselves culturally, utilize their multiple intelligences (Gardner 1983), and take control of their learning environment and their learning.

Key Ideas

✳ A warm, supportive classroom community is essential to the well-being and academic success of English language learners.

✳ Because learning and language development happen through social interaction, a classroom must support positive, production interaction between all classroom members.

✳ Classrooms facilitate the development of the literal and figurative "voice" of English language learners, and encourage ELL students to "read the world" as well as "read the word."

✳ Classrooms must become culturally democratic, where each member is able to express and explore his or her cultural identity.

✳ Classroom practice must be informed by the notion of "critical pedagogy"; learning that happens in the classroom is directly shaped by and shapes the larger world.

✳ It is up to teachers to create a classroom community that supports children academically, socially, and emotionally. Teachers share power with children, rather than assuming power over them.

✳ Effective teachers of ELL students deal with bias proactively and on an ongoing basis in the classroom.

✳ A classroom's curriculum should be relevant to students' lives, experiences, and interests.

✳ English language learners need plenty of time for purposeful talk in the classroom.

✳ Use your extensive knowledge of the children in your classroom to group them according to needs and strengths.

✳ All students need a regularly scheduled time to engage in self-directed activities around their own interests with a variety of materials.

8

Content Study

Give me a lever long enough and a fulcrum on which to place it, and I shall move the world.   —*Archimedes*

ontent study is the opportunity for teachers to move children's language from the basic playground language that comes so easily to them, to the more complex academic language that they will need in order to do well in school and to successfully navigate the world before them. For too long, educators have mistaken a mastery of conversational English for a command of academic English (Collier 1987, 1989; Cummins 1981); in this scenario, English language learners move through school less and less able to handle the ever more demanding curricular material. It is critical that we begin at the earliest level to give children sophisticated, academic language through the study of engaging content.

A Scenario: Walking to Swan Creek

"So, tomorrow we'll be walking over to Swan Creek to do some exploring and observing," informs the teacher.

"Swan Creek! Creek! I know that must be freshwater!" shouts one student proudly.

"That's right, it is a freshwater habitat. What kinds of creatures do you anticipate finding when we go to visit Swan Creek?"

"Dragonflies," says one.

"Water striders," offers another student, doing his impression of how a water strider balances on the surface of the water.

"Bullfrogs or maybe bullfrog tadpoles," suggests another boy.

"Maybe we'll see some red-headed woodpeckers or some jays, like maybe a blue jay," says another girl.

"We might see some turtles, but only the freshwater kind, not the kind that live in the ocean. Maybe a painted turtle or a snapping turtle. The snapping turtle has a pointy nose like a beak and goes 'SNAP!'"

"Wow, you know a lot of freshwater creatures to be looking for when we go to the creek tomorrow. What kinds of *predatory* animals might we encounter?" asks the teacher.

"They all predators, Ms. Cerna, they all EAT the other animals. Only the little tiny, tiny animals, they eat the plants," explains a student.

"Yeah, the bullfrogs eat the insects, and the spiders eat the insects too. YUK!"

"Maybe we see birds, they eat the worms."

"I bet we *will* see some birds, that's a good prediction. You've noticed that there are a lot of birds around here."

"Ms. Cerna, maybe we can fish and then we can be predators too!"

This conversation took place early last spring as a kindergarten class prepared to continue their study of habitats ("'habitat' is the place that has all the good things you need to live!" explained one student). They had recently embarked on a study of differences between freshwater and saltwater habitats, and were getting ready to visit a nearby freshwater habitat. Though many of them walked past the Swan Creek every day to get to school, they had only recently begun to look carefully at the details, to notice all of the wondrous plants and trees and animals and yucky bugs that lived there. They could hardly contain their excitement and pride as they became able to identify and name the inhabitants of this neighborhood ecosystem.

In this particular class, sixteen of the twenty students were English language learners, most still qualifying for ESL services. Many of them had had no experience with English before entering kindergarten; at home they spoke Russian, Ukrainian, Spanish, Cambodian, Vietnamese, and Hmong. A few of them were all but silent for the first few months of class. But, snaking down the trail to the creek, listening to their shrieks of discovery, "oooh, smell that sticky sap!" and "look at that giant anthill! Millions of ants working in their tunnels!" their limitations faded away. Instead, they were explorers, tour guides, scientists, and discoverers. And were they muddy!

Language Helps Us Negotiate the World

As we prepare to teach our English language learners, it is important to keep in mind two general principles. First, we cannot teach language as a separate entity. Language must reflect our connection to the world, our experiences within it, our feelings about it. Language without meaning is nothing more than sterile strings of letters or even words. As we teach our children language, we must also teach them about the world and their relationship to it. Rather than language learning as an end in itself, language becomes a means to learn about the world, and language learning is the equally important, simultaneous outcome. Language learning *must* therefore be embedded in content: literature, science, math, social studies, health, art, and so on. So often, when we hear teachers frustrated at their students' reading or writing progress, they are perplexed when asked, "What are you reading about? What are you writing about? What are you learning about?" Literacy for its own sake is not literacy at all, it is simply busywork that children will show little interest in.

Secondly, and similarly, language must be perceived as purposeful. In order to learn as quickly and efficiently as possible, students must have a good sense that there is important reason to learn language. We've all seen students who whip through reading or writing assignments without any real learning (some of us have even done that ourselves!). When students don't see any purpose or need to communicate, either orally or through reading or writing, they just plain don't do it, and they don't learn. In order to facilitate English language proficiency, we've got to give children some incentive. Once students *want* to communicate, they will be motivated to learn how to speak, read, and write in English.

Learning Language Through Content, Content Through Language

Rather than being a one-way progression, which is usually seen as learning English and then learning content, it is essential to reconstruct this as a more fluid process, in which children learn through language and about language simultaneously. Pauline Gibbons (2002) discusses this in her book *Scaffolding Language, Scaffolding Learning.* She uses the hourglass shape to describe the learning process for all learners, and particularly English language learners (see Figure 8–1). While using language to construct knowledge within the different disciplines, the learning process is occasionally diverted to allow the language itself to become the focus of learning. In a social studies unit about peace and justice for example, first graders made a list of things that all people need, but often don't have. As they wrote "Some people don't have enough love. Some people don't have enough money. Some people

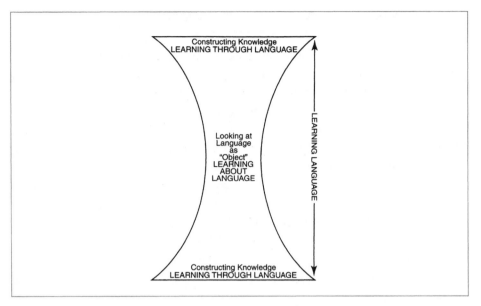

FIG. 8–1 Effective teachers weave language learning into content study.

don't have a place to live," several students noticed the word *don't* and wondered why it had an apostrophe in it. The teacher explained the concept of contractions briefly, the class brainstormed a few as the teacher charted them on paper, and the class returned to their list of "haves" and "don't haves."

Language Must Reflect Our Thinking

Jim Cummins (1981) also provides much of the theoretical framework for integrating content and language learning. Cummins asserts that language learning happens most effectively when language is learned through meaningful content activities. In the diagram in Figure 8–2, he describes teaching and learning activities in terms of their demands on the students. Tasks are either cognitively demanding or cognitively undemanding, and it is important to remember that this refers to the academic task, not the language task. Further, each task is either context-embedded, meaning that there are lots of clues to help the student understand and demonstrate proficiency, or context-reduced, meaning that there are few clues to help the student in understanding the concepts. Cummins insists that English language learners be taught at a developmentally appropriate, cognitively demanding level. That is to say, a fourth-grade English language learner should be learning

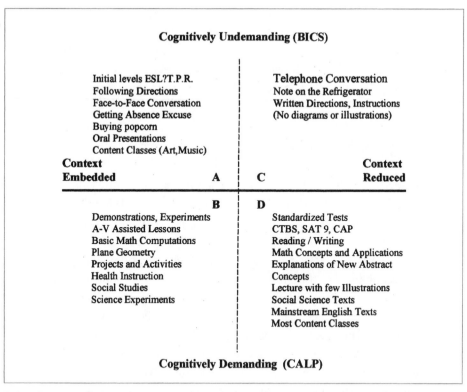

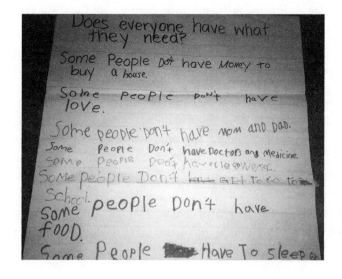

FIG. 8–2 ELLs need cognitively challenging instruction presented in a supportive, accessible context.

about state history alongside his peers, not sorting pictures of fruits and vegetables into piles. It is the teacher's responsibility to keep the student in the lower left quadrant of Cummins' model, providing high-level, high-interest academic content within a context that offers English language learners lots of scaffolding in both understanding the information presented and demonstrating comprehension.

Selecting Content Study

So what exactly does it look like to provide cognitively demanding work in a context that supports conceptual understanding and language development? Well, first, you need some content. There will likely be many sources for your decisions about what topics of study you will pursue with your children: textbooks, district standards, children's interests, and your own interests. Start with a good understanding of the district expectations, and then turn to your most important source of all teaching wisdom: the children. More often than not, district and state guidelines are written in terms of concepts rather than specific knowledge, allowing you to incorporate student interests with external expectations. For example, in Washington State, students are required to "group personal, local, state, and national events in terms of past, present, and future, and place in proper sequence on a timeline" (Washington State Office of Superintendent of Public Instruction website). This objective, while it encourages particular skills, also allows us to put the experiences of our students to use in acquiring them. When you include the children when creating curriculum, you increase their motivation to participate, you give them space to employ their prior knowledge in furthering their future learning, and you improve the cultural relevancy of your teaching and your classroom.

Combining Language and Content Goals

Once you have a good sense of the content objectives you wish to explore with your students, you will need to do some careful planning. Gibbons cites two essential questions in planning for content learning with English language learners: First, what are the language demands of the curriculum? And second, what do children currently know about language and what are their language learning needs (Gibbons 2002)?

In thinking about the language demands of curriculum, think in terms of all aspects of language. It is important to think not just about reading and writing activities for the children, but activities in which children must listen, speak, discuss, question, and otherwise explore the content *through* the language. The more varied opportunities you create for students to practice, the more you will maximize language development. As always, taking time to be conscious of the language you are using and the language tasks you are providing will mean enhanced language learning for all children, while ensuring language development and content access for English language learners. Figure 8–3 provides a set of questions to guide your thinking and planning through a content area.

Second, you will need to consider individual students' language abilities as you plan for the group. You will likely have information from many sources (language assessments, anecdotal observations, previous work samples, etc.). More information

---

Spoken Language Tasks
- What spoken language demands will there be?
- If there are currently not many opportunities for spoken language, where can oral tasks be included?

Listening Tasks
- What listening tasks will there be?
- What kind of listening do they involve: One-way? Two-way? Interpersonal? Transactional?
- If there are currently not many listening tasks, what specific listening activities could be included?

Reading Tasks
- What texts will students be reading?
- What are the possible linguistic and cultural barriers students may encounter?
- How can texts be made accessible to students?
- Do reading tasks aim to increase readers' reading strategies, and students' knowledge about language?
- If there are few reading texts, are there others that could be included?

Written Tasks
- What are the written text types that will occur, or what text types could be included?
- What is the schematic structure of text types?
- What kind of connectives occur in these text types?
- If there are few written tasks, what text types would be relevant and could be included?

Grammar Tasks
- What aspects of grammar (e.g., tense) does the topic require students to use?

Vocabulary Tasks
- What specific vocabulary does the topic require students to know?

FIG. 8–3 These questions guide us in providing appropriate, accessible language experiences within an area of content study.

about effective language assessment is provided in Chapter 11. Obviously, at the beginning of your work with a student, you will have less information about his or her language abilities. For that reason, you will want to build in as much flexibility as possible into your curriculum plans. A guiding question for any lesson in a class with English language learners should be, "In what ways are the instructional activities in the unit of study multilevel?" That may mean, for example, that you plan to begin with partnered or small-group activities, in which an English language learner could contribute at a level comfortable for him or her. Once you have worked with children for a while, you will begin to get a better picture of their language abilities and needs, and will be able to plan more precisely to meet them.

Thematic Units

Expanding content studies into broader, thematic units is one way to reinforce and maximize both language and concept learning (Enright and McCloskey 1988; Pappas, Kiefer, and Levstik 1990; Peregoy and Boyle 2001). Any area of content study can be expanded to include reading, writing, math, science, or social studies activities. When students develop a framework of content and language knowledge around a particular topic, they build up the means to support greater and greater learning in each of those areas. Ideas, concepts, vocabulary, and language structures are built and established on an increasing body of shared knowledge. Further, when concepts and vocabulary are presented in a variety of different ways for a variety of purposes, students have more opportunities to access and integrate that learning.

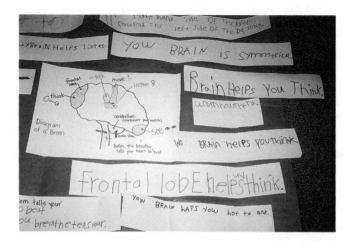

CLASSROOM MATTERS

Strategies for Differentiating Language and Content Learning

As you plan your content exploration, there are many specific strategies that you can use in order to present the information to children and guide them in their understanding of it.

* *Experiment or demonstrate*. Begin a study of properties of water by allowing an ice cube to melt or by wiping the chalkboard with a wet cloth and watching the moisture evaporate.
* *Have children demonstrate a concept*. In a discussion about attributes, the teacher divides the class into two groups, one with shoelaces and the other without shoelaces.
* *Have children role-play*. Act out the story of the *Tortoise and the Hare*.
* *Use small groups as teaching spaces*. Present a lesson in a smaller group in order to be more attuned to language issues that arise.
* *Conduct collaborative group work*. During a math lesson practice, ask one child to handle the manipulative while another interprets and records data.
* *Partner children to scaffold content and language learning*. Say, "Turn to your partner and tell them what you predict will happen next in the story."
* *Play games*. When children begin to break numbers apart play "On and Off" (from TERC's Investigations curriculum), in which they toss objects over a paper and count the number that land on and the number that land off of the paper.
* *Take field trips*. Learning about water? Take a walk through the neighborhood to discover the places that rain goes after it's fallen: gutters, puddles, storm drains, creeks, lawns, and so on.

Additional Aids to Comprehension

In addition to these specific strategies, there are a number of other tools that can and should be used in order to enhance content understanding for English language learners (and everyone else as well!).

* *Visuals*. Draw pictures of everything! (Don't worry, the kids will love your primitive scratches.) Even if you aren't an artist, it helps kids to associate some kind of symbol with a new vocabulary word or a new concept.
* *Hands-on materials*. As they study the ocean, kindergartners have the chance to try out their new words in the water table-turned-Pacific coast. Sand was packed into one half of the table and salt water filled it out. Shells, rocks,

sticks, shovels, and plastic sea animals gave children loads of opportunities to engage in plenty of ocean-talk.

* *Word banks.* These are only effective if they are generated by the class within the context of content learning.

* *Pictures.* Pictures are a great way to enhance understanding and get kids interested in a subject. Keep a picture file of good-quality, relevant pictures you find. A digital camera is also a fabulous investment for a classroom or school; that way you can take your own pictures relevant to classroom learning.

Experiencing the Content

The key is to put English language learners *into* the learning as much as possible. Rather than language being the only medium through which children are introduced to concepts, you want to create opportunities for children to see the concepts in action, to participate in them, to hear, feel, smell, taste, and touch the concepts being presented. As they *experience* the content, they will associate the accompanying language more quickly and meaningfully.

Still trying to figure out how it actually looks in a real classroom with real kids? Take a look at the following examples.

A Math Exploration: Learning About Ourselves

In a K–1 classroom, student are exploring the concepts of gathering, organizing, and interpreting data. They spend several days conducting whole-group surveys around different topics. One day, the question to be answered is "Are you bilingual?" Two clipboards hang on the wall, one labeled "Yes" and the other "Not yet." Each child has a clothespin with his or her name on it, to be placed on the appropriate clipboard. The teacher asks the group the question, and begins to match the concept of speaking more than one language to the word *bilingual.*

"Ngoc-Tran, your mommy speaks to you in Vietnamese. Do you speak to her in Vietnamese?"

"Yes," she says, nodding her head vigorously, "I talk Vietnam with my mommy."

"Wonderful! That means you are bilingual because you speak English and Vietnamese! You're going to select 'Yes.'" The teacher points to the corresponding clipboard and invites Ngoc-Tran to move her clothespin.

"Is there anyone else who speaks Vietnamese like Ngoc-Tran?"

Several children raise their hands, and Ngoc-Tran speaks to them in Vietnamese, encouraging them to respond.

"You mean you speak Vietnamese *and* English? You mean you are *bilingual*?" The children are nodding and smiling shyly. "Well you better come up and move your pins to the 'Yes' clipboard then!"

The teacher continues to invite children up to place their clothespins on the appropriate board, using her knowledge of the children's languages, and making the "bilingual" connection for them if the children don't. To a native English speaker, she says "Jeremiah, do you speak two languages? Are you bilingual?"

Jeremiah shakes his head. "I only talk English."

"Would you like to learn another language, Jeremiah?"

His eyes get big and he nods his head softly.

"Great! Then you can put your pin on the 'Not Yet' side, because you'd like to work on learning another language. Maybe Terrence will teach us how to count in Vietnamese during calendar tomorrow."

The students continue placing their pins, until all students have responded to the survey. When they finish, the teacher guides them in analyzing the data collected. She begins by asking the children what they notice.

"Dat is big one, teacher, and dat no big, teacher," one says, pointing to the respective clipboards.

"Yes, you've noticed that there are a lot of clothespins on the 'Yes' board, and not as many on the 'No' board. What a good observation. *More* students in our class are bilingual and *fewer* students are not bilingual yet. K–1 kids, share that observation with your neighbor. Explain to your neighbor what Tu just said: that there are *more* students who selected 'Yes' and *fewer* students who selected 'No.'"

The students turn to their neighbors and give them some version of what the teacher just explained. Some of them point to the clipboards and make "big" and "small" gestures with their hands.

The class continues to make and explain different observations, each time making use of the vocabulary that represents the key concepts: *more, less, how many, this group, that group, data, equal to,* and so on. The class counts and recounts the clothespins on each board, as many of the children are still learning to count or to use one-to-one correspondence.

The next day, the teacher reviews the observations that the children have made, asks the students to review them orally with each other, and then explains to them that now they will be responsible for making a representation of the data.

"That means that you're going to draw a *picture* with your partner so that someone else can know how many students in our class are bilingual and how many are not yet bilingual. You want someone to be able to look at your representation and understand our data right away. Let me show you how . . ."

After she models a representation of the data, the teacher selects partners from a cup full of popsicle sticks. The names on the sticks are written in black, reflecting greater proficiency in oral and written language, or red, reflecting less English proficiency or less writing proficiency. That way, in a red–black partnership, the students can discuss and organize the task, and at least one of them will be able to complete the written task. For the next few days, the students expand on the concepts by conducting their own surveys of their classmates. They collect information, organize it, and present their representations to the class. They learn language, they learn about each other, and they learn about gathering, organizing, and analyzing data.

Seattle Neighborhoods: A Research Project

In a fourth–fifth-grade classroom, students eagerly dive into a study of Washington state history, via their own neighborhoods. The teacher elects to focus on the following concepts in the state guidelines for social studies and history:

* Students will observe and analyze the interaction between people, the environment, and the culture.
* Students will analyze how the environment and environmental changes affect people.
* Students will examine the influence of culture on Washington state history.
* Students will examine the contributions of people from various cultural groups to the development of local and Washington state history.

Alongside these central history and social studies concepts, the teacher identifies a host of other objectives relating to math, reading, writing, language development, and so on. For example:

* Students will conduct and record interviews with prominent local citizens.
* Students will compare demographics of neighborhoods and analyze demographic information.
* Students will create written analyses of information gathered in a variety of formats. (Washington State Office of Superintendent of Public Instruction website)

The teacher begins by identifying neighborhoods where the children in the class live, and creates a list of eight neighborhoods to be studied in the unit. Students are able to create study groups of two or three students according to their own interests.

The class brainstorms about what kind of information they want to know in order to learn about each individual neighborhood, and in order to compare each one with others in the city.

From there, the teacher and students begin to gather research together. They invite community speakers into the classroom for interviews, they go to the library and gather primary source information from local archives, they analyze maps, they call on their own important knowledge of their neighborhoods, they conduct phone interviews with community members, they examine newspapers and news archives, they even take an extended tour through the city by bus in order to collect information. (See Figure 8–4.)

Throughout the unit, the class began to develop a common vocabulary that reflected the themes which were emerging in the large and small study groups: *asset, challenge, issue, demographics, landmarks, gentrification, diversity, culture, economic, intersection, civic, entrepreneur.*

Each neighborhood group was required to develop a portfolio that reflected their research and learning. The many different components of the portfolio allowed

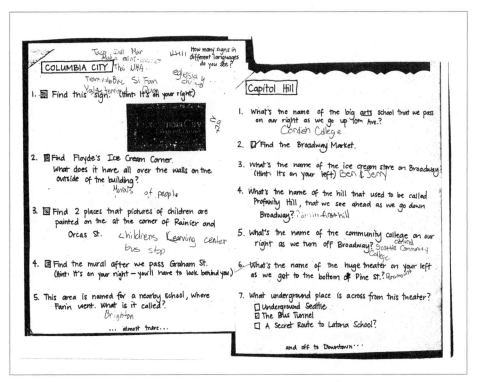

FIG. 8–4 During a Seattle history study, students traveled by bus around the city, taking in the information firsthand.

children to contribute according to their strengths and scaffold each other's learning. The students created timelines, A–Z lists, maps, a historical background, analyses of current issues, a tourist guide's description of the neighborhood, and a video clip presenting their neighborhood to the others. In their video presentations, students were encouraged to incorporate relevant art and music (the International District's group used old jazz recordings, reflecting that area's history as an early mecca for local and national jazz artists), and developed the format for presenting the information. Some students used a documentary-style, others used a news-broadcast format, and others created game shows in which contestants were quizzed on their knowledge of particular neighborhoods. (See Figure 8–5.)

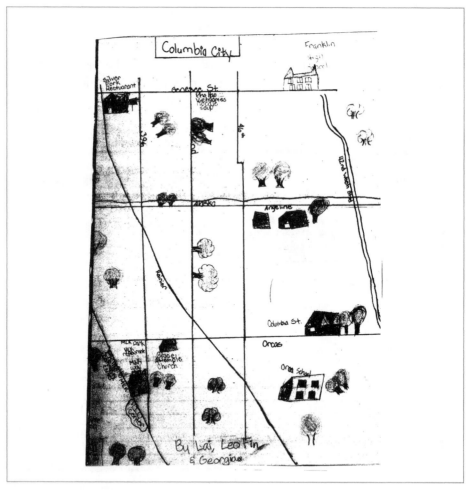

FIG. 8–5 In their research on Seattle history, students were required to produce a modern-day map, naming their own important landmarks.

CLASSROOM MATTERS

As the class worked its way through the project, the students began to incorporate the concepts and vocabulary into their discussions and their class work. The classroom community had created a tangible body of knowledge that everyone had contributed to and felt ownership of. The many English language learners in this class pushed their language and literacy learning as they read, spoke, discussed, asked questions, interviewed, wrote, analyzed, interpreted, created scripts, and presented information to different groups. The language learning was enhanced for all students as they collaborated to acquire important, intriguing, and challenging content knowledge.

Key Ideas

* Language development must be embedded in content study.

* Children learn language when they have a purpose for using it. When we build language development into engaging, meaningful content study, children are motivated to push their own language use by their desire to have access to the content.

* Factoring in children's interests when deciding on curriculum content means that children will be more interested and engaged in the learning.

* Within a content study, it's important to plan for and engineer the ways that children will speak, listen, read, and write.

* In planning a content unit, design activities that children can access and be successful in regardless of their level of literacy or language proficiency.

* Provide as much experiential learning as possible. Children learn best while they are *inside* the learning, experiencing new concepts and ideas firsthand.

9

Balanced Literacy

The man who does not read good books has no advantage over the man who cannot read them.   —*Mark Twain*

A Scenario: A Day in the Life of Balanced Literacy

Ramber is a first-grade student from Puerto Rico. He attended kindergarten with the same teacher, and is now in a multiage K–1 classroom. Ramber spent a significant part of his kindergarten year in what's called the "silent period," that time when English language learners are listening and processing language, but not quite ready to produce it independently. He was an attentive listener, but rarely spoke on his own in the classroom. All that changed in the last few months of his kindergarten year.

If we followed Ramber through one of his days later in the year, it might look something like this. Arriving in the morning, Ramber chooses a book to look at with friends until the bell rings. He cozies up in one of the library corners with a book about the deep sea, and pores over it with friends, searching out the animals detailed in the margins of the intricate illustrations. "There's the octopus!," one says. "Octopus," Ramber echoes, pointing. During the morning meeting, he watches quietly as the children generate a list of things that they've seen on a walk the day before. He watches as a student writes "I saw a," the teacher helps the child stretch out and write the letters for the word *sunflower*. The children on the carpet chime in as they hear the sounds, "s!," "n!" they shriek.

Toward the end of the morning meeting, the class works on a list of words from the day before, words that end with -*it*. One by one, the children offer new words, as the teacher walks them through the process of making new words. "*Bit*. Great! What sound do we have to put at the beginning of -*it* to make *bit*? Would you put it up there please?" Finally someone says "Spit!"; "OOOOHHH gross!" the kids shriek. Ramber laughs shyly, making a face, "Spit . . . spit . . . ," he repeats, "S . . . p . . . spit," he says as another child writes the new word on the chart.

Later in the morning, the teacher reads one of the class' favorite books, *Lilly's Purple Plastic Purse* (Henkes 1996). Ramber has heard this story before. During the story, the teacher stops to ask the children to make predictions about what will happen. When they get to the part where Lilly is bouncing along to school with her new glasses and purple plastic purse, Ramber tells his talk partner, "She gonna get trouble." After the read-aloud, Ramber selects an old favorite to read with a friend, *The Meanies Came to School* (Cowley 1995). They find a spot on the carpet in the Read Together area and begin an enthusiastic rendition of the story: "*They made a storm with paper! They made a storm with paper! They made a storm with paper! Guess what happened next?*" It hardly seems to be the same child who wouldn't speak for the first five months of school.

Before reading time is over, Ramber joins three other students with some of their "just right" books, leveled books that correspond to their particular reading levels. Together with the teacher, the group works through a new text. Today, the group will practice using initial consonants and picture cues to figure out unknown words in the text. Once they have a good grasp of that concept, they will go off to practice that strategy with other "just right" books.

After lunch, the class returns and gathers for a writer's workshop lesson. Today, the teacher is explaining how good writers tell both the inside and the outside parts of their story. She works on a story that she has created. "'I was setting the table for lunch,' that's my outside story, now let me write my inside story, 'I'm so hungry! I can't wait to eat!'" Afterward, the children begin their independent writing. Ramber is writing a story about playing basketball with a friend. On one page, he writes "*I P BB P*," and later reads it proudly to his writing partner "I played basketball at the park."

Just before the day ends, the class gathers again to read some nursery rhymes. On the carpet, the children practically burst as they follow along with the pointer. "Hickory Dickory Dock! The mouse ran up the clock!," they bellow. When they finish, the children spontaneously begin to call out words they recognize from their word wall. Ramber calls out, "Look teacher, *up*!" Another child says, "Look teacher, *ran*, that's like our list, *man, can, ran*!"

They are so proud of themselves. And as for Ramber, it looks like his "silent period" is fading into the past.

The Need for a Comprehensive, Balanced Program

This chapter discusses the importance of a balanced literacy program for English language learners. Balanced literacy is not new; in 1986, the Ohio State University Literacy Collaborative synthesized research, teacher experience, and classroom observation to create a powerful model for literacy learning that has been widely successful. They established the basic components of an effective literacy program: reading aloud, shared reading, guided reading, independent reading, shared writing, interactive writing, guided writing, independent writing, and word study. Balanced literacy is a valuable model for all students (Pressley 1998); this discussion will articulate why a balanced literacy approach is essential for English language learners.

The most important research that guides our work with English language learners is that of Brian Cambourne (1988). Cambourne spent a considerable part of his career researching the one thing that almost everyone in the world has learned successfully: how to communicate orally. How is it, he wondered, that all parents, regardless of education or wealth or social position, have successfully taught their children the complex systems required to speak a language effectively? He began to search for the conditions that allowed children to learn language naturally and seemingly effortlessly.

What emerged was a series of "learning conditions" (see Figure 9–1), which was not necessarily limited to oral language learning. The seven conditions—immersion, demonstration, expectation, responsibility, use, approximation, and response—create learner engagement, and guide students toward mastery of the learning at hand.

Cambourne (1988) subsequently applied his learning conditions to the literacy learning process. He suggested that if children could learn to speak within this context, they could also learn to read and write within a similar, carefully constructed literacy context. He sought to re-create within the classroom that natural, familiar, pleasant environment within which children learn their first language.

Cambourne's research is a cornerstone of our work with English language learners, because it speaks to the two fundamental tasks that our students face: English language learners *are* learning a brand-new language, and they are also beginning to learn how to read and write. His research gives us the framework for creating the most effective environment for our students to be successful in both areas.

A balanced literacy approach provides for all of Cambourne's conditions of learning within the classroom. Learners are immersed in all kinds of texts, they are exposed to continuous demonstrations of how to negotiate text successfully, there are many authentic purposes to which they are expected to apply their knowledge, they have

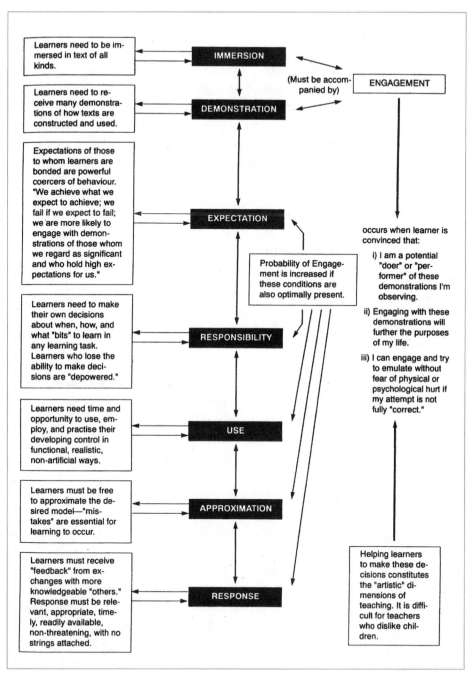

FIG. 9–1 Cambourne articulates the conditions under which authentic, meaningful learning takes place.

some freedom to direct their own literacy acquisition, the atmosphere allows children many opportunities to practice new learning without risk of failure or embarrassment, and there is regular positive feedback to guide children's performance.

English language learners need the structure of a balanced literacy program to learn the English language and to become proficient readers and writers. Fountas and Pinnell (1996) remind us that the components of balanced literacy are also integrated with the other essential building blocks of oral language development and thematic instruction. Within this comprehensive web of language development and integrated, content learning, each balanced literacy component plays an important role in guiding children toward literacy and language proficiency.

The Components of a Balanced Program

Reading Aloud

Reading aloud to children is one of the most pleasurable, effective ways to promote language and literacy development with students, and it is all the more indispensable when there are English language learners in the classroom. First of all, reading aloud demonstrates to all children the sheer delight that reading generates. As we read to children, we subtly, and sometimes explicitly, teach them concepts of text—story structure, making meaning through various strategies, character construction—but we are teaching children to *love* reading (Goodman 1984; Green and Harker 1982; Schickendanz 1978; Trelease 1990). During a read-aloud, we encourage children to relax, enjoy the story, and follow their own line of thinking and feeling through a text. This is not the time when we are giving children a test about the story; we want them to simply engage with the text on a personal level. As we read to them, we want children to see and feel how reading can change us: how it shapes our ideas, teaches us, questions us, and makes our lives bigger.

An interactive read-aloud is a strategic way to bring children into a read-aloud text, and it is a powerful tool for English language learners. In an interactive read-aloud, the teacher is not simply reading the text; rather, she has planned very intentionally how to engage the children in the text during the reading. Specifically, the teacher may have planned important questions at key points in the book, encouraging the children to think and talk about one aspect of the story or another. She may have identified vocabulary words that children may struggle with, and may plan on how to clarify those words during the reading.

The teacher may stop during a read-aloud and ask children to use a comprehension strategy to support their understanding. At the beginning of Lynne Cherry's *The Great Kapok Tree*, for example, the teacher may encourage the kids to stop at the beginning and create an image of the jungle in their minds: "Do you hear the monkeys howling? Do you feel the warm steam rising from the forest floor? Do you see the rays of sunshine poking through the thick canopy of leaves?"

Good choices for teacher read-alouds are usually somewhat beyond the independent reading level of the students. For English language learners, read-alouds are a good way to introduce them to more complex language, more sophisticated vocabulary, and more advanced concepts and ideas. Children can have access to and process these higher levels of thinking without having to be responsible for producing the surrounding language.

Finally, read-alouds provide valuable language models for English language learners. Hearing text read aloud by a competent reader is critical for ELL children: they hear how fluent language sounds, and they internalize the rhythms and tones of a new language. While we are teaching *all* of the students to create voice and expression in text, we are also communicating important elements of the English language to new language learners.

Shared Reading

Shared reading is one of the most powerful reading experiences that English language learners can have. In the example of Ramber, at the beginning of this chapter, his teacher expressed that the opportunity to do lots of shared reading, in the group and independently among friends, was the single most important contributor to Ramber's language and literacy growth. Most of all, she said, it made him look, act, and *feel* like a competent reader.

Shared reading is any reading situation where all children can either see an enlarged text or where all children have their own individual copies of a text that is being read aloud. The texts, especially in the primary grades, are usually repetitive, predictable, and fun. Big books, poems, and chants written on chart paper, songbooks, nursery rhymes written on posterboard, are all some of the many examples of shared reading opportunities. The real purpose of shared reading is to re-create "lap time" with children: that invaluable time that children spend (or not!) on a parent's lap in the early formative years, reading silly poems and repetitive stories. In the classroom, shared reading is like having all of the students on your lap, reading pleasurable materials with them for the sheer delight of it.

But beyond just the enjoyment that children get out of it, shared reading has many, many specific lessons for children, especially English language learners. During shared reading, children learn many important literacy concepts:

- ✳ One-to-one word matching
- ✳ The difference between a letter, a word, and a sentence
- ✳ Directionality of print
- ✳ Identifying words by the initial consonant
- ✳ Identifying letters and sight words in context
- ✳ Concept of rhyme
- ✳ Beginning phonics and phonemic awareness
- ✳ Punctuation and sentence construction

It should be emphasized that shared reading should begin with multiple readings of the text just for enjoyment. As with read-alouds, shared reading really helps English language learners begin to internalize the rhythms of the English language. Shared reading is also a time when many children who are new speakers of the language feel comfortable producing some language; as the group is reciting a poem, for example, a child might begin to say some parts of the poem that are familiar. During a group reading, the rest of the students will carry the child through the unfamiliar parts of the poem, and no one will notice if the child makes a mistake or doesn't pronounce a word perfectly. Shared reading is a fun, risk-free time for English language learners to push their language in a supportive environment.

When children are offered the same shared reading texts during independent reading time, English language learners will flock to them. Children can sit around a familiar big book day in and day out, "reading" the text to each other. They help each other through a text in the same way that the larger group does. As they approximate what proficient readers do, they begin to integrate particular aspects of the language and literacy into their knowledge. When Ramber first began to read the *Meanies*, for example, he began by just reciting the lines from memory. Eventually, he learned to point to the individual words, and from there, he began to recognize sight words in the text and use them as anchors during his reading. All the while, he was building confidence in himself as a proficient, powerful reader (Holdaway 1979; Martinez and Roser 1985; Snow 1983; Sulzby 1985).

After a group has read a text several times, the teacher may begin to point out certain elements of the text that children may be learning about, such as letters, punctuation, or repeated text. More likely, children will begin to spontaneously identify and call out things that they notice in the text. As in the example at the beginning of the chapter, children at all levels of language and literacy development can latch on to one or another learning opportunity in the text. While one child may be finding the first letter of her name in the text, another may be noticing that some words have the mysterious apostrophe in them, and be ready to know why. Shared reading is a great, multilevel activity that addresses many learning opportunities all at once. And, it's great fun!

Guided Reading

While guided reading looks different in different classrooms, the format and purpose are generally the same: small groups of children with similar needs come together around a carefully chosen text for the purpose of developing reading strategies and fluency. Guided reading is an important element for English language learners: it helps them build a body of texts that they can read fluently, and that support the particular strategies that they are working on at any given moment.

Guided reading is grounded in a broad set of leveled texts, which can be matched to readers depending on interest and skills being learned. The leveled texts allow us to find books that readers can mostly read; what's left for them in the text is a small bit of reading "work" that targets a specific skill or strategy. Guided reading works for English language learners because it is a developmentally appropriate way to support literacy, and because it also scaffolds language development. As teachers support children through guided reading texts, they can skillfully and purposefully "up the ante," pushing children each time a little further in their literacy growth (Clay 1991; Fountas and Pinnell 1996; Lyons, Pinnell, and DeFord 1993; Routman 1991).

Consider this example. Resep is an English language learner in first grade. He has just begun to notice (through lots of shared and independent reading) that many words end with the suffix -*ing*. Up to this point he has heard those words as *cleane* or *jumpe* (with a long *e* sound at the end), and he writes those words that same way. He has not been sure what to do with words that he finds in his books that end in -*ing*. For his guided reading lesson, the teacher chooses a book with lots of words that end with -*ing*. She explains to his small group how and why we add -*ing* to a word, and points it out to him in the text. He uses picture clues and practices each page carefully, emphasizing the -*ing* as he saw his teacher do. "Mom is cleaning. Mom is digging. Mom is painting" he reads. He smiles as he makes the connection to what he hears, what he reads, and what he now knows how to say more clearly. He takes two more books that his teacher has chosen for him and goes off to practice his new learning in the comfort of the corner beanbag.

Guided reading can be set up in many different ways. Some classrooms use reading inventories or assessments to group children homogeneously for guided reading. In this way they can choose texts that are likely to meet the needs of each particular group of children. These groups meet regularly and focus on skills and strategies that more or less correspond to that particular reading level.

In other classrooms, teachers generate lessons based on what they observe children doing, and form fluid groups around those particular lessons. This is an especially effective way to provide targeted skill and strategy instruction to English language learners. Adding in the language learning piece to children's literacy development means that sometimes the sequence of skill development may not be the same as for a child who is not simultaneously learning the English language. There may be a mismatch between what children can do orally and what they can negotiate in a text.

Take the example of a first-grade English language learner, who reads above–grade level material and speaks English fairly fluently. While he was a strong reader (he had a good foundation of oral English on which to base his reading), the teacher began to notice that he was actually missing some of the lower-level strategies that would normally be taught to more beginning readers. When faced with an unknown word in the text, for example, he was not clear about the need to use picture clues to help him figure out the new word. Thus, his teacher pulled him, along with a few other beginning readers, into a group that was focused on how to use picture clues to identify unknown words. In his normal, higher reading group, the teacher probably would not have taught that strategy specifically, assuming that those children had already mastered it.

The essential ingredients for meaningful guided reading are careful teacher observation of student reading behaviors combined with a good understanding of the stages of language and literacy development. When we know just what students are doing proficiently in their reading, it becomes easier to pick out the next teaching step more accurately. Beyond this, we need access to an extensive collection of leveled texts, which serve as the scaffold for children's literacy development.

Independent Reading

Independent reading is the time that students have to put all of their skills and strategies and excitement for learning and reading into action. It's the time when beginning or developing readers become authentic readers (Clay 1991; Krashen 1988, 1993; Pilgreen 2000). Although independent reading time often gets edged out by whole- or small-group reading instruction, it is an absolutely essential part of every student's reading diet, particularly when those students are also English language learners. Cambourne (1988) reminds us that *use* and *expectation* are important elements in creating an optimum learning environment. During independent reading time, children have the opportunity to use, practice, and develop their skills in authentic, engaging, and meaningful ways. During this important time in the classroom, we expect children to look, act, enjoy, learn, and think like real readers do.

Independent reading time may look slightly different from classroom to classroom, but there are several guidelines that will make this time most effective across the board. First, there must be a regular, uninterrupted time for children to read. Teachers have an important responsibility in promoting this time as valuable and indispensable; it shouldn't be the first thing to go if there are interruptions in the

daily schedule. Second, children should have unfettered access to a wide variety of reading materials (Krashen 1993). Leveled "just right" books, tubs of interesting content books, poetry, songbooks, big books, interactive and shared writings produced by the class, picture and chapter books, reference books, magazines and periodicals, even comic books, should all be available for children to access. Remember, this is the time that children become *real* readers, and real readers read things that are interesting and meaningful to *them*; it is key that children find these materials in the classroom.

Third, reading during this time should not be subject to intense recordkeeping or accountability. It's important to remind ourselves that all children *want* to learn and read. In our classrooms, when we find children avoiding reading, it's generally not because they don't want to read. Rather, it is usually a function of one or more of the following: children can't find or don't know how to find a text that they can read (a "just right" book), children can't find a book that they're truly interested in (yes, there *is* something for everyone!), or children have developed a veritable fear of or dislike for reading, usually because of limited reading skills and/or a history of failure at reading. In the first two instances, we realize how important it is to have a wide variety of texts available to students, and to teach them how to negotiate them. In the last instance, where kids have developed an aversion to reading, good instruction and plenty of time for independent reading become all the more essential; children will only be compelled to push themselves as readers by reading materials that are interesting, relevant, and accessible to them. And we can share with students our plan for them, explaining the ways that the different components of our reading, particularly spending lots of time with "just right" books, become stepping-stones to greater proficiency.

From the teacher's perspective, independent reading time is the time for children to put all of their developing skills and strategies to work for an authentic purpose. From the students' perspective, independent reading is the time that they use reading to pursue their own passions, questions, and interests, just like real readers (Fielding, Wilson, and Anderson 1989).

Shared Writing

Shared writing is another powerful tool for English language learners. It is another way to give children access to communication that is far beyond what they are capable of producing independently. During a shared writing exercise, children are giving ideas and creating text orally, while the teacher transcribes it onto an enlarged paper in front of the class (Goodman 1984; Holdaway 1979; Sulzby 1985). Again, this kind of activity scaffolds writing and literacy development for all children, but for English language learners, it has the added benefit of simultaneously scaffolding English language development.

Shared writing is also a fabulous way to build community in a classroom. Often, shared writing is done around common experiences that the class has had together, such as a field trip or a visitor to the class. Together, the children are developing a shared body of knowledge, and that knowledge is recorded in a way that gives all children access to it. Because the writing is done in front of the class, the children are engaged in its creation, and can often reread this writing even though it may be well beyond their independent reading level. Shared writings often become important parts of the shared reading collection.

During a shared writing activity, the teacher solicits ideas from the children around a particular topic of interest. Say, for example, a group is talking about behaviors that good readers demonstrate. The teacher asks the children to identify people in their lives that are good readers. "What do they do that makes you think that they are good readers?" she asks the students. As the children offer ideas, the teacher writes the information on a chart.

During the discussion, one of the children, an English language learner, says, "Ms. Cerna, you read good, you don't say da word bad, no you say 'no,' then you only say da word good." The teacher walks the student through the statement, using a "generous appraisal" of the student's idea, and scaffolding the child's language. "That's right! You noticed that when I'm reading and I say a word wrong, when I make a mistake, I go back and try to figure the word out! You are so smart! That's what good readers do, isn't it?!" On the paper, the teacher writes, reading out loud, "*Ms. Cerna—When she makes a mistake she goes back and tries to fix it.*"

Shared writing is such an important time to validate higher-level ideas that English language learners have and to model appropriate oral and written language for them. In this way, we give children access to so much more than what they could access on their own. And as with shared reading, shared writing allows for children to direct their attention to what they are ready to learn at each moment, something that is so important for English language learners: while one child may be hearing the /s/ sound and delighting in watching the teacher write the letter, another may be noticing that all of the first letters of each sentence begin with a capital letter. In each case, those children are ready to learn those lessons at that particular moment, and the shared writing activity gives them a powerful way to internalize those concepts.

In the context of an authentic class conversation, the teacher is modeling so many important writing skills: how sentences are structured, how you sound out words as you write them, the order of letters and words and the directionality of writing, what good handwriting looks like, how words are spaced, punctuation, and so on. As the children watch the teacher write, they are matching letters to the sounds they hear, they are identifying sight words, they are watching as a writer organizes her thoughts, they are problem solving their way through harder words (Goodman 1984; Holdaway 1979). They are watching a fluent, proficient writer in action.

Interactive Writing

Interactive writing is often done in the same space around the same kinds of classrooms discussions as shared writing, except that during an interactive writing, children are taking at least some of the responsibility for the actual writing. As the students are generating ideas and creating text together, in either a whole-group or small-group setting, the teacher is inviting the students to come up and actually write some of the words.

While students are up doing the writing, the teacher is providing guidance and feedback. This is a time for the teacher to give some "short and sweet" instruction about writing concepts and skills, in direct response to what a student is writing in the moment. Skills taught during this time range from the most basic to the more complicated: a kindergarten teacher may take the time to help the writer (and the group) notice the difference between a *b* and a *d*, while a second-grade teacher might teach kids how to combine ideas to make more sophisticated sentences. At no point, however, should the teaching of skills interrupt or supersede the real purpose at hand: to create a cohesive, meaningful text. Lessons should be concise and appropriate to what children need at any particular moment in order to proceed with the writing (Button, Johnson, and Furgerson 1996; McCarrier, Pinnell, and Fountas 1999).

The critical ingredient in interactive writing, as it is in all instruction for English language learning, is *meaning*. An interactive writing lesson is not a lesson created just to teach specific skills; rather, it is another way that teachers utilize real opportunities for writing to enhance children's development as writers. As such, teachers may employ interactive writing at different times during the day: after a walk, to capture what was seen and experienced; to write a collective thank-you to a visitor; to create captions for photographs; to retell an event or a community story; to label diagrams or artifacts; and so on. The authentic opportunities for this kind of writing should present themselves readily in any classroom that emphasizes experience- and meaning-based curriculum.

Consider this example from a kindergarten classroom. The class has created a garden together, and has spent weeks learning about plants, studying life cycles, reading poems and books about gardens, digging in the dirt, and watching with delight as their seedlings emerge. At one point the teacher asks her small reading groups to help her add captions to the photographs she has taken to chronicle the creation of the garden. She chooses a photo and calls a group to her table.

"So what can we write about this picture?" she asks. "What's happening here that we want the reader to understand?"

The children begin to talk excitedly about the day that they planted the seeds in the garden. Together, the group settles on one sentence: "We planted a surprise garden."

"Great," says the teacher. "Let's say that sentence together and hear what word we need to write first." The kids say the sentence to themselves several times, and they begin to shriek the first word. "'We'! 'We,' teacher! It's from our word wall!" One of the children takes the pen and begins to write the first word carefully. The kids then reread the first written word until they realize which word needs to follow.

"You're right," the teacher says, "Next we need *planted*. Let's really stretch that word out and see if we hear the first sound in *planted*." The kids stretch the word out as they repeat it, until they determine the first letter. One child takes the pen and begins to write *p*, right next to the *e* in *We*. "Now let me show you one important thing that writers do, and that is that they leave big spaces between their words, so people can read their writing easily. Let's say our sentence: *We planted* . . . See that? When we finish writing *we*, we're ready for the next word, *planted*, so we have to leave a big space." The teacher takes a piece of paper, glues it quickly over the misplaced *p*, and points to the space where the child needs to begin writing again.

The group continues stretching out the word, writing the corresponding sounds, until they decide that the final letter in the word *planted*, the one that comes after *t*, is *d*. Many of the English language learners in the group stopped at *t*, thinking that

April 14

They grew bigger.

the word was really *plant*. "I'm going to show you something tricky about this word *planted*," the teacher says. "When we are talking about something that we did before right now, like maybe yesterday or last week or this morning, we often have to put these two letters *-ed* at the end. I'm just going to put those two letters at the end, because that tells the reader that we planted the seeds a while ago." The teacher adds the letters quickly, and goes on to ask the kids to reread what has been written so far.

The group continues this way for about fifteen to twenty minutes, rereading, stretching words out, finding words around the room that can help them, and getting quick, instructive feedback from their teacher. Finally, they have a finished product: a page to contribute to the class garden book that they all wrote together, and that they can all read!

Guided Writing

Guided writing is any period of time in the classroom in which the teacher provides direct instruction of writing skills, which children are then expected to put to use in creating their own writing pieces. The teacher provides short, whole-group lessons, but may also work with children in small groups on particular strategies. Generally, the teacher also uses a conference format to guide children's writing one-on-one. Children usually work at their own pace during this time, beginning new pieces, conferencing, revising, and publishing as their work progresses (Calkins 1986, 2003; Graves 1983, 1994). In many classrooms, this block of time takes the form of a writer's workshop.

As in other parts of the curriculum, the guidelines for making a writer's workshop most successful for English language learners also help you maximize the benefits for all children. First and foremost, a successful writing program is one that allows children to plug in at whatever skill level they happen to be at. English language learners may often lack the language or technical skills required to produce a polished piece of writing, but it doesn't mean that they don't have great stories in their heads, and it doesn't mean that you shouldn't continue to develop that very important aspect of writing. A writer's workshop should be primarily based in articulating meaning; that is, children are taught how to come up with great ideas, how to expand on them, and how to communicate them to others. Kids need to see why writing is important and why they want to become writers.

There is a great deal that children can do in a writer's workshop that doesn't have to be slowed by limited access to English, or for that matter, lack of technical skills (i.e., kids who are not proficient with a pencil, kids who have no letter–sound knowledge to add to their writing, etc.). Pictures and sketches are perfectly suitable for telling stories, and can allow children to communicate their ideas without worrying about English language limitations. Concepts such as story structure, sequencing, adding details, even literary elements such as irony or surprise, can be effectively developed through sketching and drawing. A writing program that is based on communicating meaning allows children to develop fully as writers, even if their written and oral language skills are slower to catch up.

Further, any effective writing program for children, especially English language learners, must be designed to allow children to use themselves as their primary source of story and ideas. In other words, a writer's workshop should be a place where children are encouraged to tell their own stories, whatever they are; it's our job as teachers of writing to help children express themselves through print. After all, we all do our best writing when we are writing about something we care about (Calkins 2003).

For English language learners, self-expression is an especially important element in a writer's workshop, because it allows ELLs to draw on their extensive background knowledge, which may be overlooked at other times during the school day. During writer's workshop, children identify, articulate, and develop their own "funds of knowledge" (Moll, Amanti, Neff, and Gonzalez 1992). It's a time for children to demonstrate, for example, the joy that they find in going crabbing with a grandfather, or the combination of wonder and familiarity that they felt visiting a parent's home country. Older children especially need to be able to draw on their background knowledge; they may be perfectly capable of explaining how to make a piñata, for example, but they may not have the written English to put the words down on paper. That student needs to be able to use sketches to communicate his ideas, and can learn along with other children how to make them clearer and more interesting. When we encourage children to first develop and then write from their own interests and experiences, we set the stage for them to push themselves as writers, to seek out the skills needed to most effectively tell their own stories.

At this point, the tremendous work being done in this area by Lucy Calkins and her colleagues (2003) at the Teachers College Reading and Writing Project must be mentioned. *Units of Study for Primary Writing,* a yearlong writing curriculum for kindergarten to second grade, is an amazing guide for teachers wanting to develop and implement a meaningful writing program. Not only is this work an excellent guide

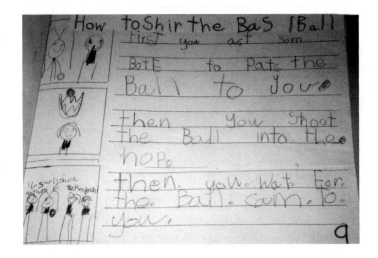

for teachers of writing, it is also exceptional in its relevance for English language learners. *Units of Study* provides all the essential elements not just for developing writers, but particularly for supporting English language learners as writers; it articulates how to teach writing in a way that circumvents language or technical limitations, while simultaneously developing the surrounding language and mechanics of writing. Most important though, this curriculum teaches children to look at their own lives as the richest source for stories and writing; children draw on their own experiences to make a "small moment" larger than life, to write a how-to book, or to create poems. In classroom after classroom that has used this curriculum, non-English speakers and nonwriters have blossomed into proficient, dynamic storytellers.

Independent Writing

Independent writing is simply a time for children to direct their own work as writers. There is no accountability during this writing, in the sense that this writing is not guided or evaluated by the teacher. Rather, children use this time to write for their own purposes (Clay 1975; Ferreiro and Teberosky 1982; Harste, Woodward, and Burke 1984). They may choose to write a letter, they might write a note to a friend, they might make a poster demonstrating some learning that has been interesting to them, they might write in a journal. As in independent reading time, it doesn't matter as much *what* children write, as long as they are writing!

In some classrooms, there may be a designated time for freewriting, like a journal writing time. In other classrooms, children might simply have access to writing materials at different times during the day in order to pursue their own writing projects. In any case, offering time and materials for children to direct their own writing experiences contributes to their perception of themselves as writers. As Brian Cambourne reminds us, we expect children to be writers, and we encourage them to find their own authentic uses for writing.

Word Study

Word study is any time during the school day when teachers and children are looking at and learning about words as individual units. Word study encompasses a range of activities, including phonics, word families, structural analysis, and spelling (Bear, Invernizzi, Templeton, and Johnston 2003; Cunningham 1995; Cunningham and Hall 1994; Pinnell and Fountas 1998; Schickendanz 1986). The developmental process for understanding how words function is similar, regardless of whether children are native English speakers or are English language learners. Although this process may seem different for older ELL children (they don't start off with the kinds of letter-learning activities that are appropriate for kindergarteners!), it is usually because those children are in the tricky process of transferring their prior knowledge of language and language systems to the English language.

Generally, children begin by learning to identify sounds with particular letters. From there, children expand to look at and integrate common spelling patterns ("chunks") and word families (*-ight*), digraphs (*th-*), and blends (*pl-*). Beyond that, children begin to look at words as being composed of different identifiable chunks of meaning; words have prefixes, suffixes, root words, common origins, and so on, that can help children identify the meaning of a word. During word study, we guide children through this process of understanding how to understand and manipulate words.

At this point, it is important to emphasize two important principles that underlie our word work with English language learners. First, as always, word study must be centered on meaning. Although there exists a clear set of blends and word families and prefixes that we want children to be able to understand and utilize, it is critical that our word study with English language learners emerge from our natural literacy work with children as much as possible. So, for example, if a group of kindergartners is reading a poem on chart paper that has lots of *-ight* words in it, and the children spontaneously begin to notice the similar word endings, that is the moment to

introduce the -*ight* word family to the children. It may be that not all of the children know all of their letters and sounds, but after several readings of that particular poem, many of them are ready to latch on to the -*ight* chunk. That's the time to finish reading the poem and make a list of -*ight* words with the children. You might say, "You noticed that a lot of words in this poem end with this spelling pattern, -*ight*. You are so observant! Can you think of some other words that *might* end with that same spelling pattern?"

Secondly, and similarly, it is important to keep in mind that this is a fluid process and that there is not necessarily a set order to guide word study with kids. In this day and age of controlled, rigid direct phonics instruction, it's important to keep in mind that children make their way through this complicated process in different ways. This becomes even more accurate when we add English language learners to the mix. Children who don't know all of their letter sounds are totally capable of integrating the -*ing* suffix into their reading and writing, if it is learned in a meaningful context.

Frequently with older ELL children, children who are quite happy and capable doing age-appropriate content material still need a bit of catch-up work in the word study area. If this is done in the context of meaningful grade-level work, and if teachers can make the connection between the students knowledge of language concepts in the first language, word study can often proceed much more quickly than with younger children. English language learners (even native English speakers) who are able to read and comprehend fairly proficiently, for example, may benefit by going back and doing some specific work with vowel sounds, for example. This work must be done as much as possible within the context of what children are already working on in the classroom.

The bottom line is that we need to become sharp observers of our children. We need to keep constant track of what children are noticing in their reading and writing, what they are experimenting with, and which next step they seem to be ready for. Beyond this, the key to guiding children's word study is for teachers at all levels to understand the elements of word study, so that they can effectively assess children's progress and suggest the next steps. It's important to do our homework outside of class time; that is, come to a clear understanding of all that we want children to know, so that when students are making moves toward particular skills, we can jump right in and give them what they need.

For example, during a read-aloud of *Stuart Little*, the teacher read in the text that Stuart was "unharmed" after his boat capsized. Several of the children in the class referred to that word *unharmed* and said that they knew it meant "not hurt" or "fine." Because the children have noticed it spontaneously, and because the teacher knows that *un-* is an important prefix to know, the teacher gave a brief, spontaneous lesson on it after the read-aloud time was over. After discussing the events of the chapter, the teacher turned the kids' attention to the prefix and asked them to brainstorm other *un-* words for a chart.

A Final Note

This chapter is not designed to provide you with the ins and outs of how to implement each component of balanced literacy in your classroom. Setting up and managing each component of a balanced literacy program takes a great deal of organization and planning. Rather, in this day and age of "scientifically based," direct instruction, this discussion emphasizes the absolutely critical need to develop a balanced literacy program for English language learners. Learning for ELLs must be based first and foremost on *meaning* and *purpose.* Only a balanced literacy approach provides for all of Cambourne's conditions for optimum learning; it is the only sensible, effective way to turn all students, and particularly English language learners, into powerful readers, writers, and thinkers.

For the real nuts and bolts of designing a balanced literacy program, consult the experts listed at the end of this book.

Key Ideas

* ✳ Cambourne (1988) has identified seven conditions for optimum learning that shape our work in developing language and literacy for ELLs: immersion, demonstration, expectation, responsibility, use, approximation, and response.

* ✳ Balanced literacy, comprised of reading aloud, shared reading and writing, guided reading and writing, independent reading and writing, interactive reading, and word study, provides for all of Cambourne's learning conditions and provides maximum language and literacy learning opportunities for English language learners.

* ✳ Reading aloud teaches as it models proficiency and the joy of reading.

* ✳ Shared reading allows children to approximate in a fun way as they slowly but surely gain more control over the reading process.

* ✳ Guided reading matches readers to leveled texts and gives them targeted instruction at their individual reading level.

* Independent reading allows readers to make decisions about their own reading and learning, and is an opportunity for them to find their own joy through reading.

* Shared writing is an opportunity for the teacher to scaffold student's ideas and translate them into proficient writing that is modeled in front of the group.

* Interactive writing gives students the opportunity to recognize and contribute what they can write, while the teacher provides additional support to complete the writing.

* Guided writing and independent writing are opportunities for children to write from their own experiences and interests, with varying levels of teacher support.

* Word study includes sound–symbol relationships, spelling patterns, word families, prefixes, suffixes, root words, any kind of activity in which *words* themselves are at the center of the learning.

10

Oral Language and Vocabulary Development

People generally quarrel because they cannot argue.   —*Gilbert K. Chesterton*

A Scenario: Word Explorers

Mrs. Flores sits in the Reading Center with a small group of fourth graders who have happily chosen to spend their recess exploring new words. The kids are "Word Explorers," always in pursuit of new and interesting words that they can integrate into their ever-expanding vocabularies.

Rigoberta notices the word *vegetarian* on the word wall in the Reading Center.

"What's a *vegetarian*?" she asks the other kids, who are milling around the classroom, looking for their own new words.

"Has anyone heard that word before? Does anyone know what that word means?" asks Mrs. Flores.

"Oh, that's a doctor for animals," says another boy.

"No, not quite," corrects Mrs. Flores, "You're thinking of a *veterinarian*. Anybody else know that word?"

None of the kids seem to know what the word means, so Mrs. Flores explains.

"A *vegetarian* is a person who eats only fruits and vegetables," she begins.

"Oh, I know," says Jesus, nonchalantly, "like an *herbivore*."

Mrs. Flores and the other teachers in the room remember back to the beginning of the year, when Jesus first began to come to the Reading Center. He, like many beginning English language learners, spoke in short choppy phrases that lacked the formalities of proper syntax and grammar. Though he seemed eager, his conversations with others were cramped by his limited vocabulary and sophistication with the English language.

His classroom teacher had referred him to the Reading Center because of the limited reading comprehension that he demonstrated in class. Jesus had so much trouble with reading that he had come to take not understanding as a given. He could decode readily, but he just expected he wouldn't understand what he was reading, and any effort to discover meaning didn't seem worth it.

As the Reading Center teachers began to work with Jesus to improve his reading comprehension, they realized that the larger obstacle was his shallow vocabulary. No matter how much mental imaging or verbalizing he did, Jesus couldn't get around the fact that he just didn't understand many of the words he was reading.

To meet the needs of Jesus and so many of his classmates who were in the same situation, the Reading Center teachers designed a program called "Word Explorers." When students came across a word that they didn't recognize, they sought out a quick, initial definition from a teacher or a classmate, and the exploration was underway. For each word, the students would enter it into their Word Explorer book, and then engage at least three adults in conversation about that particular word. "Hi, I'm a Word Explorer," they'd start. "Would you explore a word with me? My word is *wake*." From there, the student and the adult would come up with sentences using the word, and would, more often than not, get into a discussion about the word itself or its meaning. After several of these conversations with adults, the students usually had a pretty good understanding of each word.

Over the course of the year, Jesus added about 130 words to his Word Explorer book. Not only did he learn the meaning of 130 new words that were interesting to him, but, his teacher notes, that translated into about 400 engaging, purposeful conversations with adults that Jesus initiated. Jesus' oral language blossomed; not only was he learning so much more English, he was always pushing himself to talk more, to learn more, to engage others in his own learning and development. His oral language became more fluid, more grammatically and syntactically correct; he sounded like a proficient English speaker.

Once Jesus realized that he could take on any new word that came his way in a fun, engaging way, he was unstoppable. He wanted to know *every* word, and his endless questions as he read revealed just how limited his vocabulary really was. He asked about words his teachers hadn't even imagined that he wouldn't know: *lemon, fork,* and *wave* were seemingly simple words, but Jesus wasn't familiar with them, and didn't understand them in context.

The combination of purposeful conversation and explicit vocabulary development was just what Jesus needed to turn the corner in his reading and in his English.

He was no longer satisfied not understanding what he read or heard. He learned how to take control of his own learning, how to solicit the help of others for his own understanding, and how to make language work for him. His totally laid-back connection between the new word *vegetarian* and a sophisticated word that he already knew, *herbivore*, revealed a relaxed, newly found enthusiasm for the challenges of reading and speaking a second language.

The Four Domains of Language

Literacy instruction in the typical classroom is heavily focused on reading and writing development. Reading and writing are, however, only two ways that we use language to communicate. Speaking and listening are also integral parts of authentic communication, and for students learning a second language, are critical to overall language and literacy development. Peregoy and Boyle (2001) discuss the interconnectedness of the four realms of communication, describing them as "complex relationships of mutual support" (108). Boyle (1979) elaborates, "In our day-to-day lives oral and written language are interwoven like threads in a tapestry, each supporting the other" (109) to create a larger, meaningful picture.

Not only are speaking and listening essential to the process of negotiating information and making meaning in the world, but they are also essential to the process of learning a second language. When children begin to speak, they interact with others in a way that furthers their understanding of and control over language. For children and other new speakers of a language, meaning is everything. As students speak, they elicit feedback from other listeners that supports them in clarifying and refining their speech. As children listen to language, they engage in the "negotiation of meaning"; they use background knowledge, context clues, body language, tone and rhythm cues, and other clues to make meaning of what they're hearing (Long 1981; Long and Porter 1985; Peregoy and Boyle 2001). As they listen, they are making sense for themselves of the rules and conventions of language in an urgent, relevant way.

Facilitating development in any of the four processes of language "contributes to the overall reservoir of second language knowledge, which is then available for other acts of listening, speaking, reading, or writing" (Peregoy and Boyle 2001, 108). For this reason, it is important for educators to be conscious of the need to make oral language and vocabulary development specific objectives in their classrooms. Even as teachers provide opportunities for children to engage in conversations and interactions with others during the day, it is important that these occasions not be accidental or insignificant.

Oral language development and vocabulary development must be intentional, integrated components of our work with English language learners. Rather than carving out more of our already limited time with students, we must learn how to facilitate these important aspects of language into our daily work with children. Although it may seem like more work in the same limited time, oral language proficiency and vocabulary are best developed in the normal everyday happenings of classroom life. It's just a matter of focusing ourselves in the right direction.

Integrating Oral Language Development into our Classrooms

Chapter 7 focused on the importance of structuring a classroom to allow students to *talk* during the school day as much as possible. Kids need as much practice with the speaking, listening, and negotiating meaning aspects of language as they can get. This will not come through letter–sound relationship practice or through phonics drills; it will only come through meaningful, purposeful communication within the context of everyday learning.

Opportunities for oral language development should be integrated into the fabric of daily classroom life. Throughout the day, children should be encouraged to interact and communicate with each other in a purposeful way. The teacher should also be a constant source of feedback and support for children's oral language. It's critical that we are conscious of the way we talk to children. If we just grunt at kids and speak in choppy phrases all the time, our children will imitate us. If we speak clearly, using lots of descriptive and clarifying words in complete, complex sentences, our children will also replicate that precision with language.

Scaffolding Children's Language

Clearly, we must give children feedback that they are ready for; just as in reading and writing, we need to learn to recognize the "next steps" for children in their oral language. Cambourne's (1988) research illuminates the example of parents building language capacity in their very young children. When a baby points to a car and says "Ca!" we respond with something like "Yes, that's a *car*. It's a *red* car parked on the street." In any classroom, the teacher is the strongest language model, and in classes with lots of English language learners, the teacher may be the only language model. We need to maximize the opportunity to model sophisticated, precise language for ELLs. It's critical to take advantage of the many "teachable moments" throughout each day where children are ready to absorb new learning that is important to them.

When a child is excitedly telling you about how they "felled at da bed" the night before, you can respond, "Oh no! You fell out of bed! Did you hurt yourself when you fell out of bed? I hate falling out of bed!" More often than not, the child is ready to pick up on your subtle corrections and integrate them into their emerging language base. And if they don't pick it up this time, they will the next time, or the next time after that.

Chapter 7 provides some ways to build oral language into the classroom routine. It is also worthwhile to invest time in activities and lessons where oral language is both the means and the end. Especially as we work with English language learners, we need to keep in mind that we don't have to *read* or *write* everything. Sometimes our students get much more out of simply talking. The oral language that is developed and reinforced during these activities will contribute tremendously to students' overall command of English.

Strategies for Facilitating Oral Language in Your Classroom

The following suggested activities are just a few of the many lessons and strategies that you can use with all of your children to enhance language development. Wherever appropriate and possible, these strategies should be integrated into the content learning that students are already doing.

Teaching students how to help each other ✳ We can help children understand the process of oral language development, so that they can take a bit of control over the process themselves. For those who are learning (aren't we all?) we can teach them how asking questions will improve their rate of language acquisition. Giving them the actual language means that when they are confused working with a partner, they might say "I didn't understand when you said . . . Could you explain that to me?" We also teach children to help each other as they communicate with each other. We show them how to model language the way we do, so that when they hear a classmate say, "My pencil got broked," the might, one fine day, say "Oh, your pencil broke? I'm sorry your pencil is broken. Let me find you another pencil that's not broken." In this way, we teach *all* children to pay more attention to language and to listen for meaning, clarity, and accuracy.

Facilitating meaningful conversation ✳ Conversation is an art to be learned in itself (Cole 2003), and it's all the more complicated if a student is trying to do it in a second language. It's not enough to simply give children time to discuss or engage in conversation. Being explicit about such things as, "While the other person is talking, I want you to look at them and I want you to lean your head in so you can hear them properly" or "While you listen, I want you to make a mental image of what the person is saying" or "If you didn't understand, you can say 'Could you please repeat that part?'" will teach children the rules and the art of engaging in meaningful conversation. With this kind of instruction, and of course with lots of practice, children become more confident and competent speakers; they seek out conversation more often, invest more into, and get more out of conversation.

Setting up discussion groups ✳ Discussion groups can be particularly effective when they are based in content study that children are already doing. Basically, they are structured, goal-oriented conversations among children. During math, you might set up discussion groups to consider why the results of a survey turned out the way they did; rather than having to write out their ideas, students can be encourage to discuss their thoughts and share back to the rest of the group. During a morning meeting, you may set up a time to discuss current events. Children could break up into small groups and consider different aspects of a timely issue with each other. Students can be taught and encouraged to hold their own literature discussion groups, during a reader's workshop for example (Miller 2002). A tub of books with multiple copies of each title, plus lots of modeling, will facilitate this.

Encouraging students to discuss important, content-based topics in small, independent discussion groups may sound impossible. The truth is that it may be forced and limited at one moment, and noisy and distracted at another. But don't give up, children can and need to do it. Even if it seems like a waste of time to begin with, if you stick to it and continue to model your expectations and norms, even young children will begin to discuss issues and content competently on their own.

Encouraging oral presentations ✳ Rather than expecting that all knowledge and learning be demonstrated through some kind of written assignment, consider allowing children to present learning through oral presentations. They could still be expected to provide visuals to accompany their presentations, but they would spend the majority of their time explaining and demonstrating their understanding of a particular topic. Oral presentations don't always have to be in front of a large group; children can present in front of small groups, for the principal or another interested adult, or for a few kids who choose to stay in from recess to hear the presentation.

While many classrooms ask kids to do one big presentation or a final presentation that has an oral component, it's critical to normalize the process of presenting orally by asking kids to do it *all the time*. That gives students opportunities to work on their skills as public speakers: rehearsing, getting over the nervousness, speaking loudly. Putting all their efforts into one or two oral presentations may mean that children aren't as successful, and then are even less likely to enjoy or pursue opportunities to give oral presentations.

Learning through music ✳ Music is a delightful, engaging way to build fluency and confidence in a second language. Songs are repetitive, usually rhyme, and the tune helps children remember the lyrics. Music also gives the children an opportunity to join in as they feel comfortable without being nervous that anyone will hear or critique them. Many children will just mumble along happily until they gradually identify more and more of the words. You will hear students singing songs they have learned in class as they work independently, on the playground, even as they dawdle around in the bathroom. The music gives them a structure to practice language continuously, without even realizing they are getting in so much important practice! Children love playground song such as "Little Sally Walker" (Hopson and Hopson 1996) or "Miss Mary Mack." These songs encourage fluency through repetition and rhyme, and children will sing them over and over and over. Chants and shared readings of poems are similar ways to encourage fluency through repetition and rhythm.

Using drama ✳ Drama can be anything from reader's theatre to dramatizations of stories or concepts to full-scale dramatic productions. Drama gives children an authentic reason to read fluently and proficiently, and many times children who are unmotivated in other areas will challenge themselves to improve their skills for a dramatic presentation. Teachers can create all kinds of big and small, formal and informal opportunities in the classroom for drama. Materials can also be available for children to create their own dramatic presentations: puppets, puppet theatres, scarves, costumes, dress-up clothes, and so on. The more regular drama is in the classroom, the more children will turn to it, and the more it will become a tool for language development. Gibbons (2002) suggests encouraging students to "shadow" videos or audio recordings, and challenging them to re-create pronunciation, cadence, rhythm, and intonation as closely as possible.

Playing oral language games ✳ There are a number of games that are great fun at the same time that they give students a reason to build on their oral language skills. Games like Twenty Questions encourage children to listen carefully and to be precise in their thinking and language. There are many variations on the game where one child sees or even thinks of an object, while others ask questions to figure out what the object is. One game that has been a favorite with all ages is "What Happened?" in which the teacher gives the students the very last line of an elaborate story. The teacher might say only, "It disappeared," and it is up to the children to determine the rest of the story. The children ask as many yes-or-no questions as they need to re-create the story that came before the last line. In the example, where the teacher say, "It disappeared," the children ultimately determine that when Mt. St. Helen's erupted, much of the mountain was destroyed and the Toutle River disappeared.

Integrating Vocabulary Development

Cambourne's (1988) research on learning reminds us that children need to be immersed in what they are learning, the learning must be demonstrated for them, we must expect that they will practice and use their new learning without risk, and they must be free to approximate. If our objective is to increase the functional vocabulary of our students, English language learners or native English speakers, we must create the conditions within our classrooms to support this process.

Teachers are one of the most powerful language models that children will experience. The language that they learn to use will reflect the language that we use each day with them. For this reason, it is critical that we examine ourselves as language models and use language in a way that we want children to emulate. If we want children to use sophisticated vocabulary, we've got to use it in the classroom. If we want students to be interested in new words, we've got to demonstrate the excitement of finding a new word, or the relief of finding just the right word to express our thoughts. We've got to create a structure within our classrooms that supports and expects accuracy and expressiveness with language.

Infusing Your Classroom with Rich Language

While content study is rich with opportunities to interact with more complex vocabularies, the context of the classroom should be embedded with rich language throughout the school day. If we dumb down our language for kids, they won't develop strong vocabularies. Even very young children can utilize complex language with proper modeling and opportunities.

Teachers at every age level should make a conscious effort to take their classroom language up a notch or two. Rather than saying, "Give me your papers when you're done. Put your stuff away and get ready for lunch," we can say, "Once you've completed your task to the best of your ability, you can deposit your assignment on my desk. Please return all of your materials appropriately and prepare yourselves for departure. It's nearly lunchtime!" While it may feel a bit awkward at the beginning, and while you may worry that students won't know what you're talking about, taking on a more advanced vocabulary little by little is relatively easy for teachers and children. We certainly don't want to burden our speech with overly complicated words to the point that it sounds unnatural. But with a little conscientiousness, we can begin to challenge ourselves to use words like *inform, assert, distinguish, illustrate, elucidate, enlighten,* or *advise,* rather than always simply *tell.* Besides, you don't want to talk way over the children's heads; you want to use language that is just a bit beyond their independent level along with the support that makes it comprehensible. Adding more challenging vocabulary to established routines is a great way to develop language in a way that children can easily comprehend.

Consider this example. In a kindergarten class of mostly English language learners, the teacher designated a special basket to house the class' favorite read-alouds. After every read-aloud, the children were given the opportunity to suggest the book for the special basket. The class would engage in a sort of voting process to decide whether the book was really worthy. Initially, the discussion went like this:

STUDENT: Yeah, yeah, I love dat book. Put it in dere!

TEACHER: Are you suggesting that we might want to put this book in our "Books We Love" basket?

STUDENT: Yeah! Dat is a book we love!

TEACHER: Carlos says we should think about putting this in our basket. Can anyone tell me why this might be one of our favorite books? What is it that you love about it?

STUDENT: It always say, "Guess what happened next?" I like to read that part!

TEACHER: Oh yes, Ryan likes that the book is very repetitive. On every page it says, "Guess what happened next?"!

STUDENT: I don't like that book 'cuz they are too mean!

TEACHER: So not everyone loves the book. It sounds like Daniela does *not* want to put the book in our "Books We Love" basket.

The class continued this way until they finally decided that the book had enough support to become an official "Book We Love." After a few weeks of these conversations about read-alouds, it went more like this:

STUDENT: Let's put dat book in our basket, teacher!

TEACHER: You'd like to nominate that book for our special basket? Great. Can you explain to me what it is that you love about this book?

STUDENT: I like it because I laugh at the part where the naked geese are knocking on her window! That's crazy!

STUDENT: I like it because it tells you where things come from, like glass comes from sand.

TEACHER: You liked that it was funny and informative! Did anyone *not* love this book? Does anyone *object* to putting it in our "Books We Love" basket? Does anybody think it *doesn't* deserve to be one of our favorites? No objections? Great.

A few more weeks of similar discussions and this group of 95 percent ELL kindergartners sounded more like this:

STUDENT: I want to nominate dat book for our basket! I love dat book!

TEACHER: So, Tu's made a nomination. Tu, explain to us what you appreciate about this book. What are the features of this book that you really enjoy?

STUDENT: I enjoy the ending. It was a surprise ending.

TEACHER: It was a surprise, wasn't it? I never imagined what was going to happen. Boy, was I shocked!

STUDENT: I was really shocked, teacher. That make it very interesting.

TEACHER: Can anyone else justify putting this book into our special basket? Can anyone else articulate why they love this book?

STUDENT: I love it because the author make you think one thing, and then POOF! it's something else!

TEACHER: It sure was. It sounds like we have a lot of supporters recommending this book for our special basket. Are there any objectors?

STUDENTS: No, no objections. We all love this book!

TEACHER: Well then, that settles it. We can officially induct this book into our "Books We Love" basket. Christopher, would you do the honors? [The students cheer wildly.]

In this scenario, observed over a period of six or eight weeks, the teacher has used a predictable routine to introduce and scaffold new language learning. The children know the format, and each time the teacher uses a new word, the children know from the context or from their familiarity with the process exactly what she means. She doesn't introduce them all at once, and she doesn't teach the children each word explicitly, other than to say, "Oh, so you *object*, you think that it does *not* belong in the basket." The children slowly but surely begin to use the more complex terminology that the teacher has modeled.

As you introduce vocabulary within the familiar context of the classroom, it's important to reinforce new language whenever and wherever possible. Every moment is an opportunity to support students' new learning. Using the previous discussions as examples, you might say to the kids, "Does anyone *object* if I open the window?" or "I want you to *articulate* to your neighbor, that means I want you to *describe* for your neighbor the ways that you can help maintain the classroom neatly" or "You passed out the mail so efficiently today. We should induct you into the mail carriers' Hall of Fame!" The more you are conscious of the language that you use with children, and the more you are conscious of using and repeating carefully chosen new vocabulary words, the easier it will be to integrate them into your daily lexicon. You and your students will find opportunities all over the place to practice new words.

Getting Kids Excited About New Words

The exciting thing about vocabulary development, as illustrated by the example of Jesus at the beginning of this chapter, is that once children get a taste of deeper, richer vocabulary, they generate their own momentum. When language becomes a delicacy in your classroom, to be savored and explored and relished, children become language connoisseurs. They love to learn new words; it's like the switch for even *hearing* them gets turned on inside their heads. They start to ask more about words that they hear and don't understand, and they insist on "better" words when they hear boring words like *happy* or *sad*. (See Figure 10–1.)

Keep a thesaurus handy as you teach. When you hear yourself using a common word, let the kids watch what you do. "No, no, *happy* isn't enough. I was more than *happy*. I need a more appropriate synonym. Hmmm . . . I was so . . . [thumbing through the thesaurus] I was so *elated*! That's it! I was so overjoyed! I felt like I was going to just float away on a cloud!" The key to natural vocabulary development is to repeatedly use a wide variety of words in lots of different contexts, with lots of support that makes them comprehensible. Routine procedures, visual aids, tone, context clues, and demonstrations are only a few of the structures that support kids' understanding and command of more sophisticated vocabulary.

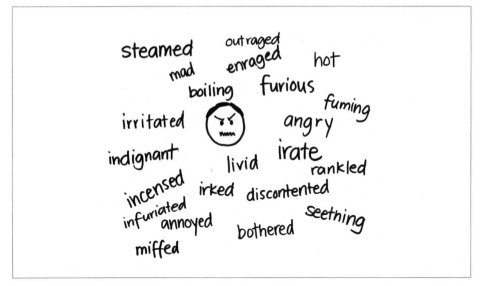

FIG. 10–1 Tired of the word *mad*, a first-grade class brainstorms interesting synonyms.

Developing Vocabulary Through Content Studies

Beyond structuring your classroom environment so that it naturally supports vocabulary development, there will be many opportunities to develop higher-level vocabulary within content areas. In all of the curricular areas, it's important to think about what new opportunities for vocabulary development present themselves, and how we are going to help students understand and integrate new vocabulary (Gibbons 2002).

It's helpful, as you plan for instruction in any area, to identify words that students might have trouble with, or even words that you *want* to include that will expand children's vocabulary base. For example, if you are doing a lesson on symmetry, your list might look something like this: *symmetry, symmetrical, equal, opposite, mirror, reflection, corresponding, axis, proportion, congruity, bilateral, trilateral, multilateral, bisect, divide, halve,* and so on. Reviewing these terms as you prepare yourself to teach means that you can be intentional about using them in your explanations and demonstrations. When children approach new words in their thinking, you can insert the right word at just the right moment. When they say, for example, "It's cut in half," you can say, "You're right! The triangle has been *bisected*, that means it's been divided into two equal parts. You are so smart!"

Strategies for Facilitating Vocabulary Development

The following suggestions are just a few of the ways that you can build vocabulary through classroom content learning. Many of them are useful across different content areas.

Thematic instruction ✳ Although the threads of content instruction and thematic learning run throughout this book, here it's important to recognize the importance of these concepts to vocabulary development specifically. Spending extended periods of time on particular topics allows children to hear vocabulary repeated extensively. In one classroom, first graders studied the human body over the course of several weeks. They became familiar with language such as: *circulate, organs, external, internal, nutrients, systems, digest, utilize,* and so on. Children used these words repeatedly, and developed a facility for adapting them to a variety of situations. When the class was ready to move on to a study of trees, many of the same words were also applicable, and the children plugged them right into their learning about trees. This gave them the confidence and the ability to push their vocabulary development even further through their tree studies.

Experiential learning ✳ There is absolutely no substitute for doing and experiencing things in order to generate and develop vocabulary. When you actually put yourself into an experience or engage in a process, vocabulary that you hadn't imagined comes up. Learning through the same process in the same environment time after time will limit available vocabulary no matter how much you try to avoid it. It's important to take students and the learning out of the familiar context on a regular basis, in order to allow new vocabulary to emerge authentically. A walking trip to the library, for example, might bring up opportunities for adding *breeze, pace, fitness, lungs, alert, orderly,* and *attentive* to children's vocabulary. During a cooking activity, the teacher asked one second grader to "arrange the squash so that the flesh of the squash is facing down in the dish." The second grader, who was always attentive and curious about new words, said immediately, "Wait, wait, hold on, what's that word *arrange*?! Tell me that word right now! I need to know it!" The teacher would have never imagined *arrange* as a target vocabulary word, but as the class engaged in the cooking experience, it came up naturally.

Word banks ✳ These are lists of words that children come up with around different themes or topics. You might create a chart of words that describe a character in a story, a list of words that pertain to worms, or a list of things that you love to do at school. As much as possible, word banks should have illustrations (they can be primitive) or even icons that remind students what the words are or what they mean. Students can also come up with word banks that contain synonyms for common words that they vow to avoid, like *good* or *mad* or *small*.

Diagrams ✳ Kids can learn to use diagrams for anything that they are interested in. (See Figure 10–2.)

One second grader was absolutely enamored of cars; he went with his dad to the dad's garage every day after school, and he just couldn't get enough of cars. His teacher finally suggested, during reader's workshop, that he research the internal and external components of a car. She encouraged him to create a diagram that he could use to teach other students about cars. The student was challenged to identify and illustrate new car terminology, and labored to make it accessible to his audience.

Graphic illustrations ✳ This term refers to illustrations used to teach or illustrate concepts. For example, a teacher or a student might make a chart showing the water cycle, and would include in that graphic the many vocabulary words that surround the particular content learning. A class-created poster of the life cycle of the mosquito would include words like: *mosquito, larva, transform, pupa, mature, habitat, adult, grow,* and so on.

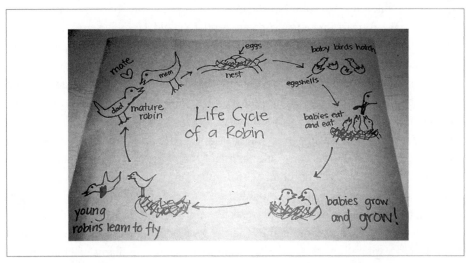

FIG. 10–2 A kindergarten class talked through the life cycle of a robin, while the teacher quickly recorded their ideas in this graphic.

Word study ✳ Word study activities include any number of activities that center on words themselves. Learning about the etymology of words, about root words, suffixes, or prefixes, and so on is one powerful way to enhance children's vocabulary. These skills are sort of like decoding for word meaning: if children know how to deconstruct multisyllabic words and are familiar with the meaning of particular parts of words, they can determine the meaning of words like *autobiography* or *prologue* with a little consideration. Word sorts are another way to expand children's understandings of words and the relationships between them (Bear, Invernizzi, Templeton, and Johnston 2003). For example, children could sort words or pictures of animals depending on whether they were insects or were not insects. As they do this, children use so much language about how insects can be distinguished from other creatures as they reinforce their conceptual understanding. Exploring synonyms, antonyms, homophones, compound words, and other kinds of "special" words are another fun way for kids to expand their vocabularies as they learn more *about* words. Even with young children, teachers can introduce these terms in a way that is accessible to students: "You're right, Terrence, there is a picture of a rock and you heard a funny word *pebble*. You know, *pebble* is just a synonym for *rock*; it's just another way of saying *rock*. Can you believe it!?" Ongoing work like this increases children's metacognition around language and gives them a sense of control over language.

Play and other self-directed activities ✳ Play is important for students of all ages (even for adults!). Even though play for older children may look different, it still expands on children's natural interests and thinking in a way that serves many purposes: to have fun, to imagine, to create, and to build language and vocabulary, among many others. *Purposeful play* is a term we use for play that encourages deep exploration and creation; a building center with blocks, a set of cars, and a set of train tracks, for example, is prime for developing purposeful play that will lead children toward natural vocabulary development. The key here is that adults or other more competent peers be available, not necessarily to play, but to scaffold children's language learning as they engage in it. A nearby adult with an eye on children who are building a city out of blocks, for example, might throw in words occasionally as they come up in the play. For the child who is planning and building the roads, the teacher can comment on what a capable *civil engineer* she is. When the cars crash together, the teacher can say "Oh no, an accident! It's an emergency! Call the authorities! Call the ambulance! Here comes the fire engine!" As older children engage in self-directed exploration, teachers can scaffold language similarly. If children are writing out words to a favorite song, for example, the teacher could suggest that the students "compose some new lyrics" and try to "innovate on the song." If children are drawing, an observing teacher might use such words as *technical, abstract, proportion,* or *composition.* The point of using playtime or free time to scaffold language is that children are usually deeply engaged in something they *love,* and that's precisely the moment that they are ready to absorb new words and new learning. Teachers must be present during this important time, however, not to direct or manage play, but to introduce and scaffold language that emerges naturally.

Games ✳ As for oral language development, games are a fun way for students to develop new vocabulary. Even games such as "I Spy," where one child has his eye on something and others are trying to figure it out through descriptions of the object, are useful in developing and reinforcing new vocabulary. Concentration is a game that can be adapted to any theme, and challenges kids to use related vocabulary. For insect concentration, for example, children have to make distinctions between the different characteristics of insects: "No, that's not a match. This one has a longer abdomen and fuzzy antenna. That one doesn't. Try again!" Pauline Gibbons (2002), in her book *Scaffolding Language, Scaffolding Learning,* has dozens of engaging games and activities that develop language and vocabulary. Games such as "Describe and Draw" (32), where one child draws something and then takes another child through detailed steps so that the other student is able to re-create the first image on his paper. In this activity, children cannot see each other's paper and must communicate all the necessary information verbally. Games that are adapted to reflect content learning are particularly valuable for developing and reinforcing target vocabulary.

Self-Selected Reading: A Natural Vocabulary Builder

Finally, it's critical to be cognizant of the impact that self-selected reading has on vocabulary growth. An extensive body of knowledge has demonstrated the relationship between free, voluntary reading and the development of vocabulary; the more kids read, the more words they incorporate (Armbruster, Lehr, and Osborn 2001; Fielding, Wilson, and Anderson 1989; Neuman 2001; Snow, Burns, and Griffin 1998). Anderson and Nagy (1992) report that students learn an average of 4,000 to 12,000 new words each year from books they've read. The key to maximizing this growth in vocabulary is also maintaining a wide variety of reading materials available to students. In order to promote depth and breadth in vocabulary, students need to have access to all kinds of genres: fiction, nonfiction, poetry, magazines, songs, comic books, reference books, picture books, chapter books, and so on (Cullinan 2000; Morrow and Gambrell 2000).

Regular self-selected reading is already such an integral part of effective classrooms for English language learners for so many reasons, another one of which is developing vocabulary. Establishing and supporting a sustained program for recreational reading is one of the easiest, most pleasurable, and most effective ways that we can support our students with their language and vocabulary development.

Key Ideas

* Oral language development is an essential component of both literacy development and second language acquisition.

* Classrooms should be structured to allow and encourage children to develop their oral language throughout the course of daily activities and routines.

* You must be conscious that you speak to children in a way that you want them to emulate. Use sophisticated, expressive, and precise language with your students in a way that they can access.

* Oral language can be a means for learning in the classroom, but it is also a worthy end in itself.

* Often students who are having trouble in reading comprehension or second language acquisition have shallow vocabularies that are limiting their progess.

* Established classroom routines provide familiarity and context for introducing more sophisticated language.

* Children easily and quickly develop their own enthusiasm and momentum for new vocabulary with the right encouragement.

* It's important to plan for vocabulary development and authentic use as content instruction is developed.

* Vocabulary development can and should be embedded in everything you do in the classroom, and can also stand alone as a primary objective in lessons or activities.

* Free, voluntary reading in the classroom has a tremendous positive impact on vocabulary development for English language learners.

11

Assessment

In the spider web of facts, many a truth is strangled. —*Paul Eldridge*

A Scenario: The Yearly Ritual

It's a familiar scene, played out year after year in schools across the country: teachers gather in the staff room, cluster by grade level, and pore over the stacks of test results. We pass around chocolates and pretzels in a vain attempt to keep our spirits up. We sift through the percentages and averages, the breakdowns and totals, the endless statistics that tell us what our children do and don't know. In some cases, there is "good" news; maybe there has been growth in particular areas, maybe reading comprehension scores have gone from 38 percent of students meeting the standard to 46 percent. We (hopefully) grasp at general upward trends so as not to be totally overwhelmed by the general deficits among the students that we've worked so hard with, all laid out so neatly in front of us.

Frequently, we get blanket statements about the numbers of kids who fail to measure up, with little, if any, information about particular strengths and weaknesses uncovered by the tests. Often, we get the results of tests months after the children have taken them, sometimes even after they have moved on to another teacher. Sometimes, after spending time simultaneously preparing for and dreading and trying to reassure kids about tests, we don't get any results back at all. Increasingly, we are required by the results of particular tests to make instructional decisions for our students that we know are inappropriate.

But across the board, when we get to the page in our stack that breaks down our population of children, we notice that our English language learners are generally behind. According to the stacks of paper, our English language learners are performing dismally, and are at grave risk of imminent failure. "But they've come so far . . ." we mumble to ourselves.

We leave these perennial sessions feeling like failures, not sure what went wrong, and fuzzy about how to even begin to make it right. Much as we try to talk ourselves out of it, our stomachs sink when we think of our children. They've worked so hard, we've worked so hard. What went wrong? Why can't they do it? We sulk out of the staff room, at the same time trying to muster up some cheer and hope with which to greet our students for the day.

The Evolution of Assessment

Assessment has become one of the most contentious areas in the field of education. While teachers and educators have always used assessment to monitor their students' progress and plan for instruction, assessment seems to have moved further and further away from those goals. Now, assessment has become a way to quickly and easily divide the "cans" from the "cannots." The hard-and-fast standards that determine where the line in the sand falls seem arbitrary and often, flat out inappropriate. Assessment, in the age of No Child Left Behind, generally refuses to take into account differences in children, differences in developmental growth and rates of growth, challenges that children face that impact their readiness to learn, substantial growth that children often make while still under the "proficiency" level, and the many other factors that influence how well children do on a particular test on a particular day. In short, assessment has become little more than noneducators setting up arbitrary standards, and chastising those children who can't or won't fit themselves neatly into the bubbles on the scan sheet.

Assessment has moved ominously away from its original goals to assess progress and plan for instruction. Through No Child Left Behind, it has become a tool for deciding who gets resources and who doesn't, who shows promise and potential and who doesn't, who gets demonized and who doesn't. Standardized testing has become a "scientifically sound" way of reinforcing our societal beliefs that some people are deserving and worthy, and others, because of their own inabilities or unwillingness, aren't. In the hierarchy created by current assessment practices, as in the parallel hierarchy created by our societal practices, English language learners are most often found at the bottom, with the most to lose.

The Power of Meaningful Assessment

We have an obligation to think through the current trends in assessing children, and to commit ourselves to becoming advocates for our English language learners. This is by no means to suggest that assessment *not* play a critical role in our work with students; rather we've got to take the lead in demanding that assessment be used appropriately with children. We need to reclaim assessment as a tool to document what our children know, how they are progressing, and what the next appropriate instructional steps for them are.

Current rhetoric in education forces us to become even better at assessment. When we get the distressing results from the state or district standardized tests, we need to be right there, ready to speak to parents and the media and the school board about exactly what our students *do* know, the progress that they have made, and the direction that their classroom instruction should move in. Even as children are subjected to more and more standardized tests, we need to recognize that taking even more time to do meaningful assessments with our students is absolutely worthwhile. Meaningful assessment gives us the critical knowledge that we need in order to work effectively with children every day, and it provides a buffer between our children and the devastating judgments about worth and potential that standardized tests produce.

What Do We Want to Know?

There are so many areas to assess children in: we want to know about their number sense, what sight words they know, what they already know about frog life cycles, if they have ever used a microscope, and on and on. This chapter focuses on assessing what children know in the realm of language and literacy learning. We need to know as much information as possible about the language and literacy development of our English language learners in order to effectively plan for their instruction in all subject areas. In the language and literacy sphere, we need crucial information in several key areas: oral English language proficiency; first language proficiency and literacy; letter names, phonics, and sight-word knowledge; independent reading level as well as reading behaviors and attitudes; and writing and spelling skills.

In each of these key areas, there are many different kinds of assessments that can be used to document children's knowledge and growth. Assessments fall into two general categories: commercially produced standardized tests, and classroom-based assessments that come out of our classroom, school, or district goals for children. The kinds of assessments that we choose to use with our students reflect our goals for them and our needs as educators.

Regardless of the kind of assessment that we utilize, it is generally an expectation that these language and literacy assessments will be conducted regularly throughout the school year. This way, we get a clear picture of a child's growth over time, and a better understanding of areas of weakness. A collection of meaningful assessments, gathered over a period of time, can give anyone interested in the child's progress, from parents to speech therapists to next year's teacher, a good grasp of where a particular child is at in his or her development.

Oral English Language Proficiency

A good place to start with English language learners is by assessing their oral language capacity in English. A good assessment will give an idea of what language children can understand and what kind of language children can produce. This is helpful in determining the kinds of content lessons and activities that children can access independently, and the kind of oral language support that might be needed in order to make those lessons and activities accessible to ELL children. Additionally, a good understanding of where English language learners are with their oral language development will give us a better idea how to go about scaffolding and extending their oral language.

There are a number of widely used tools to assess oral language development, and they vary somewhat in the kind of information that they provide. What is critical to keep in mind while choosing an oral language assessment is whether and to what extent the assessment measures cognitive academic language (CALP), and not simply day-to-day conversational English (BICS). Cummins (1981) articulates the important distinction in language proficiency between BICS (Basic Interpersonal Communication Skills) and CALP (Cognitive-Academic Language Proficiency). While it is important to measure children's language level in both of these domains, many oral language assessments focus heavily on measuring BICS. In order to make sound placement and instructional decisions, it is important to go beyond assessing BICS, and get a sense of students' proficiency with the kind of academic language that is required to be successful in school. Many times we hear students carrying on with their peers at recess or in the lunchroom, and mistakenly assume that they have the oral language skills necessary to access higher-level content in the classroom.

Commercial assessments ✳ Some of the more common commercially available oral language assessments are the LAS (Language Assessment Scales), the Bilingual

Syntax Measure, the IDEA Oral Language Proficiency Test, the Woodcock Language Proficiency Battery-Revised, and the SOLOM (Student Oral Language Observation Matrix). The LAS and the Pre-LAS are assessments that measure oral language in English and Spanish. The Pre-LAS test is available for pre–K through first grade, while the LAS can be used with students in grades two through twelve. The Bilingual Syntax Measure evaluates primarily students' knowledge of grammatical structures, and is also available in English and Spanish. The IDEA Oral Language Proficiency Test (IPT), also available in English and Spanish, uses a variety of pictures and stories to elicit oral responses from children. The Woodcock Language Proficiency Battery-Revised test can also be administered in English or Spanish to provide information about oral English proficiency. The Student Oral Language Observation Matrix (SOLOM) is a tool that teachers can use to document students' observed language in five areas: comprehension, fluency, vocabulary, pronunciation, and grammar. With the SOLOM, the teacher measures a student's language within regular classroom activities, without creating a formal situation in which a student responds to particular questions.

There are a few caveats that must be mentioned about using commercially produced English language proficiency assessments. First, for the most part, these assessments have been designed and used to make decisions about whether children qualify for or should be exited from ESL services. For this reason, these assessments may not be the best way for educators to document and measure the smaller steps and gradations of progress that ELLs demonstrate on their way to proficiency (Antunez 2003). Secondly, these assessments, with the exception of the SOLOM, measure proficiency in understanding and manipulating discrete elements of language, without much of the surrounding context that is so important for English language learners (Saville-Troike 1991). Content on these assessments, with the marginal exception of the Woodcock Language Proficiency Battery-Revised test, also falls heavily into the category of BICS speech, that is, the everyday, interpersonal language, rather than the academic language that is so crucial for success in school.

Further, these commercial assessments often fail to take into consideration cultural differences that impact student performance. A wide variety of cultural differences may result in lower scores for English language learners, from confusion at how to respond to an adult's "obvious" question ("What is this?" pointing at a dog), to divergent responses, such as "my auntie," in response to the question of "Who cuts your hair?" (credit is given only if the child answers "barber") (Faltis and Hudelson 1998). Finally, in any discussion of assessing English language learners, we must also keep in mind Krashen's (1981) affective filter hypothesis. This theory suggests a relationship between children's anxiety and self-confidence, and their language learning and production. Clearly, a formal testing environment, no matter how cheerful we try to make it, can produce high levels of stress and anxiety for children already new to the English language, and may therefore produce inaccurate results on an assessment.

Classroom-based assessments ✳ Beyond the commercially produced options, there are a number of effective ways to document children's oral language performance and growth. Oral language checklists, such as Marie Clay's (1993), can be enormously helpful in keeping track of children's growth, and can be easily customized to reflect district oral language standards, different functions of language (reporting, questioning, debating, and so on), different stages of language development, and so on.

Teacher observations, or anecdotal records, can also be used effectively to identify how and to what extent children's oral language is developing and expanding. Simply listening and recording kids' candid classroom conversations can provide a tremendous amount of information about so many things, not the least of which is their oral language functioning and development. Some teachers record children's conversations at different times during the year, either in writing as they eavesdrop or with a tape recorder. Such conversations can then be analyzed for demonstrations of the different elements of oral language. However teachers choose to observe children and record their observations, it is important that they check those observations against some kind of framework for oral language competency or development. In other words, as we observe our children so carefully, we need to be able to articulate both what they are showing us and in which direction we want to guide them.

Native language proficiency ✳ There is abundant research to support the idea that literacy in one language—speaking, listening, reading, and writing skills—can be transferred to support the development of literacy in a second language (Cummins 1981; Edelsky 1982; Faltis 1986; Hudelson and Serna 1994; Krashen 1996). Figure 11–1 (Cummins 1981) demonstrates how concepts learned in the first language provide a foundation for learning in the second language. Clearly, not everything children know in one language can or even should be transferred to the new language; what I'm talking about here are operating systems. The cognitive systems that children develop in order to speak, understand, read, and write in one language can be employed in the learning of a second (or third!) language, in this case, English. This knowledge, combined with Moll's theory of using a student's "funds of knowledge" in order to further their academic learning, compels us to investigate and identify language and literacy skills that students possess in their native languages.

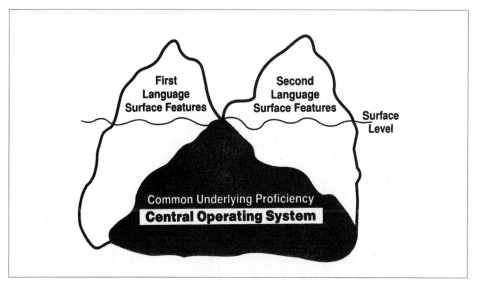

FIG. 11–1 A common underlying linguistic proficiency informs all language learning and use.

Different models and programs have different goals for English language learners, and will consequently call for different assessments. Ideally, a program's goal would be to develop literacy in a student's first language and in English; such a program would require a more comprehensive and sustained assessment process. But even if this is not the case, and the program's goal is only to facilitate proficiency in English, it is still important and valuable to document a child's proficiency in the first language. Native language proficiency information can give us tremendous insight into what underlying cognitive systems a child has already developed, what we can build on, and what language systems remain to be developed.

Commercial assessments ✳ The vast majority of commercially available assessments measuring non-English literacy are in Spanish. Standardized tests such as the SABE (Spanish Assessment of Basic Education) or APRENDA, which parallel English language standardized tests such as the SAT-9, are generally used to measure content knowledge in Spanish, and do not necessarily give useful information about a child's language functioning. August and Hakuta (1997) also suggest that these assessments are really only appropriate for children who are receiving instruction in the native language, or who come directly from school systems in their home countries. Again, children who are not schooled in the native language tend to be more proficient with BICS language rather than academic Spanish.

Nearly all of the commercially available oral language assessments have Spanish language counterparts, and most offer reading and writing assessments in Spanish as well. The LAS, the Bilingual Syntax Measure, the IDEA proficiency tests, the Woodcock Language Proficiency Battery-Revised test, and the Basic Inventory of Natural Language (BINL) are all available in Spanish formats.

The limitations of these assessments in terms of evaluating first language proficiency are similar to their limitations in measuring oral language proficiency. First, these tests tend to break language down into discrete, out-of-context elements; second language learners, who depend heavily on context for meaning, may not be able to fully demonstrate their true capacities for language use. Secondly, the wide variations within the Spanish language both outside and within the United States make it extremely different to produce a normed test that will be accessible to all Spanish speakers. Students from Puerto Rico, Mexico, and Peru may all exhibit differences in various aspects of the Spanish language, such as phonology, syntax, and vocabulary (Guerrero and Del Vecchio 1996), and a standardized assessment would require a definitive "correct" set of responses. Finally, the formality of these assessments may again create enough anxiety and stress among children as to skew their results.

Alternative assessments ✳ The limitations of these commercial assessments, combined with the general lack of assessments available in languages other than Spanish, compel us to look for other ways to evaluate what language and literacy skills children possess in their native languages. One of the most powerful ways that schools can do this is to use parents as intermediaries. Because we are looking to identify, and thus build on an underlying cognitive understanding of language as a complex system, what Cummins (1981) calls a "common underlying proficiency" with language, it makes no difference in which language children demonstrate for us their knowledge of how to use and manipulate language.

Consequently, even if we are not able to give an assessment in a child's native language, an enormous amount of helpful information can be gathered just by talking to families about their children (you will likely need a competent translator). A more formal checklist could be developed and used with parents, but the kinds of things we want to know are the same kinds of things we look for as we develop language proficiency with native English speakers:

* Can children gather information from one source and communicate it (orally or using written language) to someone else?
* Can children describe objects, events, people, and so on, in detail?
* Can children retell a story they've just heard, using similar story language?

* Can children retell an event or a story with reasonable sequencing?
* Can children engage competently in a conversation about various topics? Are they merely receptive in these conversations or do they paraphrase? Do they ask extending questions? Do they offer their own opinions and insights?
* Do children use the correct terms for everyday objects?
* Do they know and use different words for the same thing (i.e., *mad, angry, furious,* and so on)?
* Do children use correct syntax in their oral language?
* Do children read or write in their first language?
* Can they write or recognize symbols (alphabet, characters) in their first language?
* What do you hear your child talking a lot about?
* When do you feel like you can't get your child to stop talking? (Every parent has a lively answer to this question.)

Families can give us so much information about their children. Conversations like these with the families of our English language learners open many doors that ultimately support us in our work with them. Parents feel like important partners in the educational process, we collect a tremendous amount of information about what children can already do that can be used to guide their instruction, and we gather important affective information about children and families—we learn about their interests, interactions, and daily lives together.

Programs that provide native language instruction may be better positioned to provide more contextual, classroom-based assessments of first language literacy proficiency among children who speak those languages, given that they likely have staff members who are native speakers of those languages. If this is the case, many of the classroom-based assessments that are used with English speakers in English-speaking classrooms can be adapted for use with, for example, Spanish speakers in Spanish-speaking classrooms.

One note of caution, however, when it comes to adapting English literacy assessments for speakers of other languages: you may find that direct, word-for-word translations are often either unreliable or inappropriate. Other languages may not develop in the same general sequence as English, and benchmarks created for the English language may not be compatible with other languages. In Spanish, for example, even though the Spanish alphabet is similar to the English alphabet, children generally acquire writing skills in a slightly different sequence than in English (Flores 2003; Freeman and Freeman 1996). Beyond the technical aspects of translating assessments into native languages, there is also the issue of cultural relevancy. Even classroom-based assessments are created in a particular cultural context, and may not necessarily be appropriate for children who are grounded in a different culture.

Letters, Sight Words, and Phonics

Assessing children's knowledge of letters, sound–symbol relationships, sight words, and phonics is helpful in effectively guiding them through the process of becoming literate. This knowledge provides some key pieces of children's literacy progress, but it certainly cannot be considered the only source of information about students' growth and needs, particularly when those students are English language learners. Nevertheless, we do need this information to guide our instruction, and it is relatively easy to collect.

Classroom-based assessments ✳ In terms of letter names and letter sounds, any form of assessment that allows the teacher to keep track of children's responses over time is adequate. The Duthie Index, for example (see Figure 11–2), includes a space for teacher comments, which may be helpful if you've noticed ELLs demonstrating letter–sound knowledge in the greater classroom context that they can't replicate on an out-of-context form.

Monitoring sight-word knowledge is also relatively straightforward. In a one-on-one setting, teachers provide lists of high-frequency words and ask children to identify them. Districts often generate their own lists of words; otherwise, there are established lists of sight words available (Bear, Invernizzi, Templeton, and Johnston 2003; Cunningham 1995). Whichever format you choose, the essential ingredient is that you be able to show growth over a period of time. Again, it's important to keep in mind that English language learners rely heavily on context for meaning, and a list of isolated sight words may not elicit all of the words that children can actually read. For this reason it's critical to combine this information with other tools such as running records and formal reading assessments.

In terms of measuring phonics skills, there are a number of options. Some schools and districts have incorporated basic phonics concepts into their assessments of letter–sound and sight-word skills. The first grade–screening instrument developed by the Tacoma, Washington, School District, for example, asks children to identify some basic blends and digraphs. If a school or program wanted to measure these concepts outside of the context of sight-word lists and running records, it would not be difficult to create a form that asked children to identify digraphs, consonant blends, long and short vowel sounds, vowel combinations, onsets and rimes, and so on. Good analysis of running records over a period of time, along with careful

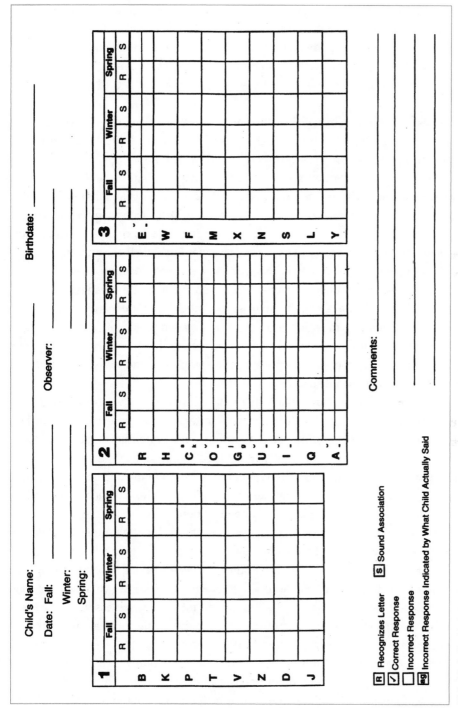

FIG. 11–2 Duthie Index Form: A simple way to record letter/sound knowledge

observation of children's shared reading and oral language, may also reveal additional information about children's phonics skills. In the case of English language learners, who must be grounded in meaning in order to learn and demonstrate learning, this kind of evaluation may be much *more* accurate that an out-of-context assessment. The key is to know what you're watching for, so pay attention, and record it!

DIBELS: Out of place in an ELL classroom ✳ Currently, there is a huge emphasis being placed on assessments such as the DIBELS (Dynamic Indicator of Basic Early Learning Skills). Assessments like the DIBELS, which are strictly timed and measure discrete, out-of-context skills, are entirely inappropriate for either measuring growth of literacy skills or for guiding our instruction of English language learners. The DIBELS claims to measure children's growth in skills such as letter sounds, initial consonant sounds, blending and segmenting, and phoneme manipulation, measured through the ability to read nonsense words. While these are certainly useful skills for children to employ in the process of authentic reading, they are useless to students, especially English language learners, outside of a meaningful context. Further, these are just a few of the many skills that children are learning to utilize in the service of making meaning from print. An overemphasis on the assessing of these particular skills will inevitably lead to an overemphasis on their teaching, with less attention given to other important reading strategies, and disastrous results for meaning-dependent English language learners.

The DIBELS does not give us information that we could not get from good analysis of children's work in the classroom and in their independent reading. In fact, this kind of assessment is more likely to give us inaccurate information because of its out-of-context nature and because it is timed so inflexibly. An effective program for English language learners helps children build skills in making sense of print. If, in our assessments, we are asking them to identify discrete, unattached bits of language, or worse, to read words that deliberately don't make sense, we confuse children tremendously. The anxiety caused by this, and by a strict timing schedule, are enough to throw a young English language learner totally off track. Children who are in or just coming out of the preproductive "silent" period of second language acquisition can't or won't be able to show us what they know within such a rigid assessment. If we're serious about accurate and informative assessments, we can't put the burden on the shoulders of our students by giving them assessments like the DIBELS; we've got to do the hard work ourselves.

If the goal of assessment is also to inform our instruction, a tool like the DIBELS has no place in a quality program for English language learners. The discrete, out-of-context skills measured by the DIBELS are exactly opposite of the skills we should be trying to develop in our English language learners. An effective literacy program for ELLs should emphasize language and vocabulary development, as well as the development of a wide variety of strategies to make meaning from print. We teach English language learners, as we teach all emergent speakers, readers, and writers, to use all available cues to make sense of the input they are receiving. With such a heavy emphasis on measuring just a few (and often not the most useful) reading strategies, we will find our reading instruction inevitably shifting to accommodate and produce better scores. Whether because of our own teacher anxiety, or from a desire that our children not be labeled inadequate, or because sources of funding demand it, we will begin to overemphasize the teaching of a few select skills in our classroom, to the unqualified detriment of our English language learners.

Finally, and beyond the instructional considerations, assessments such as the DIBELS are toxic for English language learners in an even more profound and fundamental way. Assessments that measure only discrete elements of language devoid of any meaningful context run entirely contrary to the way we know children learn languages, be they first or second languages. Cambourne's (1988) extensive research on the learning process, as well as decades of research around second language acquisition, tells us that children learn language and literacy through meaning. Knowing the research, and encouraging or even mandating an assessment that discounts it, is a deliberate setup for failure. Assessments such as the DIBELS are designed to exaggerate at best, or manufacture, at worst, shortcomings in children's literacy development. Those perceived shortcomings become generalized "risks" for complete failure, and the magical solution arrives to save the day: expensive "skills-based" programs that teach children specifically how to read out-of-sensible-context words.

This movement toward "scientifically proven" assessment such as the DIBELS and the narrow instructional programs that are subsequently called for, seems to be driven more by textbook sales and corporate publishing company profits than by what is best for English language learners. If we notice that children in our classrooms can't manipulate phonemes enough to make new words, what they need is more time reading and singing nursery rhymes together as a class ("Hickory dickory dock! The mouse ran up the _____?" *Clock!*), not drilling them on nonsense words. If they can't identify the initial sound of a word, what they need is more shared reading of fun, repetitive texts, in which they'll begin to notice and hear initial sounds, along with some carefully targeted and timed instruction—*not* meaningless exercises with unconnected words.

More and more, however, educators are latching on to the DIBELS and its corresponding "scientifically proven" instructional programs because of the need to be able to demonstrate some tangible academic success, however hollow it may be. When we see the increasing percentages on the graphs, we feel like we must be doing something right with our English language learners, where we have often felt so ineffective. We feel sure that we must be leading them in the right direction; their scores are improving, so their reading must be improving as well. But coaching kids in the discrete skills so that they can do better on an assessment such as the DIBELS is not the quality, holistic instruction that produces powerful readers. Particularly with English language learners, drilling them on meaningless bits of an unfamiliar language does not suggest in the least that we have stronger readers, it just means that we've taught kids to manipulate meaningless bits of an unfamiliar language. There is just no getting around the hard work, no shortcuts to feeling successful with our students. We need to be experts in assessing and teaching our children where it really matters.

Assessments such as the DIBELS make it sound as if children, especially early learners, are successful just by magic, and that all the "at-risk" children need is a little bit of that magic. The substantial body of research illuminating the connection between poverty and low literacy (Haberman 1995; Hart and Ridley 1995; Payne 2001) tells us that we'll have to look further than the DIBELS to understand why our English language learners aren't achieving the levels of proficiency that we'd like.

Independent Reading Development

Although the title of this section suggests that children must be reading texts independently in order to evaluate their reading progress, this area of assessment encompasses all levels of reading skills and behaviors, from the most beginning readers to the most advanced. Comprehensive reading assessment measures everything from children's attitudes about reading, to the strategies they use for reading, to what they choose to read independently.

Classroom-based assessments ✳ Independent reading assessment can begin with what Marie Clay (1993) has called "Concepts About Print." As you watch an emergent reader, you are noticing their mastery (hopefully!) of such concepts as

  ✳ The words are read from right to left.
  ✳ There is a correct way to hold the book in order to read the print.
  ✳ The words carry the meaning of the text.
  ✳ The text is made up of individual letters and words.

These kinds of observations can be done in any situation where a child is reading almost any kind of text. Watching young readers as they reread favorite big books or enlarged poems in the classroom can give a great deal of information about how children use and negotiate text.

Reading inventories, rubrics, and checklists are a good way to monitor behaviors and strategies that children are demonstrating in their reading. Figure 11–3 is an example of a form that can be used as a guide as teachers are observing children before, during, and after reading. Because these are relatively informal assessments, they are usually best conducted in an informal setting. An independent reading time in the classroom, where children are free to select any kind of reading material, is a great time to watch children reading at their best. When children are reading something that they have chosen because they are interested in it, they are most likely to put all of their reading skills and strategies to work in order to make sense of the text. As they listen, teachers can easily check off behaviors and skills that they notice children using. A reading continuum (see Figure 11–4 for an example) is one kind of checklist that can be maintained and updated over a period of time. This kind of an assessment can give us tremendous information about the not-always-straightforward journey that English language learners take to become effective readers.

Reading conferences are also a great way to observe and record children's literacy progress during independent reading time (Hill, Ruptic, and Norwick 1998; Miller 2002). Again, while children are engaged in their self-selected reading, teachers move from child to child asking basic questions in order to get children to talk about their reading. "Can you tell me what you're reading today?" or "How's your reading going today?" are nice ways to open up a conversation with children about their reading work. Children who have been taught to be conscious and reflective about their own reading process learn quickly how to proceed in a conference like this. Children may talk about the meaning of the text, whether they enjoyed it, some trouble they encountered in reading it, a new word they've figured out in the text, or some way that the reading has changed their thinking. Whatever children choose to talk about during those reading conferences gives tremendous information to a teacher about what skills children are working on independently and what new kinds of instruction they are ready for. A child who doesn't know what to talk about during a reading conference is also giving you valuable information; maybe he isn't sure how to find a "just right" book, maybe you need to teach him how to "read" the story using the pictures, or maybe you need to give him some of the language that good readers use when they're talking about their reading. In any case, you have come to understand an area of growth for that child, and you have moved them forward.

English language learners respond particularly well to a reading conference format, because it is one-on-one time with the teacher. Because the conference is more

Name:

Reading Strategies	Date: Title:	Date: Title:	Date: Title:
Rereads			
Skips/Returns			
Uses Context Clues			
Uses Picture Cues			
Uses First/Last Letters			
Uses Memory of Patterns			
Decodes by Sounding Out			
Knows Sight Words			
Miscues Preserve Meaning			
Appropriate Level			
Reads Fluently			
Literal Comprehension			
Interpretive Comprehension			
Strategy Taught/Comments			

FIG. 11-3 Reading Conference Record: Primary

Preconventional Ages 3–5	Emerging Ages 4–6	Developing Ages 5–7	Beginning Ages 6–8	Expanding Ages 7–9
• Begins to choose reading materials (e.g., books, magazines, and charts) and has favorites.	• Memorizes pattern books, poems, and familiar books.	• Reads books with simple patterns.	• Reads simple early-reader books.	• Reads beginning chapter books.
• Shows interest in reading signs, labels, and logos (environmental print).	• Begins to read signs, labels, and logos (environmental print).	• Begins to read own writing.	• Reads harder early-reader books.	• Chooses, reads, and finishes a variety of materials at appropriate level with guidance.
• Recognizes own name in print.	• Demonstrates eagerness to read.	• Begins to read independently for short periods (5–10 minutes).	• Reads and follows simple written directions with guidance.	• Begins to read aloud with fluency.
• Holds book and turns pages correctly.	• Pretends to read.	• Shares favorite reading material with others.	• Identifies basic genres (e.g., fiction, nonfiction, and poetry).	• Reads silently for increasingly longer periods (15–30 minutes).
• Shows beginning/end of book or story.	• Uses illustrations to tell stories.	• Learns information from reading and shares with others.	• Uses basic punctuation when reading orally.	• Uses reading strategies appropriately, depending on the text and purpose.
• Knows some letter names.	• Reads top to bottom, left to right, and front to back with guidance.	• Relies on illustrations and print.	• Reads independently (10–15 minutes).	• Uses word structure cues (e.g., prefixes, contractions, abbreviations).
• Listens and responds to literature.	• Knows most letter names and some letter sounds.	• Uses finger-print-voice matching.	• Chooses reading materials independently.	• Begins to use meaning cues (context) to increase vocabulary.
• Comments on illustrations in book.	• Recognizes some names and words in context.	• Knows most letter sounds.	• Uses meaning cues (context).	• Self-corrects for meaning.
• Participates in group reading (books, rhymes, poems, and songs).	• Begins to make meaningful predictions.	• Recognizes simple words.	• Uses sentence cues (grammar).	• Follows written directions.
	• Rhymes and plays with words.	• Begins to make meaningful predictions.	• Uses letter/sound cues and patterns (phonics).	• Identifies chapter titles and table of contents (text organizers).
	• Participates in reading familiar books and poems.	• Identifies titles and authors in literature.	• Recognizes many high-frequency words by sight.	• Summarizes and retells story events in sequential order.
	• Connects books read aloud to own experiences with guidance.	• Retells main event or idea in literature.	• Begins to self-correct.	• Responds to and makes personal connections with facts, characters, and situations in literature.
		• Participates in guided literature discussions.	• Retells beginning, middle, and end with guidance.	• Compares and contrasts characters and story events.
		• Sees self as reader.	• Discusses characters and story events with guidance.	• Makes predictions and "reads beyond the text" with guidance.
		• Explains why literature is liked/disliked during class discussions with guidance.	• Identifies own reading behaviors with guidance.	• Identifies own reading strategies and sets goals with guidance.

Continued on next page

FIG. 11–4 Reading Continuum

Bridging Ages 8–11	Fluent Ages 9–12	Proficient Ages 10–13	Connecting Ages 11–14	Independent
• Reads medium-level chapter books.	• Reads challenging children's literature.	• Reads complex children's literature.	• Reads complex children's literature and young adult literature.	• Reads young adult and adult literature.
• Chooses reading materials at appropriate level.	• Selects, reads, and finishes a wide varity of genres with guidance.	• Reads and understands informational texts (e.g. maps, want ads, brochures, schedules, catalogues, manuals, etc.) with guidance.	• Selects, reads, and finishes a wide variety of genres independently.	• Chooses and comprehends a wide variety of sophisticated materials with ease (e.g., newspapers, magazines, manuals, novels, poetry).
• Expands knowledge of different genres (e.g., realistic fiction, historical fiction, and fantasy).	• Begins to develop strategies and criteria for selecting reading materials.	• Develops strategies and criteria for selecting reading materials independently.	• Begins to choose challenging reading materials and projects.	• Reads and understands informational texts (i.e. maps, manuals, consumer reports, applications, forms, etc.).
• Reads aloud with expression.	• Reads aloud with fluency, expression, and confidence.	• Uses resources (e.g., encyclopedias, articles, Internet, and nonfiction texts) to locate information independently.	• Integrates nonfiction information to develop deeper understanding of a topic independently.	• Reads challenging material for pleasure independently.
• Uses resources (e.g., encyclopedias, CD-ROMs, and nonfiction texts) to locate and sort information with guidance.	• Reads silently for extended periods (30–40 minutes).	• Gathers and analyzes information from graphs, charts, tables, and maps with guidance.	• Begins to gather, analyze, and use information from graphs, charts, tables, and maps.	• Reads challenging material for information and to solve problems independently.
• Gathers information by using the glossary, captions, and index (text organizers) with guidance.	• Begins to use resources (e.g. encyclopedias, articles, Internet, and nonfiction texts) to locate information.	• Integrates information from multiple nonfiction sources to deepen understanding of a topic with guidance.	• Generates in-depth responses and sustains small group literature discussions.	• Perseveres through complex reading tasks.
• Gathers and uses information from graphs, charts, tables, and maps with guidance.	• Uses organization of nonfiction texts (e.g., titles, index, and table of contents) to locate information.	• Uses resources (e.g., dictionary, thesaurus) to increase vocabulary independently.	• Generates in-depth written responses to literature.	• Gathers, analyzes, and uses information from graphs, charts, tables, and maps independently.
				• Analyzes literary devices (e.g., metaphors, imagery, irony, and satire).

FIG. 11–4 Continued

164

Bridging Ages 8–11	Fluent Ages 9–12	Proficient Ages 10–13	Connecting Ages 11–14	Independent
• Uses context cues, other reading strategies, and resources (e.g., dictionary, thesaurus) to increase vocabulary with guidance. • Demonstrates understanding of the difference between fact and opinion. • Follows multistep written directions independently. • Discusses setting, plot, characters, and point of view (literary elements) with guidance. • Responds to issues and ideas in literature as well as facts or story events. • Makes connections to other authors, books, and perspectives. • Participates in small group literature discussions with guidance. • Uses reasons and examples to support ideas and opinions with guidance.	• Begins to use resources (e.g., dictionary, thesaurus) to increase vocabulary in different subject areas. • Begins to discuss literature with reference to setting, plot, characters, and theme (literary elements), and author's craft. • Generates thoughtful oral and written responses in small group literature discussions with guidance. • Begins to use new vocabulary in oral and written response to literature. • Begins to gain deeper meaning by reading between the lines. • Begins to set goals and identifies strategies to improve reading.	• Identifies literary devices (e.g., similes, metaphors, personification, and foreshadowing). • Discusses literature with reference to theme, author's purpose, and style (literary elements) and author's craft. • Begins to generate in-depth responses in small group literature discussions. • Begins to generate in-depth written responses to literature. • Uses increasingly complex vocabulary in oral and written responses to literature. • Uses reasons and examples to support ideas and conclusions. • Probes for deeper meaning by "reading between the lines" in response to literature.	• Begins to evaluate, interpret, and analyze reading content critically. • Begins to develop criteria for evaluating literature. • Seeks recommendations and opinions about literature from others. • Sets reading challenges and goals independently.	• Contributes unique insights and supports opinions in complex literature discussions. • Adds depth to responses to literature by making insightful connections to other reading and experiences. • Evaluates, interprets, and analyzes reading content critically. • Develops and articulates criteria for evaluating literature. • Pursues a widening community of readers independently.

FIG. 11–4 Continued

of a casual conversation about something children are interested in (the text), they may be more likely to open up and take more risks than they might be in a group setting. Looking back over notes from a series of reading conferences, you can get a clear sense of what children are interested in, what they are working on, and what instruction makes sense for them.

Anecdotal notes can be another powerful tool for documenting reading growth among English language learners. The advantage of anecdotal records is that children themselves drive them; as we watch, they show us what they are interested in, what they are working on, and what struggles they are having in their reading. This is important for English language learners because their individual paths toward literacy may look so different from that of other children, as it is impacted by oral language development, vocabulary, cultural differences, and so on. Bonnie Campbell Hill and her colleagues (1998) have developed a series of questions to guide our thinking and observations as we take anecdotal notes about students (see Figures 11–5 and 11–6). Such notes are important pieces to add to a student's profile, as they help us to document the larger skills and behaviors that may be missed in more tailored assessments (i.e., "Can the student read some environmental print?").

One of the most important and informative ways that we can assess children's reading is through miscue analysis. Taking a running record is one common example of miscue analysis. Analyzing the mistakes that children make while they are reading can be extremely useful in identifying not only readers' weaknesses but also their strengths. Running records illustrate what children can do well, and provide us with a foundation on which to improve other essential reading skills.

Generally, during a running record, teachers are listening to children read a piece of text and are noting children's reading word-for-word. The text should be appropriate in length for the reader; emergent readers will obviously have much shorter texts than more advanced readers. The text should be slightly above the reader's general independent reading level, that way we can see what children do when they come to something that is somewhat difficult for them. Teachers often have a photocopy of the text prepared in order to document the child's reading right above or below the actual text. This allows teachers to be more selective in choosing what material children will be reading for them. Running records can also be done as we listen to children during their own independent self-selected reading. In this case, a teacher uses the same notation as they would with a preprinted running record, but simply records onto a blank sheet.

However teachers choose to conduct and record running records, they can give us a terrific amount of information about students' literacy progress. Running records are particularly helpful with English language learners because they begin to

Type of Texts/Range

1. Does the student read pattern books? Beginning early-reader books? Harder early-reader books? Beginning chapter books?
2. Does the student independently choose books at an appropriate reading level?

Reading Attitude and Self-Evaluation

3. Does the student show a positive attitude toward reading?
4. Does the student listen attentively to books?
5. Does the student choose books and have favorites?
6. Does the student see him- or herself as a reader?
7. Does the student read for pleasure? Information?
8. Does the student read silently? For ten minutes? Twenty minutes? Thirty minutes? Longer?
9. Does the student reflect on his or her reading and set goals with guidance?

Reading Strategies

10. Can the student read some environmental print?
11. Does the student pretend to read books? Memorize books?
12. Does the student use illustrations to tell a story? Rely on pictures and print? Rely primarily on print?
13. Does the student recognize some or most letter names and sounds?
14. Does the student recognize some words or names in context? Simple words? Sight words?
15. Can the student match one-to-one (point to words) while reading?
16. Does the student use phonetic cues? Sentence structure cues? Meaning cues?

Comprehension/Response/Story Structure

17. Does the student participate in the reading of familiar texts?
18. Does the student share ideas during literature discussions?
19. Does the student make connections to personal experience? Other books? Other authors?
20. Does the student listen to others' ideas during literature discussions?
21. Can the student retell the main idea of the text? Plot? Characters?
22. What different forms of response does the student try (writing, art, performance arts, etc.)?

FIG. 11–5 Focus Questions for Anecdotal Notes: Reading (Primary)

give us a picture of how children's oral language impacts their reading, and what kind of instruction we can give them in order to enhance their skills in both areas. This information, combined with knowledge we have collected about students' home languages, can give us remarkable insight as to how students are processing language both in the oral and written form.

Type of Texts/Range

1. Does the student read medium chapter books? Challenging children's literature? Young adult literature?
2. Does the student independently choose books at an appropriate reading level?
3. Does the student read a variety of genres with guidance? Independently?
4. Does the student use reference materials to locate information with guidance? Independently?

Reading Attitude and Self-Evaluation

5. Does the student show a positive attitude toward reading?
6. Does the student select/read/finish a variety of materials with guidance? Independently?
7. Does the student read silently for twenty minutes? Thirty minutes? Longer?
8. Does the student reflect on his or her reading and set goals independently?

Reading Strategies

9. Does the student read and understand most words?
10. Does the student self-correct for meaning?
11. Does the student use reading strategies appropriately?
12. What strategies does the student use when encountering a new word?
13. Does the student consult a dictionary when appropriate?

Comprehension/Response/Story Structure

14. Can the student retell the main idea of the text? Plot? Characters?
15. Does the student make connections to personal experience? Other books? Other authors?
16. Does the student discuss literature in terms of genre? Writer's craft?
17. Does the student interpret deeper meaning in literature with guidance? Independently?
18. Does the student share during literature discussions when asked? Voluntarily?
19. Does the student respond to/elaborate on others' ideas during literature discussions?
20. Does the student evaluate/interpret/analyze literature critically?
21. What different forms of response does the student try (writing, art, performance arts, etc.)?

FIG. 11–6 Focus Questions for Anecdotal Notes: Reading (Intermediate)

The distinct advantage of using running records with ELL students is that we can focus on the kinds of mistakes that hinder comprehension, rather than each and every mistake for its own sake (Goodman 1973; Goodman and Burke 1972). For example, if, as frequently happens with early English language learners, the student omits common word endings such as *-ed* or *-s*, we can ask, has the omission obstructed the student's understanding of the passage? If it has, then we can take the opportunity to teach the student about how important word endings can be in communicating information. If the omission has not impeded understanding, we can still call their attention to the word endings, but in the context of a generally successful reading experience. We know at that point, however, that we need to do more work with the child so that he or she begins to notice and use word endings in the natural context of classroom oral communication and during reading and writing.

Over a period of time, it is easy to look at a series of running records and quickly identify areas that children have improved in, what their strengths as readers are, and what they are currently struggling with in their reading. This is just the kind of information that can help us put together a profile of a student that is much more accurate and informative than a single standardized assessment.

Having children retell what happened in a reading passage is another way to know just what students are able to comprehend independently. Retellings are obviously critical markers for English language learners, because we want to know how children are negotiating the language differences and if they are processing and interpreting the language accurately. Retellings can be either formal or informal, and either children or the teacher can read the selected passage. This presents a nice opportunity to get at a child's thinking beyond the language of a text. An English language learner may not be able to read a passage with enough accuracy to produce a successful running record, but he or she may be quite capable of understanding and retelling the important parts of a text. As always, we don't want language difficulties to obscure what skills and strengths children may possess.

Commercial assessments ✳ Beyond these effective classroom-based tools, there are several commercially available options for measuring children's reading progress. One that is used widely is the Developmental Reading Assessment (DRA). The DRA offers a series of leveled books corresponding with children's individual reading levels. An appropriate book is selected either by the teacher or student (the latter is preferable, and shows its own level of reading sophistication), and a running record is taken while the child reads. After the reading, the child does a retelling of the story and answers some basic questions about the text. At the end of the assessment, the teacher asks the child to respond to some general reading behavior questions, such as what books the student likes to read, who the student reads with, and what their out-of-class reading looks like. An assessment such as the DRA, when combined with other informal assessments such as informal running records, checklists, and anecdotal records, can provide a comprehensive profile of reading growth and development.

Writing and Spelling Skills

Finally, in monitoring the growth and progress of literacy learning for English language learners, it is important to keep track of their development in writing and spelling. Again, writing is one aspect of the process of being literate and proficient in the English language. It is intertwined with the other strands of literacy development, oral language, reading, vocabulary development, and so on. Writing and spelling assessments provide yet another dimension to the overall language and literacy profile of an English language learner.

Gentry and Gillet (1993) have identified five general stages of spelling development, that are, for the most part, equally valid for children learning English as a second language. The first stage is *prephonetic*, in which children make marks on the page, without any concept that the marks represent the sounds we use to make language. This includes students who write random letters, without any connection whatsoever to the correct sound–symbol relationships. The second stage is the *early phonetic stage*, as children begin to understand that the symbols they write represent spoken phonemes. Kids in this stage might write *m* for *mom*, or *lf* for *elephant*. As they become more proficient with letter–sound relationships, children move fully into the *phonetic stage*, in which they try to represent the phonemes they hear with the corresponding symbols. They may write *bot* for *bought* or *side* for *city*. In the *transitional stage*, students begin to integrate and use more conventional spelling patterns, even though they may not be entirely logical phonetically speaking. The may begin to write *light* instead of *lit* or *road* instead of *rod*. Finally, children in the *conventional stage* are spelling most words correctly, with the exceptions of more difficult, maybe multisyllabic words.

Classroom-based assessments ✷ Many of the assessments recommended for evaluating English language learners involve tracking children's writing through these stages. The form presented in Figure 11–7 is a nice way to record analyses of children's writing periodically throughout the year. Teachers can document which stage they believe the child to be in, and record notes about the student's progress. This form gives a useful profile of children's spelling growth over the course of a year.

Spelling 10 Words (Figure 11–8) is another way to evaluate children's growth over the year. A few times a year, the teacher reads a list of words (the same words each time) and asks the students to write each word. This is a powerful way to demonstrate children's progress through the stages of spelling, and also provides room for children to be reflective about their own development as spellers.

Name: _____

Date	Writing Piece	Pre-Writing WORD=זדٍٍ	Pre-Phonetic WORD= ᗺѧᴙᴙᴟ	Semi-Phonetic WORD=WD or YD	Phonetic WORD=Wᴙᴅ	Transitional WORD=Werd	Conventional WORD=WORD	Notes

FIG. 11–7 Spelling Development: Individual Profile

Name: _____   **Grade/Age:** _____

Fall	Winter	Spring

I noticed

_____

_____

FIG. 11–8 Spelling 10 Words

Beyond individual measures, teachers can look through children's writing on a more regular and frequent basis, in order to analyze what kind of mistakes children are making, and what kind of spelling instruction might be appropriate. Collecting children's writing once a week for informal analyses, asking children to write you a letter, taking anecdotal notes about what children are doing (and not doing) as they write, are all ways to get a window into children's growth in spelling and writing.

English language learners go through a similar general process as native English speakers in learning to spell and write English words. If a student is having particular trouble, it may become helpful to learn a bit about the first language. Children who come from a nonalphabetic language such as Japanese or Chinese may spend more time developing sound–symbol relationships than other children. Children who come from other alphabetic languages such as Spanish or French may be using their previous sound–symbol knowledge in the new language (Freeman and Freeman 1996). For example, a Spanish-speaking child who writes *suit* for *sweet* or *gir* for *hear* is following precisely the sound–symbol relationships of the Spanish language. The child is demonstrating, therefore, a strong adherence to letter–sound relationships: he or she just needs a little work in learning the new combinations for English!

Spelling is simply one skill involved in the complex process of learning to write, and teachers should integrate spelling assessment into the greater context of writing assessment. Writing is the complex, intimate process of communicating one's thinking to others, and children piece together the art of writing in their own individual ways. Writing assessment has moved from the more traditional, mechanical evaluations of written pieces to assessment based on children's demonstration of skills and behaviors within the various levels of writing development (a writing continuum). A continuum-based assessment allows children to drive their own progress; rather than demanding that they follow our time lines and lesson plans, this kind of assessment allows children to have some control over what kinds of skills are important to them and what aspects of their writing they are interested in developing at any given time.

As with reading, checklists, writing inventories, and rubrics can be effective ways to monitor children's growth and needs in writing. Some of these forms are used only at particular times, such as a poetry rubric, and others, such as Leanna Traill's (1993) Continuum of Written Language Development (see Figure 11–9), can be maintained and added to over time. The writing curriculum referred to in Chapter 9, *Units of Study for Primary Writing* (Calkins 2003), comes with an array of useful checklists that can accompany a holistic writing curriculum, and that can give us information about children's progress in all aspects of the writing process.

Writing conferences are one of the most powerful ways that we can monitor student's growth and instructional needs in writing. Lucy Calkins (1986) says, "Teacher-student conferences are at the heart of teaching writing; it is through them that students learn to interact with their own writing" (21). As in reading conferences, teachers move from student to student during independent writing time, observing what children are doing, and asking open-ended questions about their work. "Can you tell me what you're doing here?" or "What's next in your writing?" are examples of questions that work well to get children to talk about and reflect on their writing. Teachers keep track of writing conferences, and in looking back over a series of conference notes, can determine a great deal about where the student is at developmentally in their writing, and what areas they need guidance in.

Anecdotal notes and observations can give us a tremendous amount of information about children's writing development. Again, teachers keep observation notes, which can then be periodically (or immediately!) surveyed to determine children's

Name _____ Age _____

	Date of Entry			Comments
Preletter writing				
Writing letters, symbols, or numerals randomly				
Left-to-right sweep of letters and some words established				
Random pointing when reading back				
Letter/word pointing when reading back				
Random use of high-frequency words				
Uses initial consonants				
Partial phonetic representation for word being spelled				
Left-to-right sequential arrangement of words				
Uses a few known words appropriately				
Complete phonetic representation for word being spelled				
Uses many words appropriately				
Reads back accurately at conference				
Spells words appropriately				
Sequence ideas				
Rereads for sense				
Variety of topic choice				
Beginning to understand use of capital letters				
Beginning to hear and use medial vowels in words				
Beginning to hear and use end sounds appropriately				
Gaining control of directional movement in letter and word formation				
Writes own title				
Uses capitals correctly				
Uses periods correctly				
Marks approximations for discussion with teacher				
Developing control of systems for conventional spellings				
Maintains sequence of events over longer periods of writing				
Uses a variety of styles: • factual • imaginative • retelling • descriptive				

FIG. 11–9 Continuum of Written Language Development

strengths, areas of interest, and instructional needs. Rhodes and Dudley-Marling (1996) offer a series of questions to guide these anecdotal observations of children. As always, we need to know what we're looking for and where we want children to be headed.

* Who initiated the writing?
* Who chose the topic? Did the student have difficulty choosing an appropriate topic?
* How much did the student write and how much of the writing time was spent writing? Did the student write without prompting? What role did drawing play in the writing?
* What, if anything, did the student say aloud while writing? Did he speak first, then write, or speak during writing? Did the student's utterances give you insight into his writing strategies?
* Was there anything about the student's body language during writing that provided insight into her feelings about writing?
* Did the student reread and/or revise and edit what had been written? What sorts of revisions and/or edits?
* For what audience was the piece of writing intended?
* For what purpose was the piece written?
* How well does a piece of writing "hang together"? Is it a cohesive whole or does it read like a series of sentences related only by topic?
* How effectively does the student use language structures such as syntactic rules, word endings, and varying sentence patterns? Does the student's writing reflect the language structures of his speech or does the student use book language?
* Does the student's "voice" come through in the writing?
* Is the student's writing performance fairly consistent?
* What does the student know about punctuation, capitalization, and spelling?

Finally, collecting and analyzing writing samples from children over a period of time is the most important and informative way that we can assess children's writing development. The key to this process is to know exactly what we are looking for and what we are seeing in the student's work. Any of the checklists and continuums mentioned previously can be used as a guide to analyze pieces of writing that children have done independently. This kind of analysis can give us tremendous information about what children's strengths as writers are, and how and in which areas they have grown. It's important to be systematic in our assessment of writing samples; whichever format works for you, you should be able to quickly and clearly spell out children's progress and needs to parents, administrators, and other teachers.

Holistic Assessment

At this point, it should be clear that assessment of English language learners (and all children!) must be well planned, purposeful, and comprehensive. The purpose of assessment, first and foremost, is to provide educational guidance for teachers in their work with children. As educators of English language children, we need to understand and advocate for authentic assessment of our students. This means that rather than relying on a single, one-time test, we need to encourage the gathering of many sources of information in order to assess our students' progress, what many have called *portfolio assessment* (Clemmons, Laase, Cooper, et al. 1993; Glazer and Brown 1993). But as Regie Routman (1991) explains, "the portfolio as a particular holding place need not even exist" (330). Rather, what she calls the "portfolio approach to evaluation" refers to "using multiple indicators and data sources to inform and guide instruction and to put the learner in charge of the evaluation process" (330).

A portfolio approach gives us a dynamic picture of children's progress in a variety of areas. We get a comprehensive sense of how children are progressing over time, and what their emerging strengths and needs are. The portfolio also provides a space and purpose for including children's self-evaluations. Within a portfolio, we can ask children to look at and reflect on their own work, set goals for their own progress, and monitor their progress toward those goals. It's critical that we begin to develop within our children habits of self-reflection and goal setting. Often times, children are much more accurate at articulating their strengths and needs, and are much more ambitious and motivated when they are able to participate in setting goals for their work. Ultimately, we want children to work hard because they *want* to, and because they see the benefits over time of such an investment.

This philosophical framework is critical for the meaningful assessment of English language learners. Because their journey toward literacy can be so multifaceted, shaped by, among others, issues of second language acquisition, educational opportunity, class and ethnicity, learning styles, and each child's own individual personality, English language learners can only be effectively assessed by a variety of measures. As informative as they are, none of the assessments mentioned in this chapter can be used in isolation. Only when used together can the various assessment tools give us a complete picture of who our students are, what they can do, and what we need to teach them.

As in all other areas of our work with English language learners, we need to be vigilant advocates for appropriate assessment of our children. In the larger educational context, there is an increased effort to rely on fewer and fewer measures in judging students. More and more, we are seeing program funding, staffing, promotion and graduation, and instructional opportunities linked to the results of a very few standardized tests. This puts the education and future of English language learners at serious risk. As we put together effective systems for the assessment of English language learners, we must be conscious of this greater context, and commit ourselves, as always, to what we know is best for our students.

Key Ideas

* Assessment allows us to plan for more effective instruction and monitor the progress of our students.

* We must advocate for appropriate assessments that give us constructive information about our students.

* To plan for our English language learners, we need to know about their oral English language proficiency; their first language proficiency and literacy; their knowledge of letters, phonics, and sight words; their independent reading level; and their writing and spelling skills.

* Assessment should be ongoing in order to demonstrate growth over a period of time.

* There are a number of commercially available assessments, classroom-based assessments, and teacher-created assessments that provide information about student performance. Which assessments will be used depends on the needs of a program and the way the assessments will be used.

* Parents and families can also provide valuable information about children's literacy; this can be especially helpful for children who speak a non-English language at home.

* Educators of English language learners must advocate for assessments that provide valuable information, rather than damaging labels. We need to mitigate the potentially damaging effects that inappropriate and inflexible assessments may cause for our English language learners.

* All teachers need to become excellent observers of children. These observations, combined with solid knowledge of language, literacy, and content development, will provide a significant amount of the information we need to teach effectively.

12

This Is Political

I swore never to be silent whenever and wherever human beings endure suffering and humiliation. We must always take sides. Neutrality helps the oppressor, never the victim. Silence encourages the tormentor, never the tormented.

—*Elie Weisel*

A Scenario: Punished for Being Successful

It was a big year for the third-grade dual immersion class at Webster Elementary in Long Beach, California. It was their first year of formal reading and writing instruction, having spent their first three years developing only Spanish literacy and oral English proficiency. It would be their first year to take the state standardized test, the SAT-9. And it was the year of Proposition 227, Ron Unz's initiative to outlaw bilingual education in California. The third graders had limited understanding of the political whirlwind swirling around them. They were nervous about the test, and they knew that people were watching them. They were troopers, determined to make the best of nearly three solid weeks of testing, and went on to finish their year triumphantly, all but one reading at or above grade level. And even that one exception was nothing to feel sorry about—that particular student had advanced almost three complete grade levels in both languages.

The next year the conversation in the Long Beach Unified School District was about low test scores, and what was to be done about them. At Webster, a 99 percent free lunch school, half Latino, 40 percent African American, and 10 percent

Samoan and other ethnicities, the conversation went as follows: since the test scores for the school were low, the two-way immersion program had to go, or at least had to be modified to focus more instruction on English and test preparation.

But there were two interesting dynamics surrounding this school and its scores. First, looking at the test scores carefully, the scores of the children in the two-way immersion program, both English-dominant and Spanish-dominant, were actually *higher* than the scores of the children in the regular classrooms (based on 1998–1999 SAT-9 scores). That meant that kids who had received nearly all of their instruction for four years in Spanish, who were in their first six months of formal English instruction, and half of whom spoke primarily Spanish in their homes, scored better on a standardized test in English than children who spoke English at home and had spent their entire school careers in English-only classrooms. When the decision to forego the bilingual program in order to improve test scores was questioned, based on the fact that the program was producing better test scores than the English-only classrooms, those questions were met with a fierce tongue-lashing, and a pronouncement that the school had to be unified.

The second interesting dynamic in this scenario was the fact that another school, across town in a more affluent part of Long Beach, had similar test scores in their two-way dual immersion program. The difference was that the rest of the school, mostly white, middle-upper class children "carried" the lower scores of the dual immersion students, thus justifying the continuation of their program. It is understood and expected that scores for students in a two-way dual immersion program lag somewhat behind those of their English-only peers in the early years because of the fact that they are working toward mastery in two languages. In the later years, research shows that those scores even out, and that dual immersion scores often surpass those of English-only students (Genesee 1988; Genesee and Lambert 1983; Thomas and Collier 2002). When the question of why one school's program was spared over another's, the district responded by saying that the successful scores at the Webster two-way dual immersion program, with its black and Latino population, were no more than an "aberration," and that the future of the program wouldn't be guaranteed.

At Webster, the subsequent decision was made to change the program from a 90:10 model, where full Spanish literacy is developed before adding English literacy, to a 50:50 model, in which instruction time is divided equally between the languages, and each language group receives literacy instruction in their native language first. Thomas and Collier (2002) demonstrate that this model has proven less successful than the 90:10 model. With the new model, and little support from the district, the Webster reading specialist now reports that, where the majority of dual immersion kids used to be reading on grade level, the number now needing early reading intervention has increased significantly.

Bilingual Education: Challenging the Status Quo

Much as you might like to, there is just no getting around the fact that being an effective, transformative educator or school for English language learners is in itself a political act. In a country that has, from its earliest years, oppressed and marginalized the "other," what we are seeing in public education is nothing less than these ill effects on the newest (not so new, really) batch of "others," culturally and linguistically diverse students. But relax, you don't have to put yourself forward as the next Malcolm X or Mother Jones (unless you're compelled to!). It's just a matter of thinking a bit more thoroughly about a commitment you have likely already made: that all students deserve a meaningful education, one that gives them skills to be powerful in their personal and public lives, one that allows them to become active participants and agents of positive change in their own lives and in the world. Isn't that why we got into education in the first place?

Advocating for a meaningful education for English language learners means proposing a challenge to the traditional pedagogical model that requires students to change themselves in order to adapt to teachers and schools (Cummins 1986a, 1986b). The current system reflects larger societal values that assert that individuals should aspire to the white, middle-class prototype. We are encouraged to minimize or conceal or cast off our differences, be they cultural, ethnic, racial, linguistic, class, gender, or any other manifestations of our individuality.

Within the structure of our present society, the level of power and opportunity available are directly related to the degree of dissimilarity from the white, middle-class ideal. The more divergent individuals or communities are, the less power and fewer opportunities that are generally available to them (Giroux 1991). As people cast off their differences, language, community, religion, accent, and traditional ways of thinking and being, the more "acceptance" they receive from the mainstream society (Darder 1991).

Meaningful, transformative education for English language learners serves not only those particular students and communities, it serves us all. It is the first step in creating a society that does not thrive on the misfortune and disempowerment of some; it is a step to creating a world that values the different gifts that each of us bring to the table. Enriching, affirming, challenging, creative education should not be reserved for those children who fit a certain profile. In that context, education fails to live up to its promise as the foundation for true democracy. In that context, education fails to do right by all children: it misleads and misinforms mainstream (white, affluent) children about the source of real power and privilege, and it strips children of color, English language learners, and children of poverty of the ability to be agents for positive change in their own lives. When we begin to change our classrooms and schools in order to affirm the right of all children to be themselves and to be themselves *powerfully*, we begin to make a place for that to happen in the larger world.

Our measure for all of our educational decisions is this: would this be good enough for my child? Would I make this decision for my own children's education? The traditional model for educating English language learners has created a situation in which failure on the part of children of color, children in poverty, and English language learners is the norm, it's just what we've come to expect. But none of us wants that for our own families. Why will we allow it for other people's children (Delpit 1995)?

Challenges Will *Come Your Way*

So, if you're still reading, and you are committed to going the distance for your English language learners, prepare yourself. You don't have to get out your body armor or your bayonets. But you do have to be prepared for the challenges that will inevitably come. You will be subject to anxieties from all sides: parents, students, communities, colleagues, superiors, politicians, and the media.

Ron Unz pulled off a successful campaign to throw out bilingual education in California by exploiting the anxieties that all parents and communities have for their children. He suggested that by providing specialized instruction to English language learners (anything on the continuum from pullout ESL services to two-way dual immersion), schools were failing in their responsibilities to promote English proficiency among students. Nobody wants to put their children at risk for any kind of failure, and immigrant parents know that the stakes are even higher for their children. Unz exploited the urgency that second language communities felt for their children: if they didn't have a good command of English, how would they ever make a life for themselves in this country?

But Unz didn't understand his second language acquisition research, or maybe he just wanted to avoid it. Cummins (1981) calls it the "counterintuitive" theory: the "less is more" principle. In this case, he means that providing less English and *more* native language support early on means greater levels of English language proficiency later on. At Webster, a few parents who had been big supporters of the dual immersion program pulled their children out, "just in case," they said. They weren't willing to risk not having their kids develop fluency in English. And the evening information sessions and long phone conversations with parents about the risks to families and communities of home language loss, about the need to build English proficiency on a strong first language base, about the research that showed their children surpassing monolingual peers as they got older, were all to no avail: parents were scared. Not surprisingly, some students also expressed a fear that they wouldn't have what they needed: they knew that English was the language of power, and they were afraid that they weren't going to get it.

The Ideology of Antibilingualism

Unz is part of a larger movement urging the homogenization of U.S. society. In his article, "California and the End of White America" (1999), he insists that the future of the United States depends on "ethnic assimilation," a literal whitewashing of all linguistic and cultural differences in order to ensure a stable, productive society. He further suggests that the "politics of grievance" that minorities have espoused, in the form of affirmative action, bilingual education, and multiculturalism, will trigger a vengeful "white nationalism," if not ultimately eradicated. Other groups such as U.S. English and English First lobby against bilingual education and multiculturalism, on the basis that those movements divide our communities and our country. Groups such as these also imply that efforts to preserve cultures or native languages are at the expense of English proficiency and access to the American dream.

Rather than encourage change in a society that sets de facto parameters for people's lives based on skin color, ethnicity, language, culture, and/or sex, movements seeking an end to bilingual education and cultural pluralism prefer to lay the blame on individuals themselves. One need look no farther than the African American experience in the United States to understand the falsity of the premise that embracing the common language and culture will bring peace and prosperity. Africans brought to this country against their will were brutally, systematically, and wholly stripped of both language and culture, and it has certainly not resulted in their being recognized as full participants in our society. To this day their descendants continue to face profound marginalization and oppression in U.S. society.

Preparing Ourselves

Advocates for a meaningful, just, and theoretically sound education for English language learners must be prepared. It is critical to have a solid understanding of second language acquisition theory, in order to counter claims that the best way for children to learn English is total submersion in the language. That's why Cummins (1981) and Krashen (1987) call it "counterintuitive": colleagues, administrators, politicians, media, and even parents will point to low test scores for English language learners and respond with demands for a greater and more explicit emphasis on English, even though research has demonstrated that greater proficiency in the first language contributes to greater long-term proficiency in English. It is important to be able to articulate the complexities of language development, second language acquisition, and early literacy learning in order to either advocate for appropriate changes in policy or instruction, or to clarify where children are on the long, complex journey toward full English proficiency.

It's essential to have a comprehensive understanding of the best pedagogical practices for English language learners. That may seem redundant in a book focused on best practices for English language learners, but here it's critical to stress the social and political importance of that intentionality. If we can't articulate what we're doing and why we're doing it, we leave room for others to impose their beliefs and practices on our classrooms and students.

Experience has also shown the need to engage in this dialogue with colleagues, administrators, communities, and legislators *before* a monsoon like Proposition 227 hits. Be proactive! In your work with English language students and their families, communicate what you are doing and why. All of your interactions with parents and communities should be grounded in your clear purpose and plan for their students. Don't be afraid to share research with families at the same time you explain policies and practice; it keeps you on track and it assures parents that you understand each student's long-term needs and have a design for meeting them.

As you work with colleagues, share your beliefs and attention to the needs of English language learners. As you discuss student issues with administrators, share what you know about linguistically and culturally diverse students; many times, an issue seen in that light reveals a larger issue to be dealt with in order to facilitate student achievement. And in teaming and strategizing with other educators, take the opportunity to initiate a dialogue about the particular needs of English language learners: this may be discussing new practices you think would be appropriate for your students and why, or it may be demonstrating how practices that you already employ specifically benefit English language learners and English-only students.

The Role of Standardized Testing

The increased emphasis on standardized testing also necessitates a response from those of us advocating for English language learners. In an effort to sort out the successes from the failures, we are seeing a greater reliance on standardized tests to do just that. Politicians, the media, and communities are all being led to believe that success on a particular test means proficient, well-taught students. Conversely, failure on the same test must reflect ill-prepared, unskilled students, and inept or incompetent teaching.

As advocates for English language learners, we need to be very public about the impact of standardized testing on our students. Always grounded in our research and best practices, we need to challenge the relevancy of standardized testing for our students at all levels: school, local, state, and national (Ohanian 1999). Know the tests that your children will be required to take, and assess how suitable they are in measuring what your students know and don't know. In several parts of the country, teachers have been threatened with termination, fines, and even jail for wanting to review (*not pre*view) tests given to their students (Schmidt 2003). Be ready with your own data to show your students' growth and knowledge (see Chapter 11 for more on effective assessment and data collection). That way, if your students show dismal results on the tests, you aren't caught off guard. You can demonstrate that your students are learning and growing, you can articulate exactly what their paths to proficiency are, and you can communicate why the tests don't accurately represent your students' skills. Remember the Webster Elementary example at the beginning of this chapter? It was the misuse and misinterpretation of a standardized test that led district officials to pull the plug on their successful bilingual model; with such low scores, the district reasoned, those kids don't have time to waste learning another language.

No Child Left

And if you still aren't convinced of the importance of being ready with your purpose and plan for educating English language learners, here are four simple words: No Child Left Behind. George W. Bush's sweeping education reform legislation makes it exponentially more urgent that we elucidate and advocate for best practices for English language learners. The centerpiece of Bush's legislation is the Report of the National Reading Panel (National Institute of Child Health and Human Development 2000), a group of "experts" convened to determine how to ensure early reading success for all children. The panel conducted a supposedly thorough review of early literacy research, and concluded that an intensive, explicit emphasis on phonics and phonemic awareness was the "scientifically proven" method for teaching children to read. If teachers simply follow the formula, happily provided in multimillion dollar packages by the nation's biggest textbook publishers, all children will become proficient readers.

But the National Reading Panel (NRP) didn't earn its authority through sound research and pedagogy; even a cursory evaluation of its methodology, discussion, or ultimate findings reveals flaws and contradictions at every turn (see Allington 2002; Coles 2003; Garan 2001, 2002; and Krashen 2001 for further discussion). Rather, the Panel's findings are held up as gospel because they reflect some larger principles at work in our society, the same principles, in fact, that have created widespread educational and societal failure among the very children they purport to seek remedy for: children of color, children of poverty, and English language learners.

The NRP's prescription for failing children is based on the very same premises that have precluded their success from the beginning: a one-size-fits-all approach, with no attention to individual strengths and needs, and a belief that children are nothing more (and *should* be nothing more, that is, leave behind what you bring from home) than empty vessels, to be filled with the right combination of ingredients for success. For those followers of the National Reading Panel's advice, success is virtually guaranteed, and for those who disregard its wisdom, there's no one to blame but yourself. And predictably, the stage is set for those who do follow the NRP's guidelines and still manage to fail: first in line for blame will be teachers, schools, and most disturbing of all, students themselves. After all, you can't argue with science. Within the context of No Child Left Behind and its self-described best weapon for educational reform—shame (to say nothing of economic sanctions and loss of local control)—this new legislation is nothing more than an elaborate way of shifting the blame for widespread student failure onto the shoulders of students themselves.

Silencing Dissent

Joanne Yatvin (2000), a member of the National Reading Panel from Oregon, provided the only challenge to the NRP's findings and recommendations. Yatvin noted that the panel did not fulfill its obligations to review all research relevant to early literacy learning: "From the beginning, the Panel chose to conceptualize and review the field narrowly, in accordance with the philosophical orientation and the research interests of the majority of its members" (1). In short, the NRP manufactured the results it wanted. One of Yatvin's biggest contentions with the report was that it refused to include ethnographic research that would have considered cultural and linguistic differences. Yatvin's "Minority View," although printed on the last pages of the NRP's report, is not even properly referenced in the document's contents.

Denying the Social and Political Context

In his brilliant discussion of the philosophical underpinnings of forces like the National Reading Panel and No Child Left Behind, Gerald Coles (1998) illuminates the purpose of legislating pedagogically unsound practices for children. He describes the institution of ". . . a managerial, minimally democratic, predetermined, do-as-you're-told-because-it-will-be-good-for-you form of instruction" (3). It is, in his words, "a scripted pedagogy for producing compliant, conformist, competitive students and adults" (3). In other words, it provides children of color, children of poverty, and English language learners with an education that corresponds magnificently to their well-established, low-level niches in our society (Ohanian 2004).

Coles goes on to describe why social and political conservatives so enthusiastically embrace a traditional, one-size-fits-all pedagogy: it gives them a way to disregard "the influence of political, economic, and social forces on literary achievement . . . It makes no challenges to the distribution of wealth and power, and the resources available to schools, classrooms, children, and their families" (38). Those in social and political control thus abdicate their responsibility to provide for the success of students, in this case children of color, children of poverty, and English language learners in particular. The everlasting message is "Do it our way or fail."

It is imperative, if we are to be successful educators of English language learners, that we keep abreast of the social and political contexts surrounding our work. We've got to know the research and best practices for second language learners, not simply to guide our efforts with them in the classroom. It's not enough to go into our classrooms and close the doors. Our students need us to advocate for them at all levels. We must take these issues into the larger forum, and speak with loud and clear voices. It's *our* obligation and our children are counting on us.

Key Ideas

* Providing a meaningful, liberatory education for English language learners runs counter to the de facto role of schools to sort children into their prescribed places in U.S. society.

* As educators of English language learners, we cannot avoid the political nature of our work.

* Being effective with English language learners requires vision, humility, persistence, self-reflection, and a commitment to ongoing learning and professional growth.

* ELL teachers must know the research behind their work backward and forward, in order to meet the challenges to their practice that will inevitably arise. We should be confident and ready to explain our philosophy and practice to anyone who's interested.

* Teachers need to be transparent in their work with parents and families: we must talk with parents regularly about what we are doing and why.

* The stakes for English language learners are high—their futures depend on the important work that we do with them every day.

13

Program and Policy Development

Injustice anywhere is a threat to justice everywhere. We are caught in an escapable network of mutuality, tied in a single garment of destiny. Whatever affects one directly, affects all indirectly.   —*Martin Luther King Jr.*

Beyond the Classroom

My work with English language learners has been driven and inspired by the children that I work with. Each day when the bright, eager faces arrive, I am touched deeply by my responsibility to them and my hope for them. For this reason, I, like most other teachers, have spent the majority of my time and energy researching and reflecting how I can be most effective with my students every day. But often, I've realized that the work I do in my classroom is not always enough to provide for the complex needs of my English language learners. I've realized that some of the factors that impact the lives and experiences of my students are beyond my reach within my classroom. Many times, I've felt my obligations to my students pulling me out of the confines of my classroom and into the larger educational and societal context.

Becoming an effective teacher is a long, arduous, intense process. We can only absorb and integrate so much new learning about our teaching at any given time. New teachers spend considerable time at the beginning of their careers just surviving each day, before they feel ready to take on bigger pieces of the puzzle. But many teachers, after considerable time reflecting on and refining their work with English language learners, are aware of the need to take their work further in order to truly impact the lives of their students, and ready for the next step. For this reason, this book includes a discussion of what those next steps might be. You will decide when and in what form you'll be ready to take on some of these larger issues. In any case, I offer them to provoke your thinking. Opportunities to address these bigger issues come to us in large and small ways constantly. It's critical to know what they are, so that when you come face-to-face with some of them (which you will, whether you want to or not!), you may be a little more prepared to know how to advocate for your English language learners.

Educational Issues

Quality Bilingual Programs

Clearly, the best possible scenario for English language learners is one that draws on and supports their connections to their first language and culture, while at the same time providing access and skills both in the English language and the dominant culture. The specifics of a "best model" depend greatly on the first language proficiency of English language learners, the age, and the needs and desires of the families and communities. There will be different "best models" for different groups of children. What counts is an ongoing commitment to assessing the needs of the children that we serve, and matching those needs with what we know about language acquisition, literacy development, bilingualism, and biculturalism.

It's crucial that any effort to create bilingual programs be sincere, well-planned, based on sound learning theory and literacy research, and developed in partnership with the communities that will be served. Anything less is not only not worth the effort, but is actually damaging to the cause of bilingualism and the prospects for English language learners. One trend almost as disturbing as the English-only and the anti-immigrant, antibilingual movements is the proliferation of hastily designed, poorly planned bilingual programs that are not grounded in solid research or theory. These kinds of programs, which are inevitably unsuccessful, frustrate and discourage educators; dilute the potency of true bilingualism, biliteracy, and biculturalism; confuse and misguide students; and most disturbing of all, provide fodder for those anxious to prove that bilingualism really can't work and isn't sensible educational policy. If you're not going to do it well, don't do it at all.

This can be a very unpopular perspective, particularly within circles of progressive educators who may be inclined to support any efforts to provide specialized programs for English language learners. "It's better than no program at all," they'll say. These comments certainly reflect good intentions, but good intentions are just the beginning, and must be followed by partnerships with families and communities, extensive examination of the community and the language and literacy research, and substantial investments of time and resources in initial planning.

When we see programs being created that lack these essential elements, it's our obligation to students to ask hard questions and to hold our colleagues accountable. There are no shortcuts, no magic formulas for a high-quality education. It takes work, sweat, organization, time, money, planning, planning, and more planning. As educators and advocates for English language learners, we need to challenge ourselves to do this hard work, and we need to challenge and support our colleagues in their responsibilities as well.

High-quality, well-planned programs produce results that speak for themselves (see Thomas and Collier 2002, for a discussion of the effectiveness of different bilingual programs). Our students don't need us to gloss over the complexities of their lives or their possibilities; if we build a solid framework, they will offer us inestimable returns on our investment, and our hard work will have been well worth the effort.

Dual Language Programs

Dual language programs, also called two-way immersion programs, hold the highest promise for a substantial majority of English language learners today. Dual language programs (see Chapter 3 for a more detailed description of this model) are based on solid language acquisition and learning theory; address the complex dimensions of and connections between language and culture; and promote bilingualism, biliteracy, and biculturalism for all children, all within the context of a rigorous, academic curriculum.

As advocates for English language learners, we are obligated by the research and the results of these programs to examine the potential of dual language programs for our students (Christian 1994; Lindholm 1990; Lindholm and Gavlek 1994; Peregoy 1991; Peregoy and Boyle 1990; Thomas and Collier 2002). Because dual language programs are so comprehensive, policy makers are often initially hesitant to jump into a discussion of whether a program is possible or even desirable. It takes persistence, diplomacy, a wealth of ready information, lots of alliance-building, and maybe, a great deal of time.

We can start by talking with parents, colleagues, administrators, and community members about the research behind dual language programs. Many times the problems and challenges that we face as we work with English language learners are effectively addressed in a dual language program; those are the opportunities to campaign for dual language programs as not only desirable but necessary. For example, one problem that comes up frequently with English language learners is how to access background knowledge. A dual language program accesses background knowledge through teachers who speak the children's first language, and an emphasis on *culture* as well as language. When colleagues come upon these issues in their work with English language learners, it's time for us to pull out our research and offer some effective possibilities.

In many situations where successful dual language programs have developed, they have emerged from a groundswell of support and energy from within the families and communities of the students; they have often been responses to a community's demand for appropriate and effective education of English language learners. This is frequently the most efficient road to educational reform; sometimes school districts that rebuff the efforts of educators to implement more effective policies will take more seriously an organized, goal-oriented community effort.

Higher-Level Policies

Frequently, schools are limited in the kinds of support and services that they can offer English language learners because of decisions made at the district level. Particularly in districts where ELLs are not present in significant numbers (but also often in districts where they are), district decisions seem to be based on a long list of factors that don't necessarily reflect what is best for English language learners. Budget concerns, staffing issues, school board priorities, special interest groups, and even political "correctness" tend to distract districts away from decisions and policies that would be beneficial for English language learners.

No more excuses ✳ Time and time again, in response to efforts to provide effective services for English language learners, those efforts have been shut down quickly and decisively with two common refrains: "We don't have the money" and "We don't have the staff." These seem to be almost instinctual responses on the part of policy makers, and can be difficult for educators to counter. We need to challenge district decisions that disregard the needs of our students in a way that is diplomatic, organized, and persistent.

Budget issues are frequently cited as reasons why effective programs and services cannot be offered for English language learners. It's important to emphasize the need to invest in the long-term growth and success of our students, rather than short-term band-aid solutions. Effective, research-based programs can be expensive and labor-intensive to implement (but not always), but the eventual payoff in terms of student success should outweigh the initial investment. Rather than bringing in a new, expensive cure-all for underperforming students, which will inevitably have to be replaced in a year or two when it doesn't really solve the problem, districts would be wiser to invest in programs and services that have been proven over time to be successful with English language learners.

Putting the resources where they belong ✳ Secondly, school districts do have money, even during lean times, and they also have remarkable discretion over how that money is spent. The key is to press districts to make spending decisions that provide the most benefit for all students, including English language learners (Krashen 1993). Is an investment in computer upgrades the most pedagogically sound way to allocate money, or could that money be used to hire a few more bilingual classroom aides? As districts go about making these decisions, we've got to be there with the research that acknowledges the limited utility of technology (Chu 1995; Krashen 2003; Krendl and Williams 1990; Lance, Welborn, and Hamilton-Pennell 1993) versus the importance of bilingual teachers in a classroom and a low teacher–student ratio. Do all staff members, including librarians, music teachers, and so on, need to be trained in a new math adoption, or could that money be better spent on more high-quality classroom library books? Districts need to be held accountable for their spending decisions and the impact that they have on the day-to-day experiences of students (Krashen 1993).

Additionally, there are a number of decisions that districts can make that do not involve huge investments of money. Consolidating resources, the primary one being personnel, is one significant way that districts could provide better services without additional spending. Rather than having one Spanish-speaking teacher at one school, another at a different school, and two bilingual aides working at still another school, why not bring those resources together into one building in order to support a more comprehensive program for English language learners? Frequently, a district's desire to spread out resources dilutes the very value of those resources.

Sometimes, a district's reluctance to "segregate" children prevents a situation where students themselves could constitute a resource. Rather than spreading out Cambodian-speaking children among four elementary schools, for example, why not consolidate resources and efforts at one school to provide an effective language and literacy development program for those students? While pressuring students from particular backgrounds to accept choices that they don't want does suggest segregation, providing and encouraging students to take advantage of effective programs that put their real needs before the demands of "political correctness" is an entirely different proposition. Often districts present some vague reference to "diversity" in order to avoid taking on the complex tasks of actually meeting students' needs.

Finding the resources we need ✳ In response to districts that claim they don't have the staff to support quality programs and services for English language learners, we must insist that districts examine and plan for the changing demographics of their students. It's *not OK* for policy makers to continue to say, "We don't have teachers who speak those languages, so we can't offer that program or that support." In some cases, it may be just a matter of bringing teachers who do speak a particular language into one building, as mentioned earlier. If it is in fact the case that there are no staff who speak the languages of the children, *that* is the problem that needs to be addressed. Districts need to be compelled to develop a staff that can meet the needs of the student population. Whether districts support promising classroom aides or even parents in becoming credentialed teachers, or they specifically recruit credentialed teachers who speak the languages of the students, districts must be proactive in addressing a staff–student mismatch. Districts need to adapt to meet the needs of students, not the other way around.

Finally, even if a district possesses the resources to meet the needs of English language learners, it may not possess the will to do so. Again, we need to hold policy makers accountable for this. In one district in Washington, when there were budget cuts to be made, district officials routinely and openly (at least to their staff) made them "where they would encounter the least resistance." This meant that programs and services for English language learners and for schools that served them, located in one isolated corner of the city, were first to be cut. ESL teachers were asked by the Director of ESL services to "explain to parents that the changes were good for them," and to discourage families from protesting cuts. "The superintendent will not appreciate a bunch of calls to his office," teachers were told. As advocates for English language students, we've got to step up. When programs and services are sacrificed based on the social and economic clout that students' communities possess (or don't possess), we are obligated to expose and challenge those policies.

Our question for policy makers must be consistent: "How will we meet the needs of our students?" Programs and policies that are developed by the district must be accountable to that question; we have the opportunity and the obligation to be at the forefront of an effort to make sure that districts fulfill their mandate to our students.

School Reform

We are currently in the midst of a top-down effort to overhaul education. The No Child Left Behind legislation is the centerpiece of a long-gathering effort to reform public schools. There is no doubt that significant reform is necessary; the significant number of children who are performing below their potential is indisputable. What's troubling about current reform efforts, particularly for English language learners, is that the failings of the current system have been misdiagnosed, and subsequent educational policies have been at best, ineffective, and in many cases, injurious.

Flawed "science" ✳ Much of today's reading reform stems from numerous studies designed to identify those factors that effect good reading performance, which are presumably missing in the experiences of poor readers. Gerald Coles, in his book *Misreading Reading: The Bad Science That Hurts Children* (2000), refers to them as the "social class studies." In these studies, researcher after researcher examined the literacy histories of strong and poor readers, and developed what can be considered profiles of the lives and experiences of good readers. Middle-class students, the vast majority of whom were more proficient readers, had, for the most part, extensive literacy experiences that were natural, pleasurable, and integrated into their preschool lives. Poor families, the vast majority of whom were struggling readers, had not had these early literacy experiences.

But rather than prescribing a re-creation of the rich, literate environment that guided middle-class children toward reading success, these researchers mysteriously concluded that the decisive factor in the success of the middle-class students had been their parents' emphasis on developing phonological awareness. All that was missing from the experiences of poor readers was the specific training that taught children to match sounds to symbols, to blend and segment phonemes, or to substitute one sound for another to make a new word. All poor readers needed to become proficient was direct, systematic training in these critical skills.

The resulting legislation and educational policies have followed this general line of thinking: provide explicit, methodical training in the "scientifically based" requisite skills, and children will become proficient readers. A massive industry ready and willing to provide the keys to reading proficiency, in the form of "scientifically based" direct reading programs has, not coincidentally, merged, and in fact become questionably intertwined with the efforts to reform public instruction and produce higher levels of success among underperforming children (Garan 2004; Goodman, Shannon, Goodman, and Rapoport 2004; Ohanian 2002).

If it is clear that children who are surrounded with extensive natural literacy experiences are better prepared for and have more success in reading, why would we not design classrooms that re-create those experiences for children who've not had them at home? If we know that strong readers typically have been raised on lots of books in the home, lots of "lap time" with caregivers, fun language games, songs, poems, and rhymes, and an underlying structure that supports, reinforces, and guides children toward authentic reading and writing, why do we not embrace this context as a solution for struggling readers (Allington 2002; Graves 2002; Smith 2003)? The answers to these critical questions speak to the profound conflict between recent trends in school reform and the needs of English language learners.

Rather than acknowledge the intricate web of behaviors and circumstances that lead to reading success, educational policy makers have chosen to focus on a very few, easily quantifiable factors that they have elevated to panacea status. Phonemic awareness and phonics have become the centerpiece of federal reading initiatives and mandates. The emphasis on a specific set of discrete skills has made it easy for policy makers to legislate public school policy and classroom instruction. They have presented their policies as foolproof, teacher-proof, and student-proof. Failing schools, failing teachers, and failing students just haven't followed the secret recipe and are to blame for their own subsequent shortcomings.

Noneducators making education policy ✳ It's no accident that the new trends in school reform are also so easily marketable. Federal initiatives for school improvement have been quickly transformed into a windfall for major textbook and publishing companies, who have been more than eager to promote their products as a cure-all for struggling students. In fact, the partnership between corporate interests and public policy makers has become so interconnected that in many cases, it is difficult to distinguish one from the other (Garan 2004; Ohanian 2002). Easily packaged remedies for failing students are also appealing to school districts and educators who are looking for a fast and easy way out of their academic calamities. The educational interests of English language learners have, needless to say, been lost in the shuffle.

For English language learners, a one-size-fits-all solution that is centered on a highly controlled sequencing of discrete skills couldn't be more off the mark. Long-term research into second language acquisition tells us that language learning must be meaning based. Cambourne's (1988) years of research about the nature of the learning process tell us that real language and literacy development happen within a natural, purposeful, supportive context that is personally meaningful to each learner. Indeed, in schools that serve English language learners there is a disturbing trend toward eliminating "extraneous" subjects such as art, music, and even science and social studies, even recess, in order to spend as much time as possible on the mastery of basic math and the out-of-context, discrete reading skills that make up popular, federally supported reading curricula.

There is just no getting around the fact that there is no precise science that gives us a magic formula for teaching children. Although we have decades of research to guide us, the bottom line is that children are different, children's varied backgrounds have prepared each one of them a little bit differently, and children's needs on any given day may be different from other kids down the hall or down the street. We've got to focus on efforts that respond to the different strengths and needs of students. We cannot short circuit the complexities of becoming literate, much less of becoming *biliterate* or becoming literate in a second language. This means that any real efforts to improve the education of English language learners must center on developing teachers' skills in identifying and responding to the wide and varied needs of students. Rather than packaging up illusory miracle cures, our educational reform should be targeted at developing teachers as professionals, so that every teacher in every classroom is able to identify and meet the needs of each student in the class.

The importance of high-quality teachers cannot be overstated, for all children, but particularly when children face the additional challenges of poverty, low levels of family literacy in English, and/or linguistic and cultural dissimilarity from schools and mainstream culture (Haberman 1995; Hart and Ridley 1995). Current trends in education reform are decidedly antiteacher; this is especially problematic for students who depend on teachers to be attentive to the special needs that language

learners have and to respond with effective instruction. Recent reforms suggest that children are better off when teachers have less discretion and judgment in the classroom decisions on a day-to-day basis. On any given day, for any given child, what makes a difference is the quality of the instructional judgments that teachers make. We are professionals, not robots.

Keeping our vision clear ✳ By oversimplifying and misinterpreting the causes of widespread underperformance by poor and/or ELL students, policy makers have been able to avoid confronting the complex academic and instructional needs of these children. Though there are particulars to working with English language learners, the changes needed to bring about greater academic success are changes that would mean more effective instruction and schools for *all* children.

When school reform comes to our schools and our classrooms, as it inevitably will, we've got to make sure that new programs and policies make sense for our students. If we know clearly the research that supports the work we do with students, and if we can articulate the comprehensive needs of our students, we will be in a good position to determine a sensible course for our programs and schools.

Standardized Testing

Parallel to the current school reform movement has emerged the frenzy of standardized testing. Widespread standardized testing is just another manifestation of the push to homogenize students, micromanage schools and classrooms, and differentiate the "cans" from the "cannots." While the supposed aim is to improve instruction and academic performance, standardized testing has served primarily to stratify schools and label students. Within the context of the No Child Left Behind legislation, standardized testing has also become the mechanism for meting out the punitive measures that follow poor test results. Efforts to actually improve real academic results are either absent or empty (Ohanian 2002).

Standardized testing is a disaster waiting to happen (or one that is already happening) for students outside of the mainstream, dominant culture. Students who do not fit neatly into the bubbles on the scan sheet, those who don't speak English proficiently, those who don't take tests well, those who don't relate to white, middle-class American culture, or those who are differently abled are destined to be misrepresented by standardized tests. By their very nature, standardized tests emphasize and reward a very limited amount of skills, that must be effectively presented on one or two days in a child's school career.

Standardized testing in general, especially when it includes a high-stakes component (students must pass in order to graduate, for example), narrows the scope of what's considered worthwhile learning, and puts tremendous emphasis on the test itself. Rather than developing long-term, high-level thinking skills, in this age of high-stakes testing, students and teachers are increasingly focused on doing whatever it takes to *pass the test* (Doyon 2003; Ohanian 1999, 2002). Attention to students' interests, special needs, cultural differences, multiple intelligences, and nonlinear strengths go more and more by the wayside. For English language learners, this emphasis on testing rather than teaching means an erosion of the very practices that are most effective and impending castigation for the disappointing results that will inevitably follow.

Chapter 12 described the devastating toll that standardized testing took on a thriving, highly promising dual language program. The overemphasis on standardized testing created a total disregard for the terrific results that the program was producing. It didn't matter that poor, minority children were becoming bilingual and biliterate, it didn't matter that the vast majority of them were performing at or above grade level, it didn't even matter that they were outperforming native English speakers in all-English classrooms; the deciding factor in the fate of the program was their lower-than-average performance on the state, English language standardized test. The toll was heavy not only for the program, but also for the students who began to internalize the widespread portrayal of their supposed "failure."

Standardized tests do not provide an accurate picture of what our students know at any given moment. They do not allow us to see the gradations in their development, they do not put ELLs' progress in perspective (i.e., a student who has made two years' growth in six months but continues to be below grade level), and they do not give us good information about the strengths that our students can use as a basis for new learning.

As advocates for English language learners, we've got to be vigilant about the effects that standardized tests have on our students and on their education. We can't stand by while our children are condemned by mismatched tests and we can't allow their educational opportunities to be limited by or driven by assessment that doesn't take their needs into consideration. We need to be ready to buffer our children from the impact. This means knowing our students well, being able to articulate clearly what they know and where they are headed, advocating for sound assessment, and negotiating and defending against inappropriate standardized testing.

Valuing Bilingualism and Biliteracy as Goals for All

Americans are easy to spot traveling abroad; they're the only ones who don't speak more than one language. The United States is one of the few countries in the world that uses and teaches one language exclusively (or presumes to). While most other countries are busy teaching their students two, three, or more languages, the United States has been belligerent in clinging to its monolingualism. We stamp out first languages in young children and then encourage students to try to learn it (or a different language) for a few semesters in high school.

It's time for us to revamp our thinking about bilingualism and biliteracy. The extensive research that documents the cognitive and creative advantages of learning more than one language, as well as the research that supports maintaining a first language while learning a second, should give us the confidence to support and advocate for bilingualism as a goal for all children. The remarkable successes that have been demonstrated in dual language models show us that children are capable of doing rigorous academic work while they become bilingual and biliterate, and often outperform their English-only peers.

As educators, we have a significant vantage point from which to advocate for bilingualism and biliteracy as sensible educational policy. The tremendous growth of English language learners in our public school system gives us the perfect opportunity to capitalize on the strengths of different groups of children for the good of all. Once we make the philosophical shift to encourage bilingualism, our approaches to the needs of students tends to shift as well. Rather than perceiving an English language learner as having a deficit, we talk about how exciting it is that he or she is becoming bilingual. Rather than being troubled by having 30 percent of the school population speaking Spanish at home, we begin to see expanded educational possibilities for all students.

Encouraging bilingualism in our country will only make our nation stronger. We will not see the demise of the English language, nor the carving up of our country because of linguistic differences. A national appreciation for bilingualism and bilingual people will mean better educated, more resourceful citizens who can facilitate cooperation and collaboration within our borders and who are more effective participants in the global society.

Outside of the Sphere of Public Education

Beyond what we may believe to be "our issues" in education, there are a number of other factors that shape tremendously the experience of our English language learners. By addressing these larger issues, we impact the lives of our students for better or for worse. It is essential to integrate these greater issues into our work to improve the education and prospects of English language learners. Although we have tremendous power within our classrooms to influence the lives of our students, the scope of that work is limited if we confine it to our classrooms. If we want our children to be powerful, creative, whole human beings capable of and ready for greatness, we've got to make sure that our society is ready to support and embrace them.

Antibias, Antiracism

Knowing the way that bias works to limit the lives of our students within the school system, we are compelled to address that same bias outside of our classrooms as well. If we work to create an effective, culturally responsive program for our students in our schools, and take no notice of the work that needs to be done outside of our schools, we undermine all of our hard work.

Racism, classism, anti-immigrant, and antibilingual sentiment are all powerful forces in the greater society. They are manifested when cities build freeways through poor communities, when police brutalize rather than protect minority communities, when some neighborhoods have more liquor stores than libraries, when third-generation Mexican Americans are told to "go back to where they came from," when poor people pay a greater percentage of their incomes in taxes than wealthy people, the list goes on and on. We may think that these are not our issues, but we cannot ignore the effect that these public policies have on our students. Although our primary responsibility as educators is to meet the day-to-day needs of our students, when we are confronted with bias in our own lives, the action (or inaction) we take makes a difference in the bigger picture for the students we serve (Kozol 1981).

When we as individuals and as a society begin to confront actions and behaviors that oppress others, we will change the landscape for English language learners and their families. Working toward these goals in the greater societal context is part of the effort to build stronger families and communities, and more confident and capable students. The more work that we do outside of our classrooms to eliminate bias and oppression, the less work we will ultimately have to do within our classrooms.

Quality of Life Issues

Quality of life issues is a general term for all of the bigger public policy issues that affect the students that we serve. Again, we may be tempted to believe that our work stops at the classroom door, but we must be cognizant of the impact of local and national social policies on the students that we teach. High-quality affordable housing, health care (or lack of it), immigration policies, the absence or presence of living-wage jobs, parenting support and child abuse prevention, quality child care, mental health services, and substance abuse treatment and control, are, among others, issues that have tremendous influence over the lives of our children (Kozol 1967, 1988, 1991, 1995).

We know what it's like to work with children whose families are struggling to meet basic needs. Without underestimating the differences that we *can* make by providing children with a powerful, transformative education, we recognize that our work can be undercut by bigger factors that play out in the lives of English language learners.

We must be conscious of how the decisions we make in the rest of our lives affect the students and communities that we work with. If we struggle to develop relevant, effective programs for English language learners at school, and then we go home and support cuts in health care and affordable housing, we are diluting the hard work that we do each day. If we modify our classroom practice to meet the needs of English language learners and then vote for candidates who want to erode social services or who support punitive immigration policies, we're being inconsistent.

All of our actions have consequences, both inside and outside of our classrooms. I believe that it is incumbent upon each of us to consider how the decisions we make in our own lives affect the lives of the students we work with. Rather than negating our daily efforts in the classroom, a comprehensive effort to support the needs of English language learners, their families, and their communities will ultimately make our jobs as educators a little easier.

Key Ideas

* The classroom is one of many places that we must advocate for the education and future of English language learners. There are many other factors that impact the lives of ELL students and communities and that must be also be addressed in order to maximize the future prospects for our students.

* We must advocate for high-quality, well-designed bilingual programs, and challenge the proliferation of hastily implemented programs that are not set up for success.

* If circumstances exist or can be arranged, dual language programs provide the most effective model for language acquisition, literacy development, cross-cultural competence, and the development of biculturalism.

* Educators must begin to address the larger district policies that impact their classroom work with English language learners.

* We need to be critical in assessing the value of school reform efforts and standardized testing.

* Bilingualism and biliteracy are goals we should hold for all children, not just English language learners.

* As advocates for English language learners, we must address bias within our school settings *and* in the larger society.

* Societal issues such as poverty, affordable housing, job training, and so on, have a tremendous impact on the lives of our students. Our work in the classroom must be complemented by congruent activism around these issues outside of our classroom.

References

Agra Deedy, C. 1991. *Agatha's Feather Bed*. Miami: Santillana.

Allington, R. L. 2002. *Big Brother and the National Reading Curriculum: How Ideology Trumped Evidence*. Portsmouth, NH: Heinemann.

Allington, R. L., and P. M. Cunningham. 2002. *Schools That Work: Where All Children Read and Write*. Boston: Allyn and Bacon.

Anderson, R., P. Wilson, and L. Fielding. 1988. "Growth in Reading and How Children Spend Their Time Outside of School." *Reading Research Quarterly* 23: 285–303.

Anderson, R. C., and W. E. Nagy. 1992. "The Vocabulary Conundrum." *American Educator* 14 (18): 44–46.

Antunez, B. 2003. *Assessing English Language Learners in the Great City Schools*. Washington, DC: Council of the Great City Schools.

Applebee, A. N., J. A. Langer, and V. S. Mullis. 1988. *Who Reads Best? Factors Related to Reading Achievement in Grades 3, 5, and 11*. Princeton, NJ: Educational Testing Service.

Armbruster, B. B., F. Lehr, and J. M. Osborn, eds. 2001. *Put Reading First: The Research Building Blocks for Teaching Children to Read*. Washington, DC: The National Institute for Literacy.

Ascher, C. 1988. "Improving the School–Home Connection for Low-Income Urban Parents." New York: ERIC Clearinghouse on Urban Education.

Ashton-Warner, S. 1963. *Teacher*. New York: Simon and Schuster.

Aspiazu, G. G., S. C. Bauer, and M. D. Spillett. 1998. "Improving the Academic Performance of Hispanic Youth: A Community Education Model." *Bilingual Research Journal* 22 (2): 1–20.

Au, K. H. 1993. *Literacy Instruction in Multicultural Settings*. Fort Worth, TX: Harcourt Brace.

August, D., and C. Pease-Alvarez, L. 1996. *Assessment System for Schools and Teachers of English Language Learners*. Santa Cruz, CA, and Washington, DC: National Center for Research on Cultural Diversity and Second Language Learning.

August, D., and K. Hakuta. 1997. *Improving Schooling for Language Minority Children*. Washington, DC: National Academy Press.

Baker, C. 1995. *A Parents' and Teachers' Guide to Bilingualism*. Bristol, PA: Multilingual Matters.

Bear, D. R., M. Invernizzi, S. R. Templeton, and F. Johnston. 2003. *Words Their Way* 3d ed. Englewood Cliffs, NJ: Prentice-Hall.

Berman, P., S. Aburto, B. Nelson, C. Minicucci, and G. Burkart. 2000. *Going Schoolwide—Comprehensive School Reform Inclusive of Limited English Proficient Students: A Resource Guide*. Washington, DC: Center for the Study of Language and Education, George Washington University.

Berman, P., C. Minicucci, B. McLaughlin, B. Nelson, and K. Woodworth. 1997. *School Reform and Student Diversity: Case Studies of Exemplary Practices for LEP Students*. Washington, DC: National Clearinghouse for Bilingual Education.

Bissett, D. 1969. The Amount and Effect of Recreational Reading in Selected Fifth-Grade Classes. Doctoral diss., Syracuse University.

Boyle, O. F. 1979. "Oral Language, Reading and Writing: An Integrated Approach." In *Writing Lessons That Work, Volume I*, edited by O. F. Boyle. Berkeley: University of California/Bay Area Writing Project.

Brown, H. D. 1987. *Principles of Language Learning and Teaching* 2d ed. Englewood Cliffs, NJ: Prentice-Hall.

Bruner, J. 1978. "The Role of Dialogue in Language Acquisition." In *The Child's Conception of Language*, edited by A. Sinclair, R. J. Jarvella, and W. J. M. Levelt. New York: Springer-Verlag.

Button, K. M., M. Johnson, and P. Furgerson. 1996. "Interactive Writing in a Primary Classroom." *The Reading Teacher* 49 (6): 446–54.

Calkins, L. M. 1986. *The Art of Teaching Writing*. Portsmouth, NH: Heinemann.

———. 2003. *Units of Study for Primary Writing: A Yearlong Curriculum*. Portsmouth, NH: Heinemann.

Cambourne, B. 1988. *The Whole Story: Natural Learning and the Acquisition of Literacy in the Classroom*. Auckland, NZ: Ashton Scholastic.

Carger, C. L. 1997. "Attending to New Voices." *Educational Leadership* 54 (7): 39–43.

Carle, E. 1969. *The Very Hungry Caterpillar*. New York: Putnam.

Carter, T., and M. Chatfield. 1986. "Effective Bilingual Schools: Implications for Policy and Practice." *American Journal of Education* 90: 200–32.

Cary, S. 2000. *Working with Second Language Learners: Answers to Teachers' Top Ten Questions*. Portsmouth, NH: Heinemann.

Chavkin, N. F. 1991. "Family Lives and Parental Involvement in Migrant Students' Education." Charleston, WV: ERIC Clearinghouse on Rural Education and Small Schools.

———. 1993. *Families and Schools in a Pluralistic Society*. New York: State University of New York Press.

Chavkin, N. F., and D. L. Gonzalez. 1995. "Forging Partnerships Between Mexican American Parents and the Schools." Charleston, WV: ERIC Clearinghouse on Rural Education and Small Schools.

Cherry, L. 1990. *The Great Kapok Tree*. San Diego: Harcourt Brace.

Christian, D. 1994. *Two-Way Bilingual Education: Students Learning Through Two Languages*. Santa Cruz, CA, and Washington, DC: National Center for Research on Cultural Diversity and Second Language Learning.

Christian, D., and F. Genesee. 1998. "Two-Way Immersion." *Talking Leaves* 2 (2): 7.

Chu, M.-L. 1995. "Reader Response to Interactive Computer Books: Examining Literary Responses in a Non-Traditional Reading Setting." *Reading Research and Instruction* 34: 352.

Clark, C. T., P. A. Moss, S. Goering, R. Herter, B. Lamar, D. Leonard, S. Robbins, M. Russell, M. Templin, and K. Wascha. 1996. "Collaboration as Dialogue: Teachers and Researchers Engaged in Conversation and Professional Development." *American Educational Research Journal* 35 (1): 193–231.

Clay, M. 1975. *What Did I Write?* Portsmouth, NH: Heinemann.

———. 1991. *Becoming Literate: The Construction of Inner Control*. Portsmouth, NH: Heinemann.

———. 1993. *An Observation Survey of Early Literacy Achievement*. Portsmouth, NH: Heinemann.

Clemmons, J., L. Laase, D. Cooper, N. Areglado, and M. Dill. 1993. *Portfolios in the Classroom: A Teacher's Sourcebook*. New York: Scholastic.

Cloud, N. 1994. "Special Education Needs of Second Language Students." In *Educating Second Language Children: The Whole Child, the Whole Curriculum, the Whole Community*, edited by F. Genesee. Cambridge, UK: Cambridge University Press.

Cole, A. 2003. *Knee to Knee, Eye to Eye: Circling In on Comprehension.* Portsmouth, NH: Heinemann.

Coles, G. 1998. "No End to the Reading Wars." *Education Week* 18 (14): 38, 52.

———. 2000. *Misreading Reading: The Bad Science That Hurts Children.* Portsmouth, NH: Heinemann.

———. 2003. *Reading the Naked Truth: Literacy, Legislation, and Lies.* Portsmouth, NH: Heinemann.

Collier, V. P. 1987. "Age and Rate of Acquisition of Second Language for Academic Purposes." *TESOL Quarterly* 21: 617–41.

———. 1989. "How Long? A Synthesis of Research on Academic Achievement in a Second Language." *TESOL Quarterly* 23: 509–31.

Comer, J. 1988. "Educating Poor Minority Children." *Scientific American* 259 (5): 42–48.

Costa, A. L., and B. Kallick. 1995. "Process Design: Shared Vision." In *Student Assessment in the Context of Systemic Reform*. Newton, MA: Education Development Center.

Cotton, K., and K. R. Wikelund. 1989. *Parent Involvement in Education.* Portland, OR: Northwest Educational Regional Lab.

Cowley, J. 1995. *The Meanies Came to School*. Bothell, WA: Wright Group.

Cullinan, B. 2000. "Independent Reading and School Achievement." *School Library Media Research* 3.

Cummins, J. 1979. "Cognitive/Academic Language Proficiency, Linguistic Interdependence, the Optimum Age Question, and Some Other Matters." *Working Papers on Bilingualism* 19: 121–29.

———. 1981. "The Role of Primary Language Development in Promoting Educational Success for Language Minority Students." In *Schooling and Language Minority Students: A Theoretical Framework*, 3–49. Los Angeles: California State Department of Education.

———. 1984. *Bilingualism and Special Education: Issues in Assessment and Pedagogy.* Clevedon, UK: Multilingual Matters.

———. 1986a. "Bilingual Education and Anti-Racist Education." *Interracial Books for Children Bulletin* 17 (3 and 4): 9–12.

———. 1986b. "Empowering Minority Students: A Framework for Intervention." *Harvard Educational Review* 56 (1): 18–36.

———. 1994. "Knowledge, Power, and Identity in Teaching English as a Second Language." In *Educating Second Language Children: The Whole Child, the Whole Curriculum, the Whole Community*, edited by F. Genesee. Cambridge, UK: Cambridge University Press.

Cunningham, P. M. 1995. *Phonics They Use*. New York: HarperCollins.

Cunningham, P. M., and D. P. Hall. 1994. *Making Words: Multilevel, Hands-On Developmentally Appropriate Spelling and Phonics Activities Grades 1–3*. Parsippany, NJ: Good Apple.

Cunningham, P. M., D. P. Hall, and J. W. Cunningham. 2000. *Guided Reading the Four Blocks Way: With Building Blocks and Big Blocks Variations.* Greensboro, NC: Carson-Dellosa.

Cunningham, P. M., D. P. Hall, and L. B. Gambrell. 2002. *Self-Selected Reading the Four Blocks Way.* Greensboro, NC: Carson-Dellosa.

Cunningham, P. M., and R. L. Allington. 1999. *Classrooms That Work: They Can All Read and Write.* New York: Longman.

Cunningham, P. M., and K. E. Stanovich. 1998. "The Impact of Print Exposure on Word Recognition." In *Word Recognition in Beginning Literacy,* edited by J. Metsala and L. Ehri. Mahwah, NJ: Lawrence Erlbaum.

Darder, A. 1991. *Culture and Power in the Classroom.* Westport, CT: Bergin and Garvey.

Delgado-Gaitan, C. 2001. *The Power of Community: Mobilizing for Family and Schooling.* Lanham, MD: Rowman and Littlefield.

Delpit, L. 1995. *Other People's Children.* New York: New Press.

De Paola, T. 1975. *Strega Nona.* New York: Simon and Schuster.

Derman-Sparks, L. 1989. *Anti-Bias Curriculum: Tools for Empowering Young Children.* Washington, DC: National Association for the Education of Young Children.

Diaz Soto, L. 1997. *Language, Culture, and Power: Bilingual Families and the Struggle for Quality Education.* Albany: State University of New York Press.

Doyon, J. 2003. *Not with Our Kids You Don't: Ten Strategies to Save Our Schools.* Portsmouth, NH: Heinemann.

Dreher, M. J. 1998. "Motivating Children to Read More Nonfiction." *The Reading Teacher* 42: 414–17.

Edelsky, C. 1982. *Writing in a Bilingual Program: Habia una Vez.* Norwood, NJ: Ablex.

Elley, W. B. 1998. *Raising Literacy Levels in Third World Countries: A Method That Works.* Culver City, CA: Language Education Associates.

———. 1992. *How in the World Do Students Read? IEA Study of Reading Literacy.* The Hague, Netherlands: International Association for the Evaluation of Educational Achievement.

Enright, D. S., and M. L. McCloskey. 1988. *Integrating English: Developing English Language and Literacy in the Multilingual Classroom.* Reading, MA: Addison-Wesley.

Entwisle, D. R., K. L. Alexander, and L. S. Olson. 1997. *Children, Schools, and Inequality.* Boulder, CO: Westview.

Espinosa, L. M. 1995. "Hispanic Parent Involvement in Early Childhood Programs." New York: ERIC Clearinghouse on Elementary and Early Childhood Education.

Faltis, C. 1986. "Initial Cross-Lingual Reading Transfer in Bilingual Second Grade Classrooms." In *Language and Literacy Research in Bilingual Education*, edited by E. Garcia and B. Flores. Tempe: Arizona State University Press.

———. 1997. *Joinfostering: Adapting Teaching Strategies in the Multilingual Classroom* 2d ed. New York: Merrill.

Faltis, C. J., and S. J. Hudelson. 1998. *Bilingual Education in Elementary and Secondary School Communities: Toward Understanding and Caring*. Boston: Allyn and Bacon.

Ferreiro, E., and A. Teberosky. 1982. *Literacy Before Schooling*. Portsmouth, NH: Heinemann.

Fielding, L. G., P. T. Wilson, and R. C. Anderson. 1989. "A New Focus on Free Reading: The Role of Trade Books in Reading Instruction." In *Contexts of Literacy*, edited by T. E. Raphael and R. Reynolds. White Plains, NY: Longman.

Fine, M. 1987. "Silence and Nurturing Voice in an Improbable Context: Urban Adolescents in Public School." *Language Arts* 64 (2): 157–74.

Flores, W. 2003. "The Development of Spanish Language Literacy." In *Soy Bilingue: Language, Culture, and Young Latino Children*, edited by S. Cronin and C. S. Masso. Seattle: Center for Linguistic and Cultural Democracy.

Fountas, I. C., and G. S. Pinnell. 1996. *Guided Reading: Good First Teaching for All Children*. Portsmouth, NH: Heinemann.

———. 1999. *Matching Books to Readers: Using Leveled Books in Guided Reading, K–3*. Portsmouth, NH: Heinemann.

Fox, M. 1988. *Koala Lou*. San Diego: Harcourt Brace Jovanovich.

Freeman, Y. S., and D. E. Freeman. 1996. *Teaching Reading and Writing in Spanish in the Bilingual Classroom*. Portsmouth, NH: Heinemann.

Freeman, Y. S., D. E. Freeman, and S. P. Mercuri. 2002. *Closing the Achievement Gap: How to Reach Limited-Formal-Schooling and Long-Term English Learners*. Portsmouth, NH: Heinemann.

Freire, P. 1970. *Pedagogy of the Oppressed*. New York: Seabury.

———. 1985. *The Politics of Education: Culture, Power, and Liberation*. Granby, MA: Bergin and Garvey.

Freire, P., and D. Macedo. 1987. *Literacy: Reading the Word and Reading the World*. New York: Bergin and Garvey.

Galdone, P. 1974. *The Little Red Hen*. New York: Clarion Books.

Garan, E. 2001. "Beyond the Smoke and Mirrors: A Critique of the National Reading Panel Report on Phonics." *Phi Delta Kappan* 82 (7): 500–506.

———. 2002. *Resisting Reading Mandates: How to Triumph with the Truth*. Portsmouth, NH: Heinemann.

———. 2004. *In Defense of Our Children: When Politics, Profit, and Education Collide.* Portsmouth, NH: Heinemann.

Garcia, E. 1988. "Attributes of Effective Teachers for Language Minority Students." *Education and Urban Society* 20 (4): 387–99.

———. 1994. *Understanding and Meeting the Challenge of Student Cultural Diversity.* Boston: Houghton Mifflin.

Gardner, H. 1983. *Frames of Mind: The Theory of Multiple Intelligences.* New York: Basic Books.

Gardner, R. C., and W. E. Lambert. 1972. *Attitudes and Motivation in Second Language Learning.* Rowley, MA: Newbury House.

Gay, G. 1988. "Designing Relevant Curriculum for Diverse Learners." *Education and Urban Society* 20 (4): 327–40.

Genesee, F. 1988. "The Canadian Second Language Immersion Program." In *International Handbook of Bilingualism and Bilingual Education,* edited by C. B. Paulson. Westport, CT: Greenwood.

Genesee, F., and W. E. Lambert. 1983. "Trilingual Education for Majority Language Children." *Child Development* 54: 104–14.

Genesee, F., ed. 1994. *Educating Second Language Children: The Whole Child, the Whole Curriculum, the Whole Community.* Cambridge, UK: Cambridge University Press.

Gentry, J. R., and J. Gillet. 1993. *Teaching Kids to Spell.* Portsmouth, NH: Heinemann.

Gibbons, P. 1993. *Learning to Learn in a Second Language.* Portsmouth, NH: Heinemann.

———. 2002. *Scaffolding Language, Scaffolding Learning: Teaching Second Language Learners in the Mainstream Classroom.* Portsmouth, NH: Heinemann.

Giroux, H. 1981. *Ideology, Culture, and the Process of Schooling.* Philadelphia: Temple University Press.

Giroux, H. 1983. *Theory and Resistance in Education.* New York: Bergin and Garvey.

———. 1988. *Teachers as Intellectuals.* New York: Bergin and Garvey.

———. 1991. "Rethinking the Pedagogy of Voice, Difference and Cultural Struggle." In *Pedagogy and the Struggle for Voice: Issues of Language, Power, and Schooling for Puerto Ricans,* edited by C. E. Walsh. Toronto: OISE Press.

Glazer, S. M., and C. S. Brown. 1993. *Portfolios and Beyond: Collaborative Assessment in Reading and Writing.* Norwood, MA: Christopher-Gordon.

Goodman, K, ed. 1973. *Miscue Analysis: Application to Reading Instruction.* Urbana, IL: National Council of Teachers of English.

Goodman, K., P. Shannon, Y. Goodman, and R. Rapoport. 2004. *Saving Our Schools: The Case for Public Education, Saying No to "No Child Left Behind."* Berkeley, CA: RDR Books.

Goodman, Y. 1984. "The Development of Initial Literacy." In *Awakening to Literacy*, edited by H. Goelman, A. Oberg, and F. Smith. Portsmouth, NH: Heinemann.

Goodman, Y. M., and C. L. Burke. 1972. *Reading Miscue Inventory Manual: Procedure for Diagnosis and Evaluation*. New York: Macmillan.

Gramsci, A. 1971. *Selections from Prison Notebooks*. New York: International Publications.

Graves, D. 1983. *Writing: Teachers and Children at Work*. Portsmouth, NH: Heinemann.

———. 1994. *A Fresh Look at Writing*. Portsmouth, NH: Heinemann.

———. 1999. *Bring Life into Learning: Create a Lasting Literacy*. Portsmouth, NH: Heinemann.

———. 2002. *Testing Is Not Teaching: What* Should *Count in Education*. Portsmouth, NH: Heinemann.

Green, J. L., and J. O. Harker. 1982. "Reading to Children: A Communicative Process." In *Reader Meets Author/Bridging the Gap: A Psycholinguistic and Sociolinguistic Perspective*, edited by J. A. Langer and M. T. Smith-Burke. Newark, DE: International Reading Association.

Guerrero, M., and A. Del Vecchio. 1996. *Handbook of Spanish Language Proficiency Tests*. Washington, DC: National Clearinghouse for Bilingual Education.

Gutherie, J. T., W. D. Schafer, C. Vaon Secker, and T. Alban. 2000. "Contributions of Integrated Reading Instruction and Text Resources to Achievement and Engagement in Statewide School Improvement Program." *Journal of Educational Research* 93: 211–26.

Haberman, M. 1995. *Star Teachers of Children in Poverty*. Bloomington, IN: Kappa Delta Pi.

Handscombe, J. 1989. "A Quality Program for Learners of English as a Second Language." In *When They Don't All Speak English*, edited by P. Rigg and V. G. Allen. Urbana, IL: National Council of Teachers of English.

Harste, J. E., V. A. Woodward, and C. L. Burke. 1984. *Language Stories and Literacy Lessons*. Portsmouth, NH: Heinemann.

Hart, B., and T. R. Ridley. 1995. *Meaningful Differences in Children's Everyday Lives*. Baltimore: Brookes.

Hayes, D. P., and J. Grether. 1983. "The School Year and Vacations: When So Students Learn?" *Cornell Journal of Social Relations* 17: 56–71.

Henderson, A. 1987. *The Evidence Continues to Grow: Parent Involvement Improves Student Achievement—An Annotated Bibliography*. Columbia, MD: National Committee for Citizens in Education.

Henkes, K. 1993. *Owen*. New York: Greenwillow.

———. 1996. *Lilly's Purple Plastic Purse*. New York: Greenwillow.

———. 2000. *Wemberly Worried*. New York: Greenwillow.

Hill, B. C., and C. Ruptic. 1994. *Practical Aspects of Authentic Assessment: Putting the Pieces Together.* Norwood, MA: Christopher-Gordon.

Hill, B. C., C. Ruptic, and L. Norwick. 1998. *Classroom-Based Assessment.* Norwood, MA: Christopher-Gordon.

Holdaway, D. 1979. *The Foundations of Literacy.* Sydney, Australia: Ashton Scholastic.

Hopson, D., and D. Hopson. 1996. *Juba This and Juba That: 100 African-American Games for Children.* Columbus, OH: Fireside.

Hudelson, S. 1989. *Write On: Children Writing in ESL.* Englewood Cliffs, NJ: Prentice-Hall.

Hudelson, S., and I. Serna. 1994. "Beginning Literacy in English in a Whole Language Bilingual Program." In *Under the Whole Language Umbrella: Many Cultures, Many Voices,* edited by A. Flurkey and R. Meyer. Urbana, IL: National Council of Teachers of English.

Inger, M. 1992. "Increasing the School Involvement of Hispanic Parents." New York: ERIC Clearinghouse on Urban Education.

Jones, E., and J. Nimmo. 1994. *Emergent Curriculum.* Washington, DC: National Association for the Education of Young Children.

Jones, T. G., and W. Velez. 1997. Effects of Latino Parent Involvement on Academic Achievement. Paper presented at the annual meeting of the American Educational Research Association, 24–28 March, Chicago, IL.

Joyce, B., and B. Showers. 1988. *Student Achievement Through Staff Development.* New York: Longman.

Joyce, B., and E. Calhoun. 1995. "School Renewal: An Inquiry, Not a Formula." *Educational Leadership* 52 (7): 51–55.

Kozol, J. 1967. *Death at an Early Age: The Destruction of the Hearts and Minds of Negro Children in the Boston Public Schools.* New York: Penguin.

———. 1981. *On Being a Teacher.* New York: Continuum.

———. 1988. *Rachel and Her Children: Homeless Families in America.* New York: Fawcett.

———. 1991. *Savage Inequalities.* New York: Crown.

———. 1995. *Amazing Grace: The Lives of Children and the Conscience of a Nation.* New York: Crown.

Krashen, S. 1981. *Second Language Acquisition and Second Language Learning.* Oxford: Pergamon.

———. 1982. "Bilingual Education and Second Language Acquisition Theory." In *Schooling and Language Minority Students: A Theoretical Framework,* edited by California State Department of Education. Los Angeles: Evaluation, Dissemination and Assessment Center, California State University.

————. 1987. *Principles and Practice in Second Language Acquisition.* New York: Prentice-Hall.

————. 1988. "Do We Learn to Read by Reading? The Relationship Between Free Reading and Reading Ability." In *Linguistics in Context: Connecting Observation and Understanding,* edited by D. Tannen. Norwood, NJ: Ablex.

————. 1993. *The Power of Reading.* Englewood, CO: Libraries Unlimited.

————. 1996. *Under Attack: The Case Against Bilingual Education.* Culver City, CA: Language Education Associates.

————. 2001. "More Smoke and Mirrors: A Critique of the National Reading Panel Report on Fluency." *Phi Delta Kappan* 83 (2): 119–23.

————. 2003. "Does Accelerated Reader Work?" *Journal of Children's Literature* 29 (2): 9, 16–30.

Krendl, K., and R. Williams. 1990. "The Importance of Being Rigorous: Research on Writing to Read." *Journal of Computer Based Instruction* 17: 81–86.

Kuykendall, C. 1992. *From Rage to Hope: Strategies for Reclaiming Black and Hispanic Students.* Bloomington, IN: National Educational Service.

Ladson-Billings, G. 1994. *The Dreamkeepers: Successful Teachers of African-American Children.* San Francisco: Jossey-Bass.

Ladson-Billings, G., and M. L. Gomez. 2001. "Just Showing Up: Supporting Early Literacy Through Teachers' Professional Communities." *Phi Delta Kappan* 82 (9): 675–80.

Lance, K. C., L. Welborn, and C. Hamilton-Pennell. 1993. *The Impact of School Library Media Centers on Academic Achievement.* Castle Rock, CO: Hi Willow Research and Publishing.

Levin, H. M. 1987. "Accelerated Schools for Disadvantaged Students." *Educational Leadership* 44: 19–21.

Lindholm, K. J. 1990. "Bilingual Immersion Education: Criteria for Program Development." In *Bilingual Education: Issues and Strategies,* edited by A. Padilla, H. Fairchild, and C. Valadez. Newbury Park, CA: Sage.

Lindholm, K. J., and K. Gavlek. 1994. *California DBE Projects: Projectwide Evaluation Report, 1992—1993.* San Jose, CA: Author.

Lindholm-Leary, K. 2001. *Dual Language Education.* Clevedon, UK: Multilingual Matters.

Little, J. W. 1990. "The Persistence of Privacy: Autonomy and Initiative in Teachers' Professional Relations." *Teacher College Record* 91 (4): 509–36.

Long, M. 1981. "Input, Interaction, and Second Language Acquisition." *Native Language and Foreign Language Acquisition, Annals of the New York Academy of Science* 379: 259–78.

Long, M., and P. Porter. 1985. "Group Work, Interlanguage Talk, and Second Language Acquisition." *TESOL Quarterly* 18: 207–27.

Lopez, G.R. 2001. "The Value of Hard Work: Lessons on Parent Involvement from an (Im)migrant Household." *Harvard Educational Review* 71 (3): 417–37.

Louis, K. S., and S. Kruse. 1995. *Professionalism and Community: Perspectives on Reforming Urban Schools.* Thousand Oaks, CA: Corwin.

Lucas, T., R. Henze, and R. Donato. 1990. "Promoting the Success of Latino Language-Minority Students: An Exploratory Study of Six High Schools." *Harvard Educational Review* 60 (3): 315–40.

Lyons, C. A., G. S. Pinnell, and D. E. DeFord. 1993. *Partners in Learning: Teachers and Children in Reading Recovery.* New York: Teachers College Press.

Mace, A. 1997. "Organizing the Instructional Resource Room." In *Inside Learning Network Schools,* edited by M. Herzog. Katonah, NY: Richard C. Owen.

MacIntosh, P. 1988. *White Privilege and Male Privilege: A Personal Account of Coming to See Correspondences Through Work in Women's Studies.* Wellesley, MA: Wellesley College Center for Research on Women.

Marks, H. M., and K. S. Louis. 1997. "Does Teacher Empowerment Affect the Classroom? The Implications of Teacher Empowerment for Instructional Practice and Student Academic Performance." *Educational Evaluation and Policy Analysis* 19 (3): 245–67.

Martinez, M., and N. Roser. 1985. "Read It Again: The Value of Repeated Readings During Storytime." *Reading Teacher* 38: 782–86.

McCarrier, A., G. S. Pinnell, and I. C. Fountas. 1999. *Interactive Writing: How Language and Literacy Come Together, K–2.* Portsmouth, NH: Heinemann.

Miller, D. 2002. *Reading with Meaning: Teaching Comprehension in the Primary Grades.* Portland, ME: Stenhouse.

Moll, L. 1992. "Bilingual Classroom Studies and Community Analysis: Some Recent Trends." *Educational Researcher* 21 (2): 20–24.

Moll, L. C., C. Amanti, D. Neff, and N. Gonzalez. 1992. "Funds of Knowledge for Teaching: Using a Qualitative Approach to Connect Homes and Classrooms." *Theory into Practice* 31 (2): 132–41.

Morrow, L. M., and L. B. Gambrell. 2000. "Literature-Based Reading Instruction." In *Handbook of Reading Research,* vol. 3, edited by M. Kamil, P. Mosenthal, P. D. Pearson, and R. Barr. Mahwah, NJ: Lawrence Erlbaum.

National Institute of Child Health and Human Development. 2000. *Report of the National Reading Panel: Teaching Children to Read.* Washington, DC: NIH Publication 00-4654.

Neuman, S. B. 1999. "Books Make a Difference: A Study of Access to Literacy." *Reading Research Quarterly* 34: 286–311.

———. 2001. "Books Aloud: A Campaign to Put Books in Children's Hands." *Reading Teacher* 54: 554–57.

Neuman, S., and D. Celano. 2001. "Access to Print in Low-Income and Middle-Income Communities." *Reading Research Quarterly* 36: 8–26.

Newmann, F., and G. Wehlage. 1995. *Successful School Restructuring: A Report to the Public and Educators.* Madison: University of Wisconsin, Center on Organization and Restructuring of Schools.

Nieto, S. 1999. "Multiculturalism, Social Justice, and Critical Teaching." In *Education Is Politics: Critical Teaching Across Differences, K–12,* edited by I. Shor and C. Pari. Portsmouth, NH: Boynton/Cook.

North Central Regional Educational Laboratory. 1994. "Funds of Knowledge: A Look at Luis Moll's Research into Hidden Family Resources." *CITYSCHOOLS* 1 (1): 19–21.

Ogbu, J. 1978. *Minority Education and Caste.* New York: Academic.

Ohanian, S. 1999. *One Size Fits Few: The Folly of Educational Standards.* Portsmouth, NH: Heinemann.

———. 2002. *What Happened to Recess and Why Are Our Children Struggling in Kindergarten?* New York: McGraw Hill.

———. 2004. *Why Is Corporate America Bashing Our Public Schools?* Portsmouth, NH: Heinemann.

Owocki, G. 1999. *Literacy Through Play.* Portsmouth, NH: Heinemann.

Pappas, C., B. Kiefer, and L. Levstik. 1990. *An Integrated Language Perspective in the Elementary School: Theory into Action.* White Plains, NY: Longman.

Payne, R. K. 2001. *A Framework for Understanding Poverty.* Highlands, TX: Aha Process.

Peregoy, S. 1991. "Environmental Scaffolds and Learner Responses in a Two-Way Spanish Immersion Kindergarten." *Canadian Modern Language Review* 47 (3): 463–76.

Peregoy, S., and O. Boyle. 1990. "Kindergartners Write! Emergent Literacy of Mexican American Children in a Two-Way Spanish Immersion Program." *Journal of the Association of Mexican American Educators*: 6–18.

———. 2001. *Reading, Writing, and Learning in ESL: A Resource Book for K–12 Teachers.* New York: Longman.

Perry, T., and L. Delpit, eds. 1998. *The Real Ebonics Debate: Power, Language, and the Education of African American Children.* Boston: Beacon Press.

Peterson, B. 1999. "My Journey as a Critical Teacher: Creating Schools as Laboratories for Social Justice." In *Education Is Politics: Critical Teaching Across Difference, K–12,* edited by I. Shor and C. Pari. Portsmouth, NH: Boynton/Cook.

Pilgreen, J. 2000. *The SSR Handbook: How to Organize and Maintain a Sustained Silent Reading Program.* Portsmouth, NH: Heinemann.

Pinnell, G. S., and I. C. Fountas. 1998. *Word Matters: Teaching Phonics and Spelling in the Reading/Writing Classroom.* Portsmouth, NH: Heinemann.

Pressley, M. 1998. *Reading Instruction That Works: The Case for Balanced Teaching*. New York: Guilford.

Ramirez, M., and A. Castaneda. 1974. *Cultural Democracy: Bicognitive Development and Education*. New York: Academic.

Revicki, D. A. 1981. *The Relationship Among Socioeconomic Status, Home Environment, Parent Involvement, Child Self-Concept, and Child Achievement*. Chapel Hill: University of North Carolina.

Rhodes, L. K., and C. Dudley-Marling. 1996. *Readers and Writers with a Difference* 2d ed. Portsmouth, NH: Heinemann.

Routman, R. 1991. *Invitations: Changing as Teachers and Learners K–12*. Portsmouth, NH: Heinemann.

Samway, K. D., and D. McKeon. 1999. *Myths and Realities: Best Practices for Language Minority Students*. Portsmouth, NH: Heinemann.

Saville-Troike, M. 1991. *Teaching and Testing for Academic Achievement: The Role of Language Development*. NCBE Focus: Occasional Papers in Bilingual Education, 4. Washington, DC: National Clearinghouse for Bilingual Education, George Washington University.

Schickendanz, J. 1978. "'Please Read That Story Again!' Exploring Relationships Between Story Reading and Learning to Read." *Young Children* 33: 48–55.

———. 1986. *More Than ABCs: The Early Stages of Reading and Writing*. Washington, DC: National Association for the Education of Young Children.

Schmidt, G. 2003. Victory in Chicago! Press Conference. Chicago, IL.

Scribner, A. P. 1999. "High Performing Hispanic Schools: An Introduction." In *Lessons from High-Performing Hispanic Schools: Creating Learning Communities*, edited by P. Reyes, J. D. Scribner, and A. P. Scribner. New York: Teachers College Press.

Scribner, J. D., M. D. Young, and A. Pedroza. 1999. "Building Collaborative Relationships with Parents." In *Lessons from High-Performing Hispanic Schools: Creating Learning Communities*, edited by P. Reyes, J. D. Scribner, and A. P. Scribner. New York: Teachers College Press.

Seuss, Dr. 1960. *One Fish, Two Fish, Red Fish, Blue Fish*. New York: Random House.

Shor, I., and C. Pari, eds. 1999. *Education Is Politics: Critical Teaching Across Differences, K–12*. Portsmouth, NH: Boynton/Cook.

Smith, F. 2003. *Unspeakable Acts, Unnatural Practices: Flaws and Fallacies in Scientific Reading Instruction*. Portsmouth, NH: Heinemann.

Smitherman, G. 1977. *Talkin' and Testifyin'*. Detroit: Wayne State University Press.

Snow, C. E. 1983. "Literacy and Language: Relationships During the Preschool Years." *Harvard Educational Review* 53 (2): 165–89.

Snow, C. E., S. M. Burns, and P. Griffin, eds. 1998. *Preventing Reading Difficulties in Young Children.* Washington, DC: National Academy Press.

Sosa, A. S. 1997. "Involving Hispanic Parents in Educational Activities Through Collaborative Relationships." *Bilingual Research Journal* 21 (2): 1–8.

Sulzby, E. 1985. "Children's Emergent Reading of Favorite Storybooks: A Developmental Study." *Reading Research Quarterly* 20: 458–81.

Swain, M. 1985. "Communicative Competence: Some Roles for Comprehensible Input and Comprehensible Output in Its Development." In *Input in Second Language Acquisition,* edited by S. Goss and C. Madden. Rowley, MA: Newbury House.

Thomas, W. P., and V. P. Collier. 2002. *A National Study of School Effectiveness for Language Minority Students' Long-Term Academic Achievement.* Santa Cruz, CA: Center for Research on Education, Diversity, and Excellence.

Traill, L. 1993. *Highlight My Strengths: Assessment and Evaluation of Literacy Learning.* Barrington, IL: Rigby.

Trelease, J. 1990. *The New Read-Aloud Handbook.* New York: Penguin.

Trumbull, E., C. Rothstein-Fisch, P. M. Greenfield, and B. Quiroz. 2001. *Bridging Cultures Between Home and Schools: A Guide for Teachers.* Mahwah, NJ: Lawrence Erlbaum.

Unz, R. 1999. "California and the End of White America." *Commentary Magazine* 108 (4).

Van Hoorn, J., P. M. Nourot, and B. Scales. 1992. *Play at the Center of the Curriculum.* Princeton, NJ: Prentice-Hall.

Velez-Ibanez, C., and J. Greenberg. 1992. "Formation and Transformation of Funds of Knowledge Among U.S. Mexican Households." *Anthropology and Education Quarterly* 23 (4): 313–35.

Vygotsky, L. 1962. *Thought and Language.* Cambridge, MA: MIT Press.

Walberg, H., R. Bole, and H. Waxman. 1980. "School-Based Family Socialization and Reading Achievement in the Inner City." In *Psychology in the Schools.* Santa Monica, CA: Rand.

Walsh, C. E. 1991. *Pedagogy and the Struggle for Voice: Issues of Language, Power, and Schooling for Puerto Ricans.* Toronto: OISE Press.

Wasserman, S. 1990. *Serious Players in the Primary Classroom.* New York: Teachers College Press.

White, E. B. 1945. *Stuart Little.* New York: Scholastic.

Yatvin, J. 2000. "Minority View." In *Report of the National Reading Panel: Teaching Children to Read.* Washington, DC: National Institute of Child Health and Human Development.

Index

Content-embedded tasks, 96
Content study, 93–107
  combining language and content goals,
    98–100
  defined, 93
  developing vocabulary through, 141
  differentiating language and, strategies for,
    101–102
  experiencing the content, value of, 102
  language, content study and, 95–96
  language, negotiating the world through,
    95–98
  math exploration (sample), 102–104
  Seattle Neighborhoods research project,
    104–107
  selecting, 98–100
  thematic units, 100
  walking to Swan Creek (scenario), 93–94
Context-reduced tasks, 96
Continuum of Written Language Development, 173–74
Conventional stage of spelling development,
  170
Conversations. *See* Oral language
Cotton, Kathleen, 60
Counterintuitive principle, 89, 182–83, 184
Critical pedagogy, 79
Cruz, Celia, 73
Cultural backgrounds, importance of knowing
  students', 13–15
Cultural democracy
  in classroom, creating, 78
  commitment to, 18
  establishing, 11–12
  true multicultural education, 79
Culture
  biculturalism, valuing, 16–17
  inseparability of language and, 41
  oppressive societal structures, classrooms
    mirroring, 77
  oppressive societal structures, classrooms
    that challenge, 77–78
  staffs that reflect cultural diversity of stu-
    dents, importance of, 35–36
Culture of poverty, 42
Culture of questioning, 19–20
Cummins, Jim
  content learning and, 96, 98–99
  counterintuitive principle and, 89, 182, 184
  dual iceberg theory and, 39
  oral language assessment and, 150, 152, 154
  student empowerment and, 77–78
  on zone of proximal development, 76
Cunningham, Patricia, 54, 68, 69, 70, 90

Curriculum
  creating thinkers with, 85–86
  making talk purposeful in, 87–88
  play, value of, 90–91
  relevance and, 84–85
  talking, importance of, 86–88

Darder, Antonia, 78
Data
  in ELL planning process, 28
  math exploration (sample), 102–104
Demonstration, learning condition, 110, 111
Demonstrations, in content study, 101
Describe and Draw (game), 145
Developmental Reading Assessment (DRA),
  169
Diagrams, vocabulary development and, 143
Diaz Soto, Lourdes, 83–84
Discipline of magic, 10–11
Discussion groups, setting up, 135
Dissent, silencing, 186
Drama, learning oral language through,
  136–37
Dual iceberg theory, 39
Dual language immersion model, 31–32,
  180–81
Dual language programs, 191–92
Dudley-Marling, Curt, 175
Duthie Index, 156, 157
Dynamic Indicator of Basic Early Learning
  Skills (DIBELS), 158–60

Early-exit and late-exit transitional programs,
  30
Early phonetic stage of spelling development,
  170
Ebonics, 11
Eldridge, Paul, 147
Elley, Warwick, 47
Emergent curriculum, 84
English as a second language (ESL), 1
English First, 183
English immersion model, 22–23, 30
English language. *See also* Language
  traditional, 1
  type of, 1
English language learner (ELL)
  budget issues and, 192–94
  challenging the status quo, 181–85
  defined, 1
  effective teaching of, 6–7
  first-generation students, 2
  home–school communication, strategies for
    developing, 65–67

Interpersonal space, 76
IPT (IDEA Oral Language Proficiency Test), 151, 154
I Spy (game), 145

Jones, Elizabeth, 84
Just right books, 109

Kaiser, Henry, 1
King, Martin Luther Jr., 33, 189
Koala Lou, 53
Krashen, Stephen, 76, 151, 184

Language
combining language and content goals, 98–100
content learning and, 95–96
differentiating content study and, strategies for, 101–102
domains of, 132–33
inseparability of culture and, 41
negotiating the world through, 95–98
oral (*see* Oral language)
play in language development, 91
as reflecting thinking, 96–98
rich language, infusing classroom with, 138–40
teaching, principles for, 95
thematic units, 100
Language Assessment Scales (LAS), 150–51, 154
Language development
ideal settings for, 5–6
limiting factors, 4–5
Larson, Kathy, 22, 23, 24
Leadership, effective, 19–20
Learners, teachers becoming, 43
Learning community. *See also* Classroom environments
creating an effective, 79–91
Letter knowledge, assessing, 156–60
Librarians, value of, 48
Libraries
classroom, 48–50
family lending libraries, 51–52
library at center of a community (scenario), 45–46
school libraries, 46–48
Lilly's Purple Plastic Purse, 109
Limited English proficient (LEP), 1
Limited English speaking (LES), 1
Lincoln Elementary School (Olympia, Washington), 9–10, 15–16, 17–18, 19–20, 63

Linguistic backgrounds, importance of knowing students', 13–15
Linguistics
bilingualism, valuing, 16–17
staffs that reflect linguistic diversity of students, importance of, 35–36
Listening
as domain of language, 132–33
importance of, 132
Listening tasks in content study, 99
Lister Elementary (Tacoma, Washington), 50–51, 61
Literacy, balanced, 108–28
components of balanced program, 112–28
a day in the life of balanced literacy (scenario), 108–109
guided reading, 110, 115–17
guided writing, 110, 122–25
importance of a balanced program, 110–12
independent reading, 110, 117–18
independent writing, 110, 125
interactive writing, 110, 120–22
model for literacy learning, 110
reading aloud, 110, 112–13
shared reading, 110, 113–15
shared writing, 110, 118–20
word study, 110, 125–28
Little Red Hen, The, 53
Long Beach Unified School District (California), 179–80
Long's Interaction Model, 86
Lopez, Gerardo R., 62
Lowell, James Russell, 45

MacIntosh, Peggy, 42
Malcolm X, 181
Marginalization of students, 5–6
Math exploration (sample), 102–104
Meanies Came to School, The, 109, 115
Meaning, in interactive writing, 121
Mentoring services, 71
Miller, Debbie, 90
Minnich, Elizabeth, 42
"Minority View," 186
Miscue analysis, 166, 167, 168
Misreading Reading: The Bad Science That Hurts Children, 195
Mixtec, 2, 4
Models, in ELL planning process, 29
Moll, L., 152
Mother Jones, 181
Multicultural education, true, 79
Music, learning oral language through, 136

Tacoma School District (Washington), 156
Talk. *See* Oral language
Teacher
    authority and student empowerment, nego-
        tiating, 82–83
    training (*see* Staff development)
Teachers
    becoming learners, 43
    continuing education (*see* Staff development)
    high-quality, importance of, 197–98
    learning community, creating an effective,
        80–81
    as resources, 40–41
    rethinking roles and remodeling structures
        for, 42–43
    staffing (*see* Staffing)
    strong, value of, 83–84
    teacher needs *versus* student needs, 38
Teachers College Reading and Writing Project
    (Columbia University), 85–86, 124
Teaching organically, 84
Team teaching, effectiveness of, 24
Thematic instruction, vocabulary develop-
    ment and, 142
Thematic units, 100
Theory
    grounding philosophy in, 41–42
    grounding practice in, importance of, 39
    turning theory into action, 40
Theresa, Mother, 73
Thinking
    goals, 10
    language as reflecting, 96–98
Thinking behaviors, 10
Thomas, Wayne P., 180–81
Thoreau, Henry David, 9
Time
    assessing the payoff, 55
    cutting summer losses, 55–56
    every second counts, 54
    as resource, 54–56
Title I remedial reading program, 23, 52
Traill, Leanna, 173
Transitional programs, early-exit and late-exit,
    30
Transitional stage of spelling development, 170
Twain, Mark, 108
Twenty Questions (game), 137
Two-way immersion model, 31–32

Units of Study for Primary Writing, 85–86,
    124–25, 173
Unz, Ron, 179, 182–83

U.S. English, 183
Use, learning condition, 110, 111, 117

Very Hungry Caterpillar, The, 58
Videos, shadowing, 137
Vision
    living by schoolwide, 17–19
    in successful ELL programs, 10–11
Visuals, in content study, 101
Vocabulary development
    content studies, developing vocabulary
        through, 141
    diagrams, 143
    experiential learning, 142
    games, 145
    graphic illustrations, 143
    integrating, 137–45
    new words, getting students excited about,
        140–41
    play, 144–45
    rich language, infusing classroom with,
        138–40
    with self-selected reading, 145–46
    strategies for facilitating, 142–45
    thematic instruction, 142
    word banks, 142–43
    word study, 144
Vocabulary tasks in content study, 99
Voice, 78, 81
Vygotsky, Lev, 76

Washington State Office of Superintendent of
    Public Instruction website, 98, 104
Webster Elementary School (west Long Beach,
    California), 45, 47, 48, 51–52, 179–81, 185
Weisel, Elie, 179
What Happened (game), 137
White nationalism, 183
Wikelund, Karen Reed, 60
Women, Infants, and Children (WIC) program,
    69
Woodburn School District (Oregon), 22–27
Woodcock Language Proficiency Battery-
    Revised, 151, 154
Word banks
    in content study, 102
    vocabulary development and, 142–43
Word explorers (scenario), 130–32
Word study
    in balanced literacy program, 110, 125–28
    vocabulary development and, 144
Work, recognizing students' hard, 15–16
Work activity time, 90